CHESHIRE IN PHOTOGRAPHS

MARK HELLIWELL

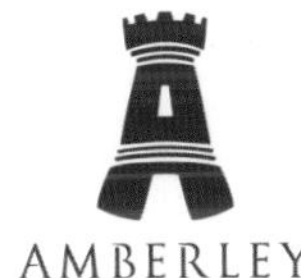

AMBERLEY

First published 2019

Amberley Publishing
The Hill, Stroud
Gloucestershire, GL5 4EP

www.amberley-books.com

ISBN 978 1 4456 9300 2 (print)
ISBN 978 1 4456 9301 9 (ebook)

British Library Cataloguing in Publication Data.
A catalogue record for this book is available from the British Library.

Typesetting by Aura Technology and Software Services, India.
Printed in the UK.

ABOUT CHESHIRE

Cheshire is a mid-sized county in the north-west of England, covering approximately 900 square miles with a population of around 1 million. It is said that the county of Cheshire was created by Edward the Elder some 1,100 years ago. It is bordered by six counties (one in Wales) and comprises four unitary districts: Cheshire East, Cheshire West and Chester, Warrington and Halton. The county extends from Disley in the east to Chester and parts of the Wirral in the west, and from Warrington in the north to Crewe in the south.

The Cheshire landscape is varied and characterised by an expanse of central flat plains bordered by the gritstone hills of the Peak District in the east and a sandstone ridge in the west. The county has a strong industrial heritage, home to the silk and cotton mills of the late Middle Ages towards the east of the county and salt mines largely in the centre of the county. Heavy industry, such as chemical plants and power stations, are typically found in the north, where there is easy access to major waterways (e.g. the Manchester Ship Canal and River Mersey) and road networks (M6 and M56). Although agriculture and dairy farming (Cheshire cheese) are present throughout Cheshire, these industries are concentrated in the central and lower plains.

Cheshire is also awash with market towns, picture-postcard villages, stately homes and gardens, churches, museums, sporting venues and castles. For those who enjoy the outdoors, there is an expansive network of walking and cycling routes that provide views of the many canals, rivers, ridges and monuments throughout the county.

This book is organised into the following four chapters: City of Chester, Cheshire Towns and Villages, Cheshire Countryside, and Visiting Cheshire.

Chester is the county town of Cheshire and has had city status for nearly 500 years. It was founded as a Roman fort, evidenced by remains of the castle, an amphitheatre, Roman gardens and medieval buildings, but more impressively by the mostly continuous wall enclosing the city, which can be walked along. The famous Eastgate Clock is situated on a section of the wall, overlooking the busiest shopping street in Chester. Four central streets are flanked by the Rows – two-storey terraces of shops and restaurants dating from Tudor times. In the heart of the city is the impressive Chester Cathedral, dating from at least the eleventh century. To the south of the city there is a university, racecourse (The Roodee) and the fast-flowing River Dee. This area is popular with tourists, with ample riverside seating, boating, a bandstand and ice-cream parlours, not to mention pleasant walking on both sides of the river, accessed by an old sandstone bridge and a newer suspension bridge.

Given the area and population of Cheshire, it is not surprising there are numerous towns and villages. Old cotton mills are still in existence in Macclesfield and Bollington, many of which have been converted to business premises and apartments. Places such as Prestbury, Knutsford, Wilmslow and Alderley Edge boast expensive residences, partly a result of an influx of professional footballers from the two Manchester teams. Cheshire has a number of market towns including Macclesfield, Frodsham, Nantwich and Sandbach, the latter of which proudly displays two Anglo-Saxon crosses in the town centre. The larger towns tend to be situated to the north, with Warrington, Runcorn, Widnes and Ellesmere Port having an industrial feel to them. Many of the villages have impressive churches, cottages and inviting pubs, often close to established countryside walking routes. Daresbury was the birthplace of Lewis Carroll; an outline of the Cheshire Cat can be seen in the design of the village sign. Cheshire also has a small coastline thanks to the Mersey and Dee estuaries.

Two main forests feature in the Cheshire countryside: one at Macclesfield and one at Delamere. The largest hills – Shining Tor and Shutlingsloe (also known as the Cheshire Matterhorn) – are close to Macclesfield and look fantastic in winter when covered with snow. There is a large network of canals across the whole county, a few with splendid locks (e.g. Bunbury) and marinas and many rivers, meres and reservoirs, often close to country parks. There are three main walking trails offering exceptional views: the Sandstone Trail in the west, the Gritstone Trail in the east, and the North/South Cheshire Way in between. Hilltop follies pop up here and there, most notably White Nancy in Bollington, as do ancient monuments, such as the Neolithic Bridestones near Timbersbrook. The Cheshire countryside is home to abundant wildlife, and if you're lucky you can get a fairly close look at stags roaming free in Tatton Park.

Cheshire attracts many tourists. For those interested in astronomy and astrophysics, there is the observatory at Jodrell Bank, recently declared a UNESCO World Heritage Site. There are several castles and stately homes with beautifully manicured gardens (e.g. Capesthorne Hall), and some host open-air plays and music/comedy events (e.g. Gawsworth Hall). Museums are aplenty, many celebrating the silk, cotton and salt industries of yesteryear, and the National Waterways Museum is housed at Ellesmere Port. Several dairy farms produce their own ice cream (e.g. Snugburys in Hurleston), and there is even a boutique gin and whisky distillery in Wildboarclough (Forest Distillery).

In this book I have attempted to capture the identity, heritage and character of Cheshire. Although I have travelled close to 10,000 miles in bringing you the images of Cheshire in this book, I feel I have barely scratched the surface. I could easily travel the same distance over and discover many new viewpoints.

ABOUT THE PHOTOGRAPHER

I am a landscape photographer based in Macclesfield. I believe passionately that some of the greatest landscape photographs exist on your doorstep, and so I focus much of my time exploring the landscapes of Cheshire and neighbouring Derbyshire, both of which share large areas of the Peak District.

My landscape work has been recognised in several regional, national and international photography competitions. In 2011, I won a *Sunday Telegraph* competition with a winter theme, and in 2013 was the overall winner of the Macclesfield Barnaby Festival photography competition. In 2014 I decided to challenge myself in other genres of photography, and entered the international Amateur Photographer of the Year competition, coming second place overall from a total of ten disparate themes. Success followed in 2015 and beyond in the prestigious Landscape Photographer of the Year competition, with several commendations leading to publication and exhibitions in London.

I am a regular contributor and author to *Outdoor Photography* magazine, and offer individual tuition in landscape photography and digital processing. I sell my landscape images through my website (www.markhelliwell.com) and take on commissions. I like to support local events, and so often exhibit my work at art fairs and shows in Cheshire.

CITY OF CHESTER

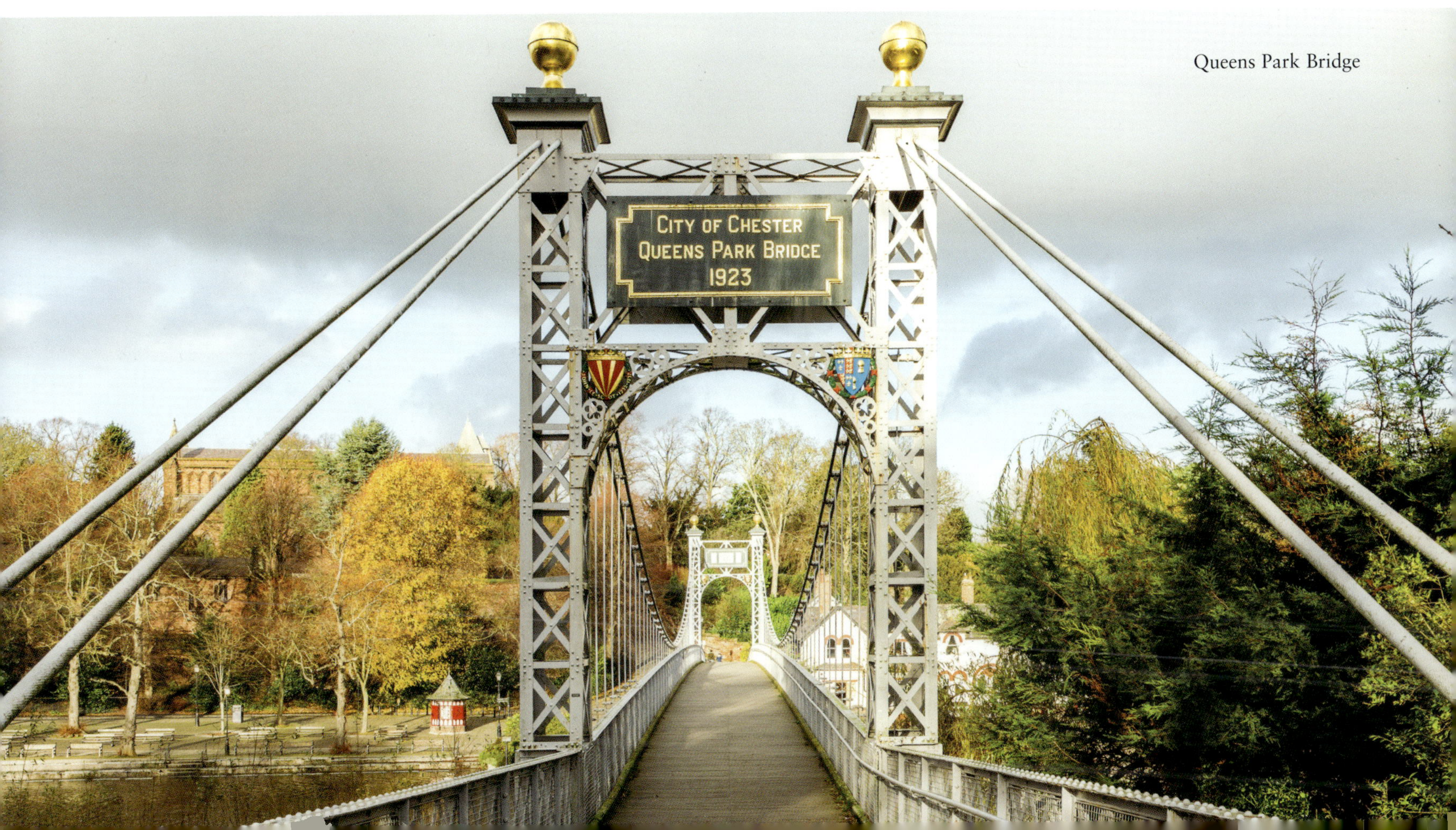

Queens Park Bridge

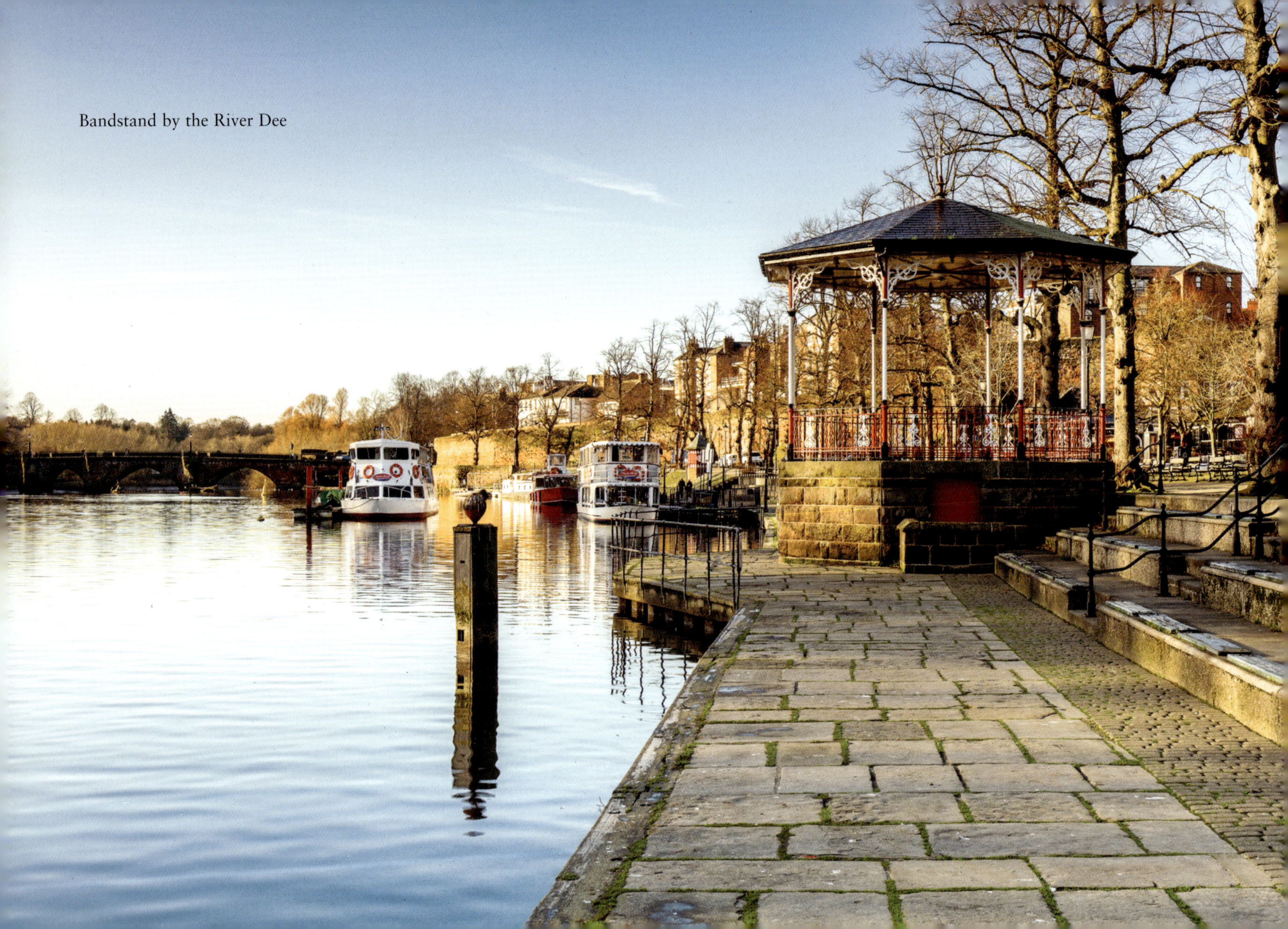

Bandstand by the River Dee

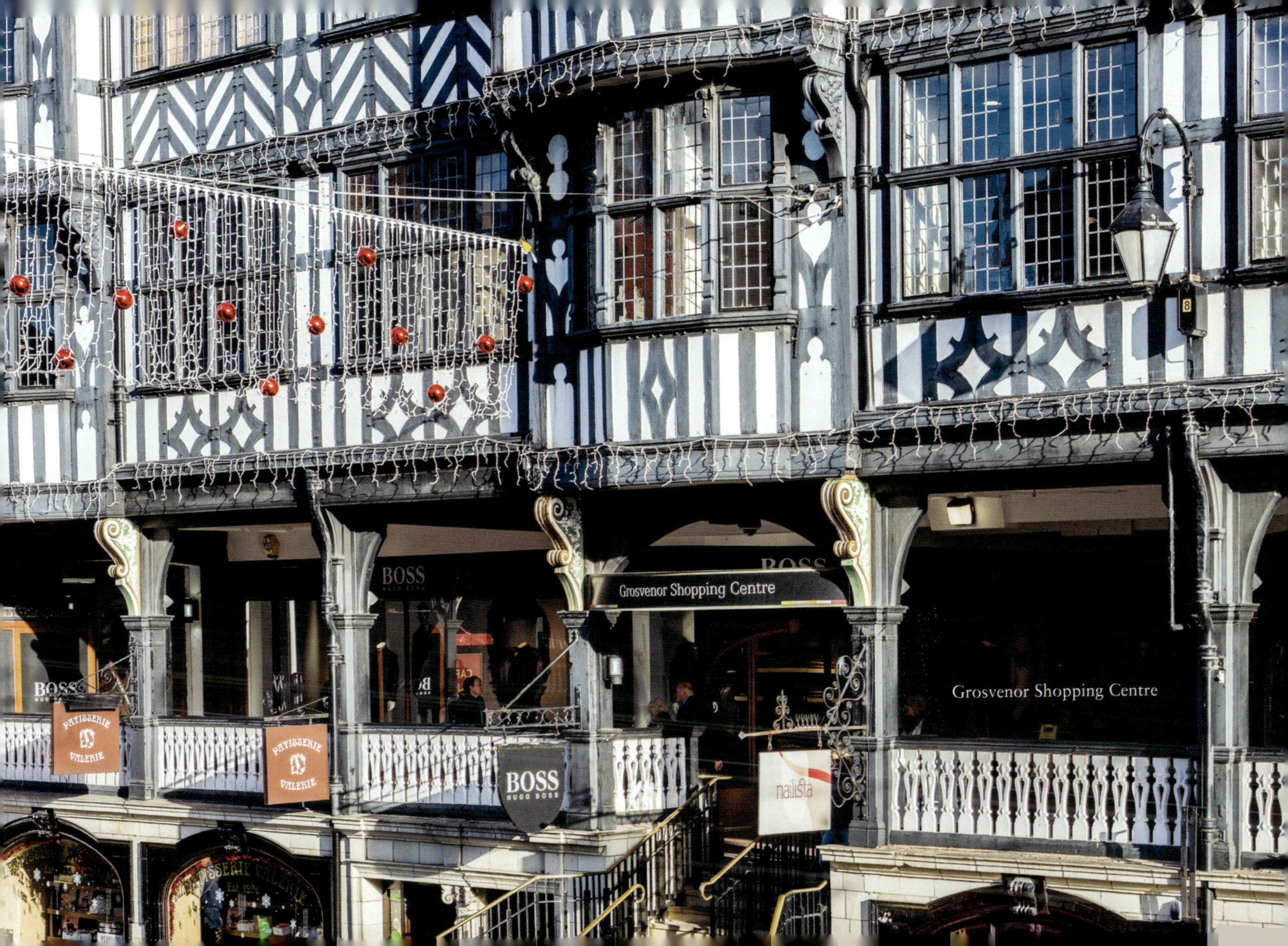

BOSS
Grosvenor Shopping Centre
Grosvenor Shopping Centre
PATISSERIE VALERIE
PATISSERIE VALERIE
BOSS
HUGO BOSS
nailista

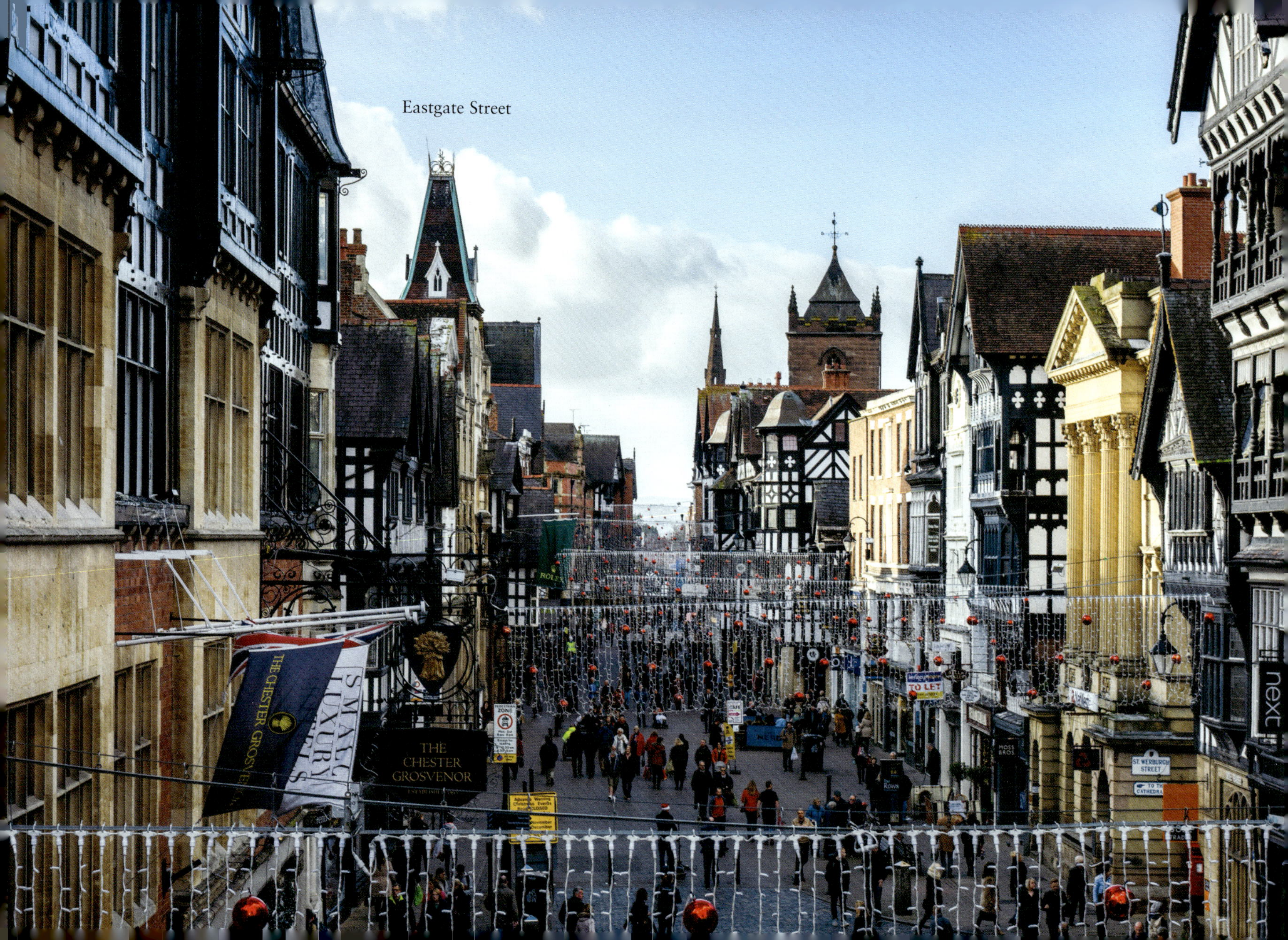

Eastgate Street

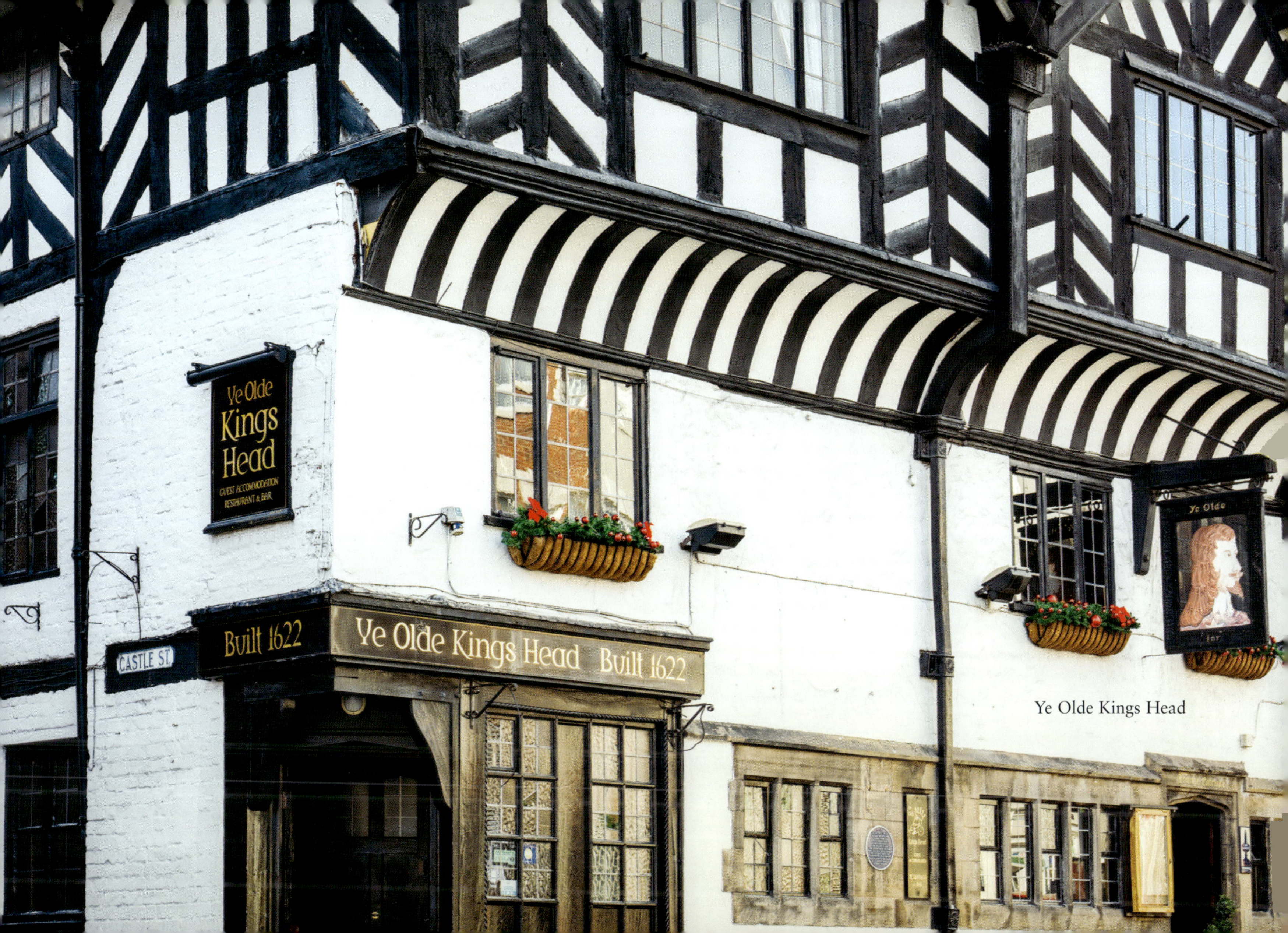

Ye Olde Kings Head

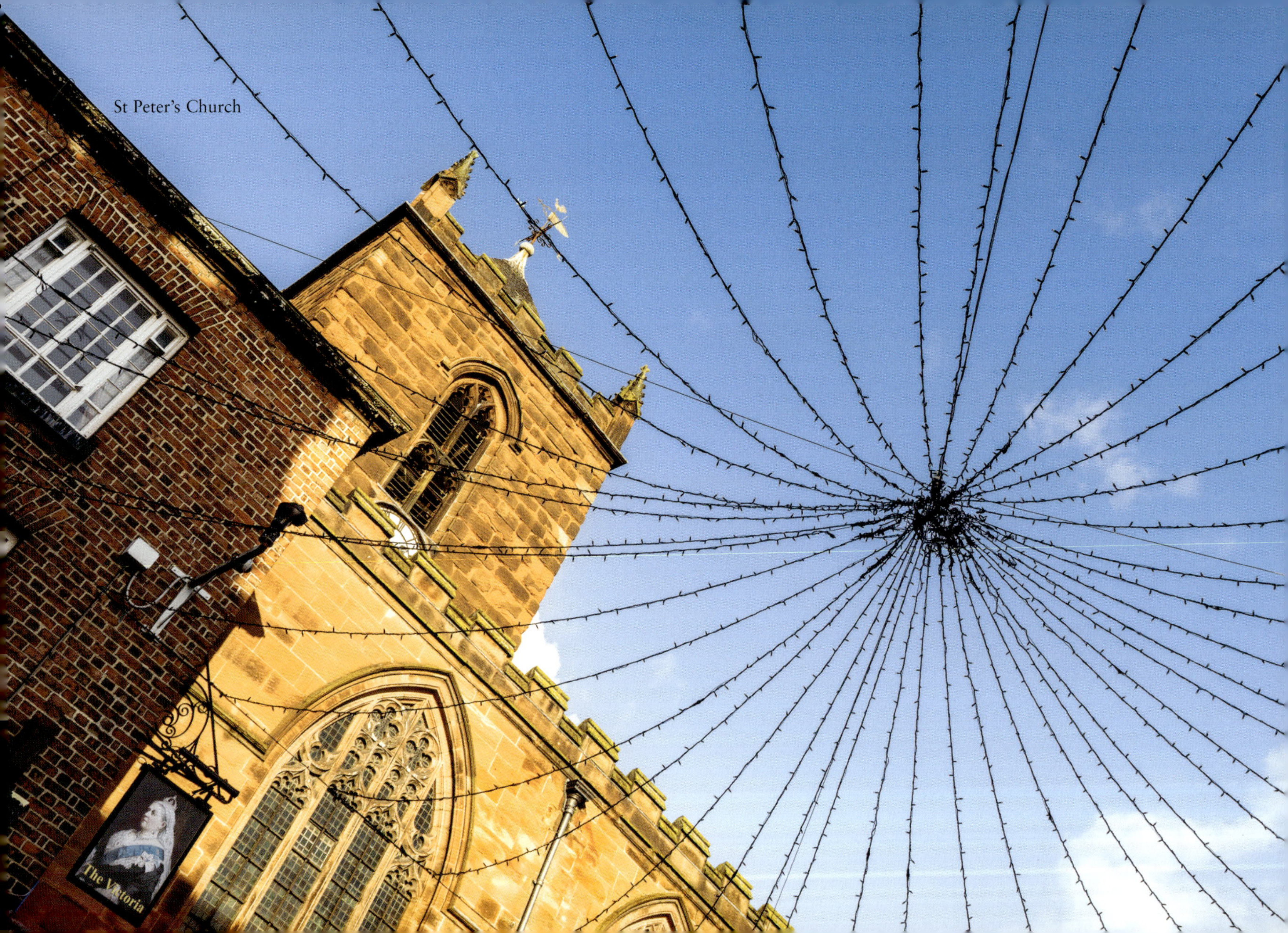

St Peter's Church

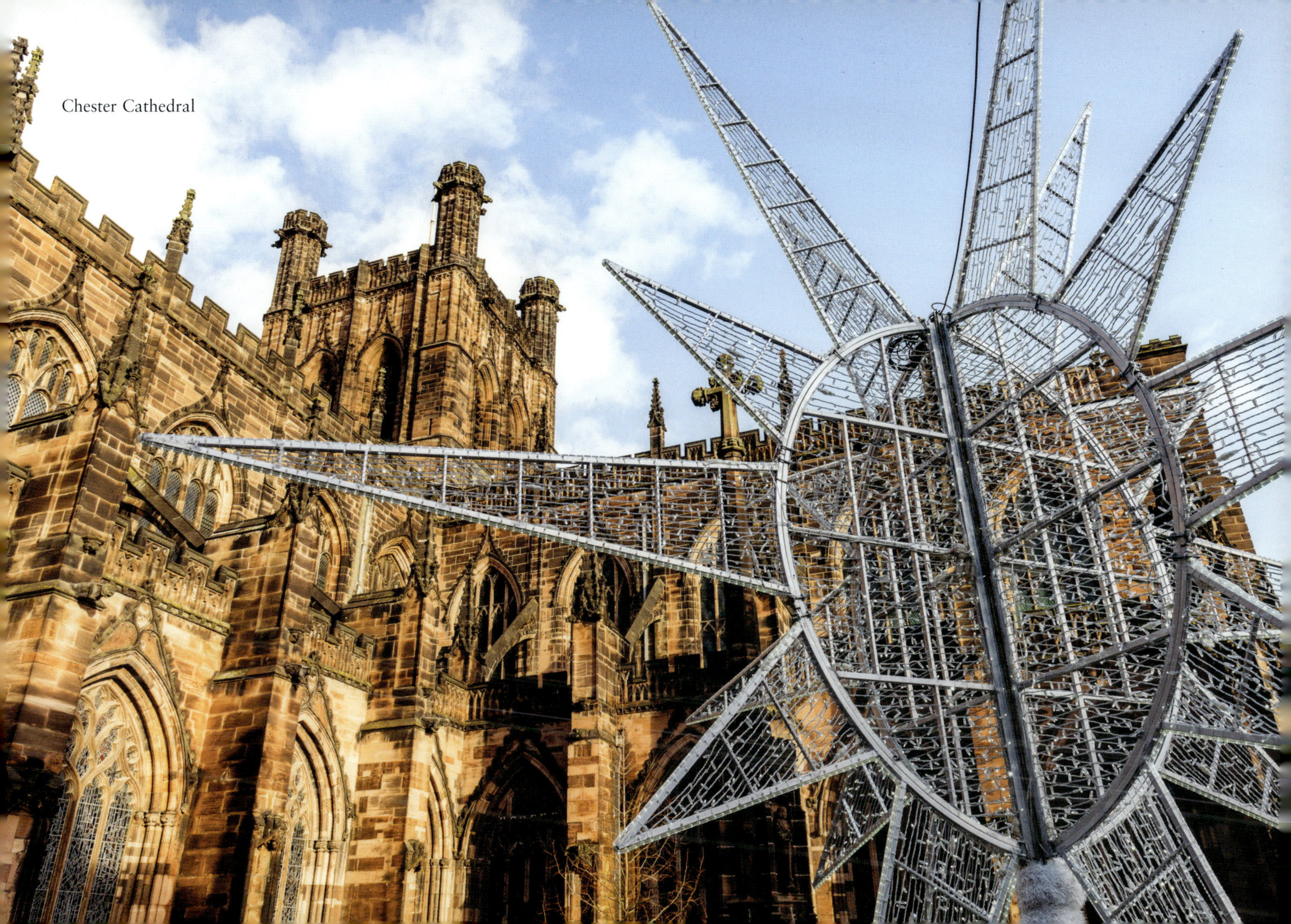

Chester Cathedral

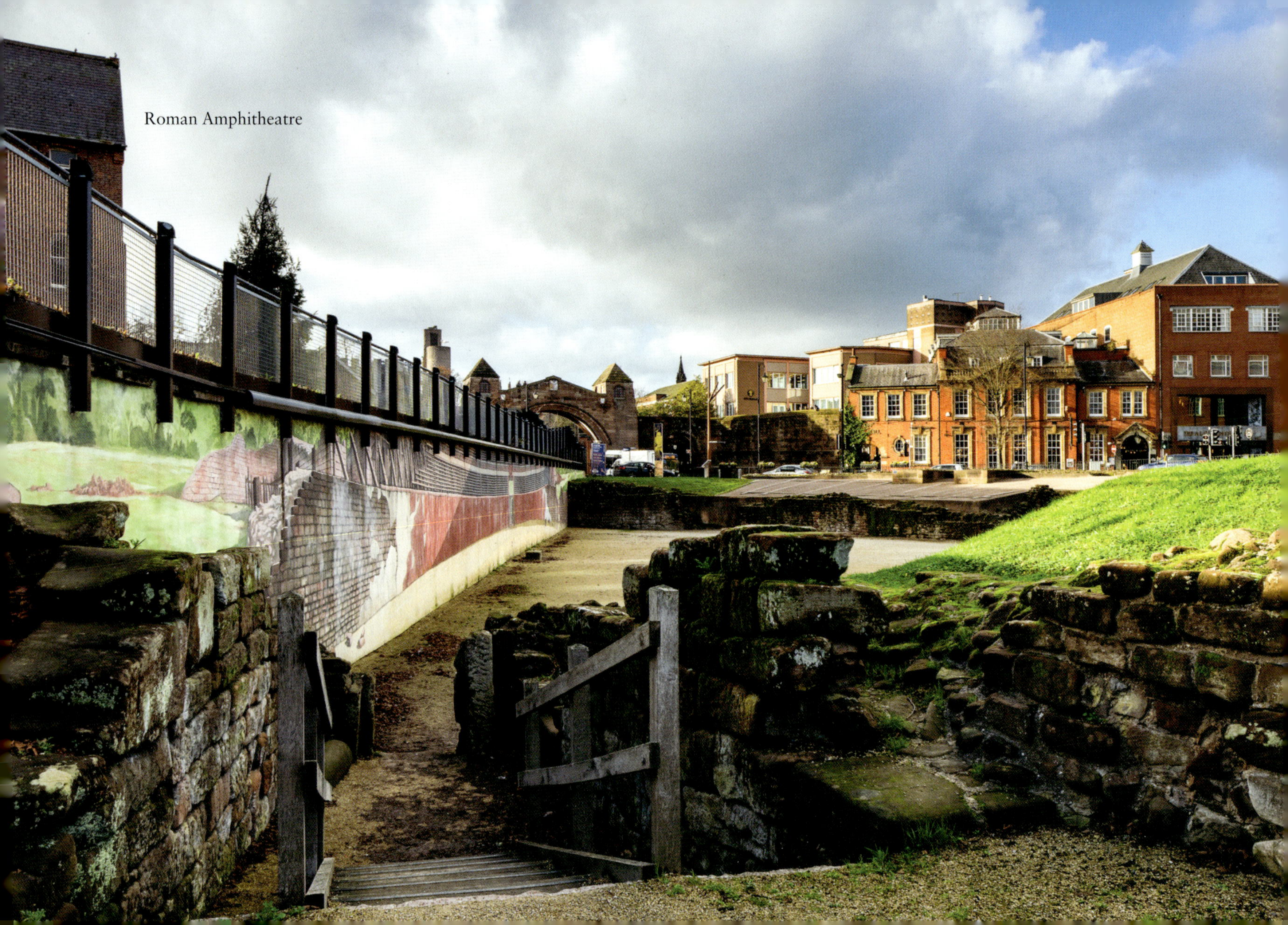

Roman Amphitheatre

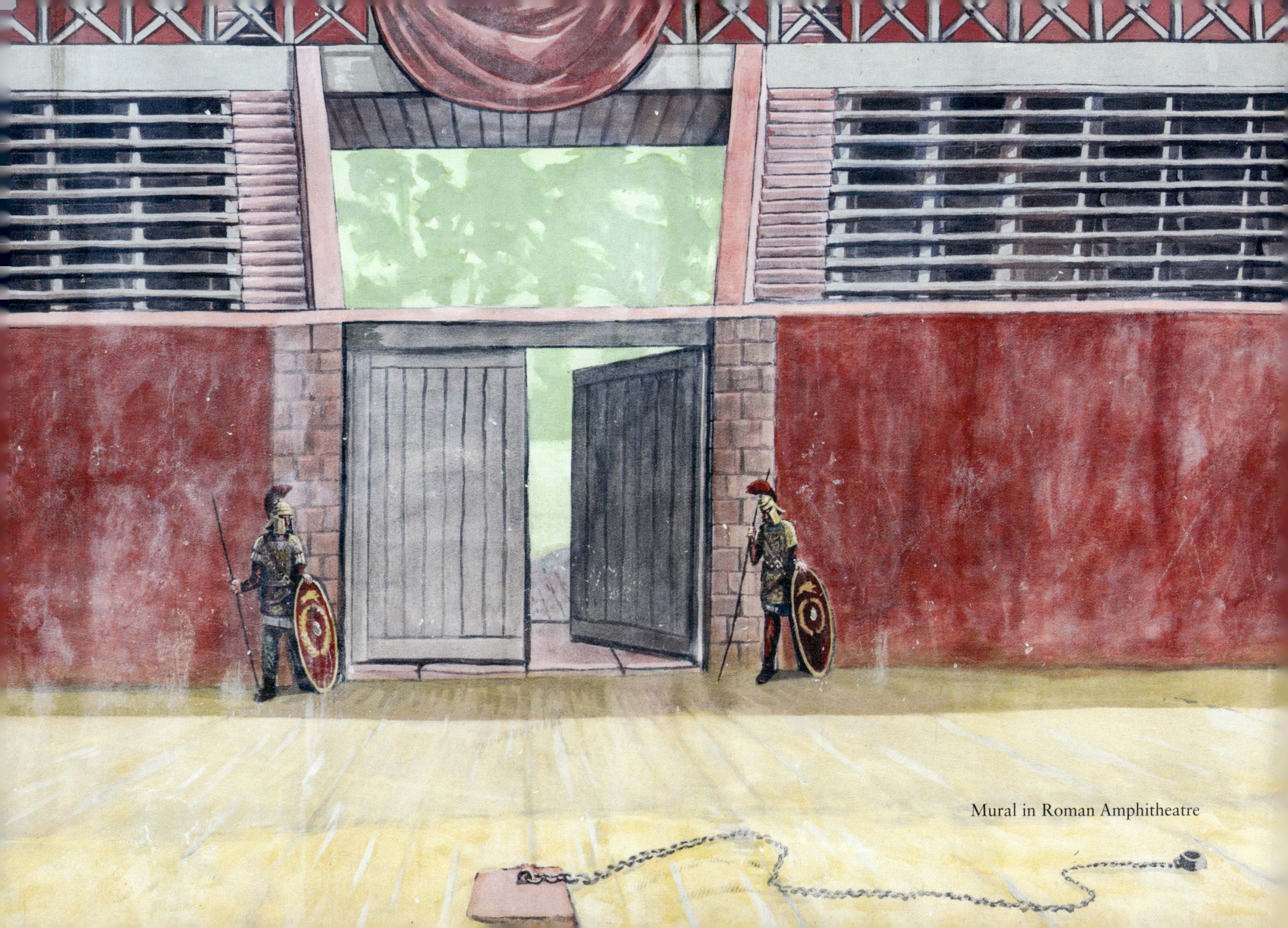

Mural in Roman Amphitheatre

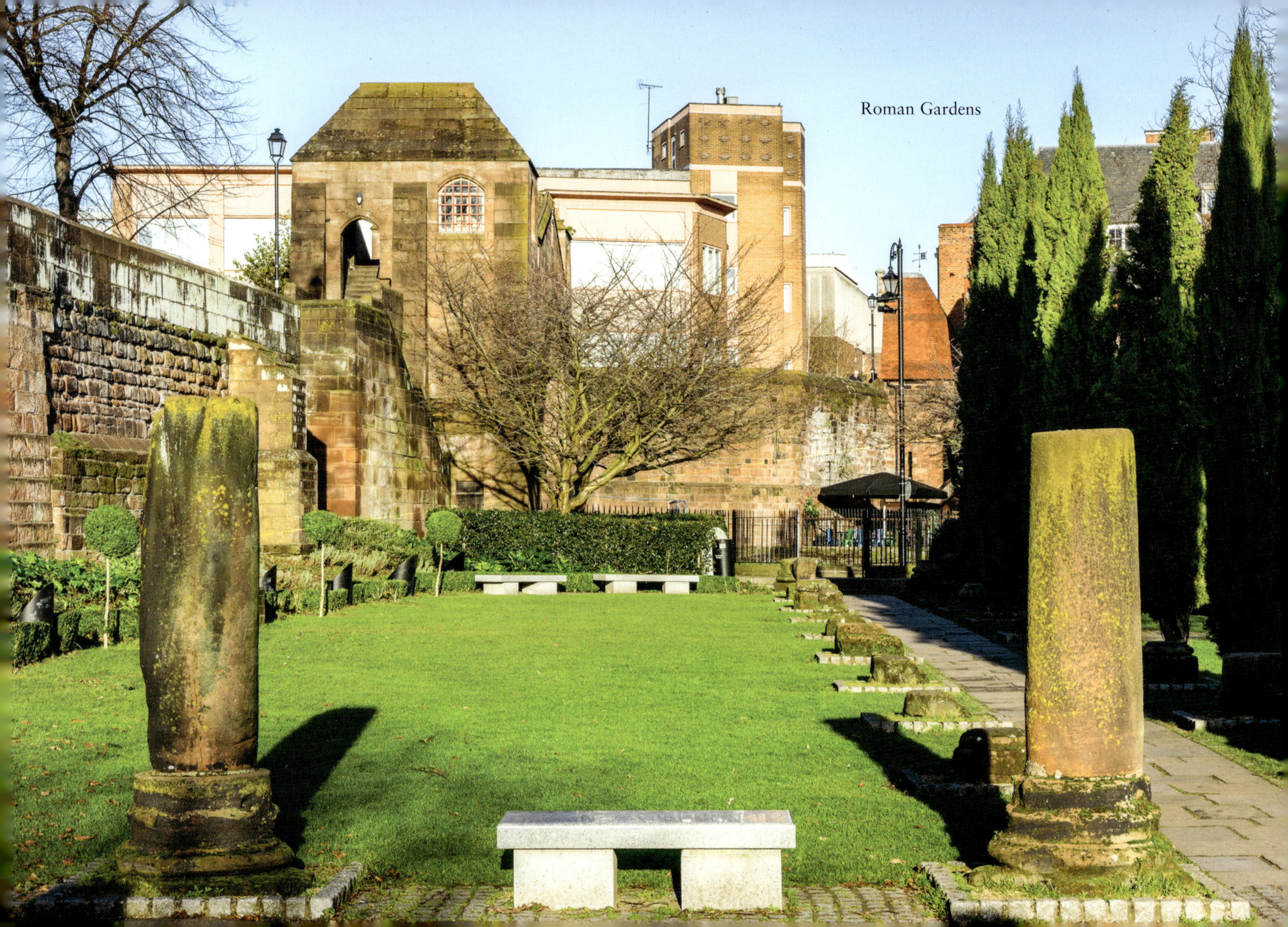

Roman Gardens

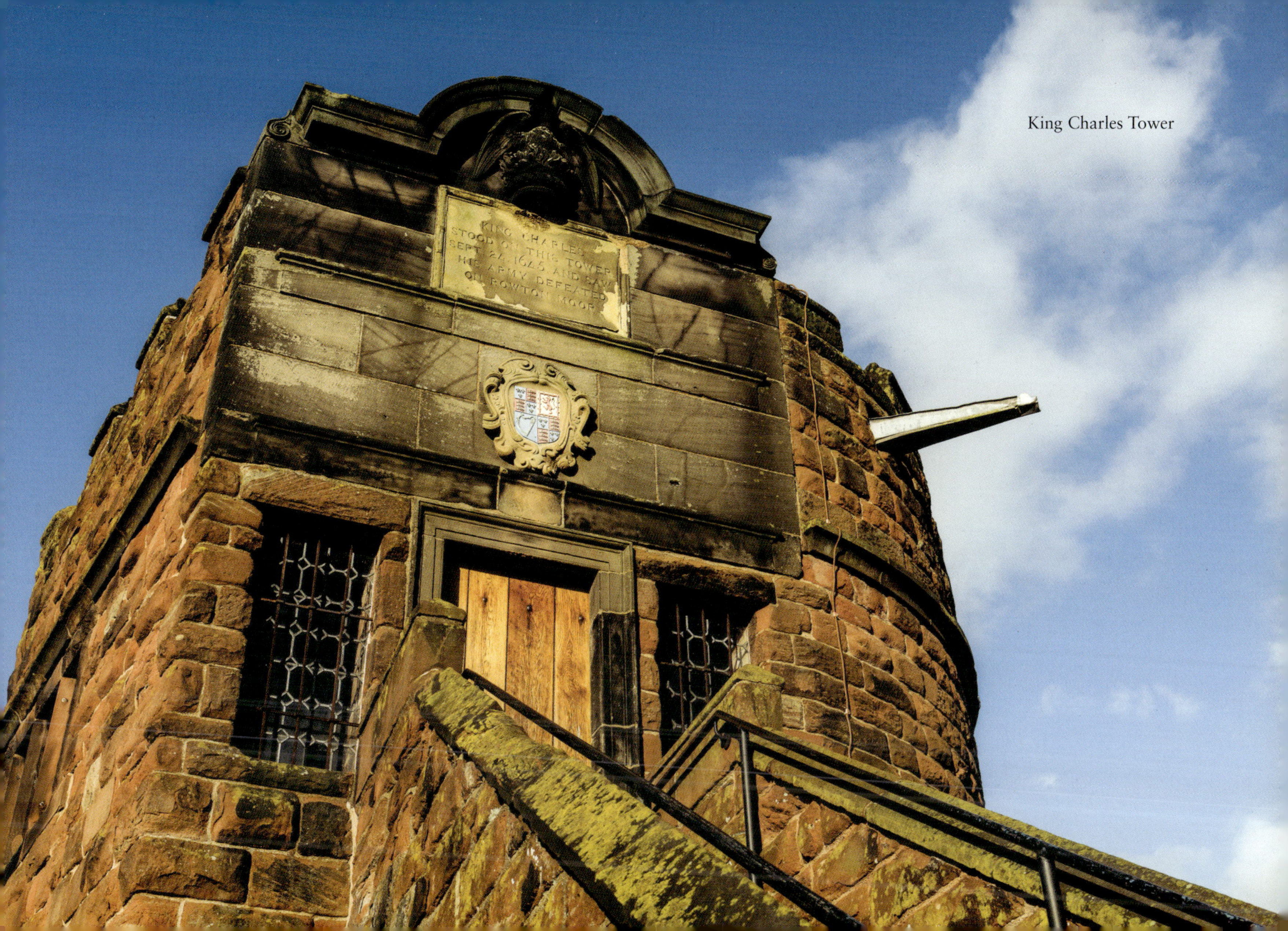

King Charles Tower

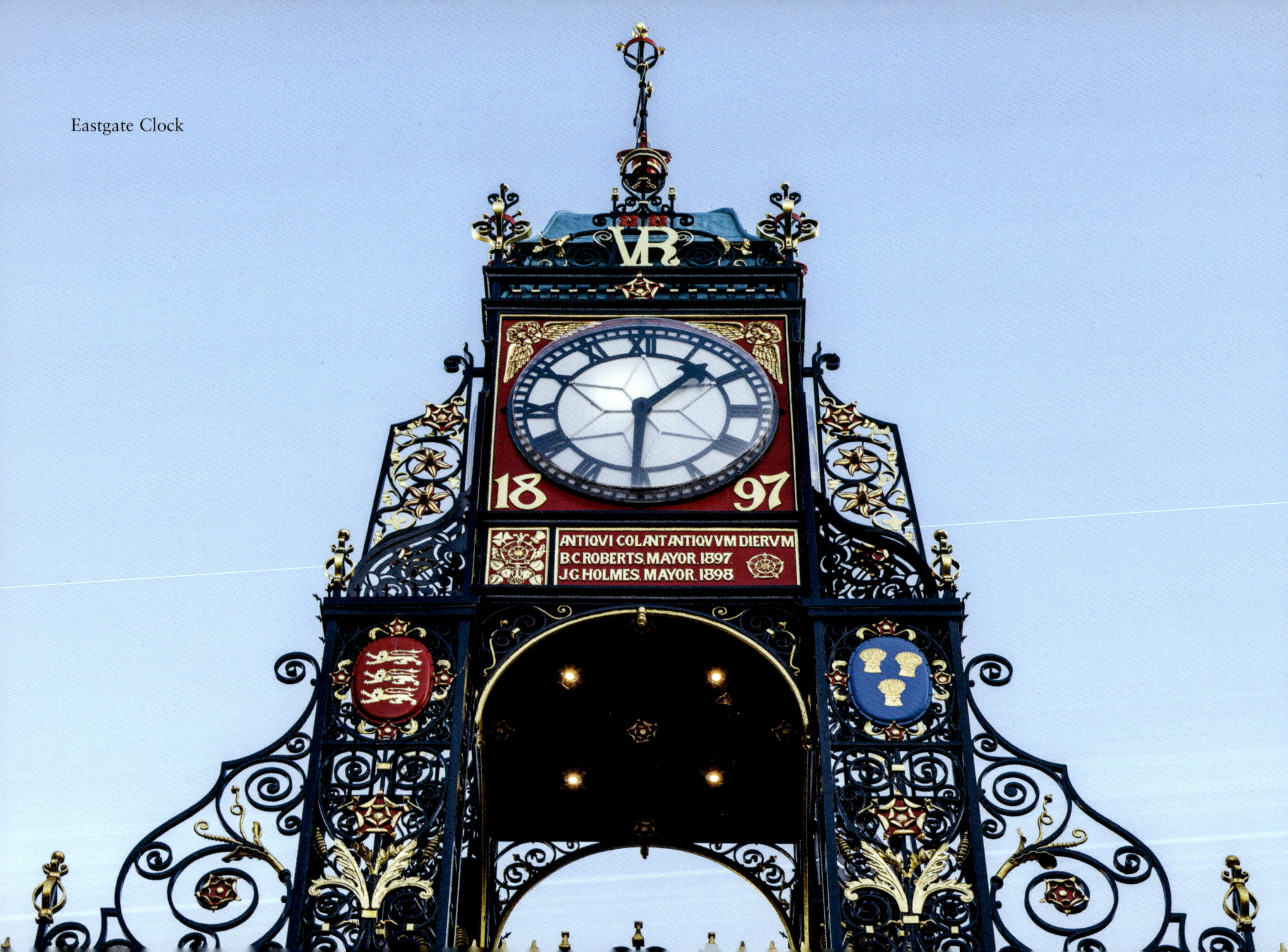

Eastgate Clock

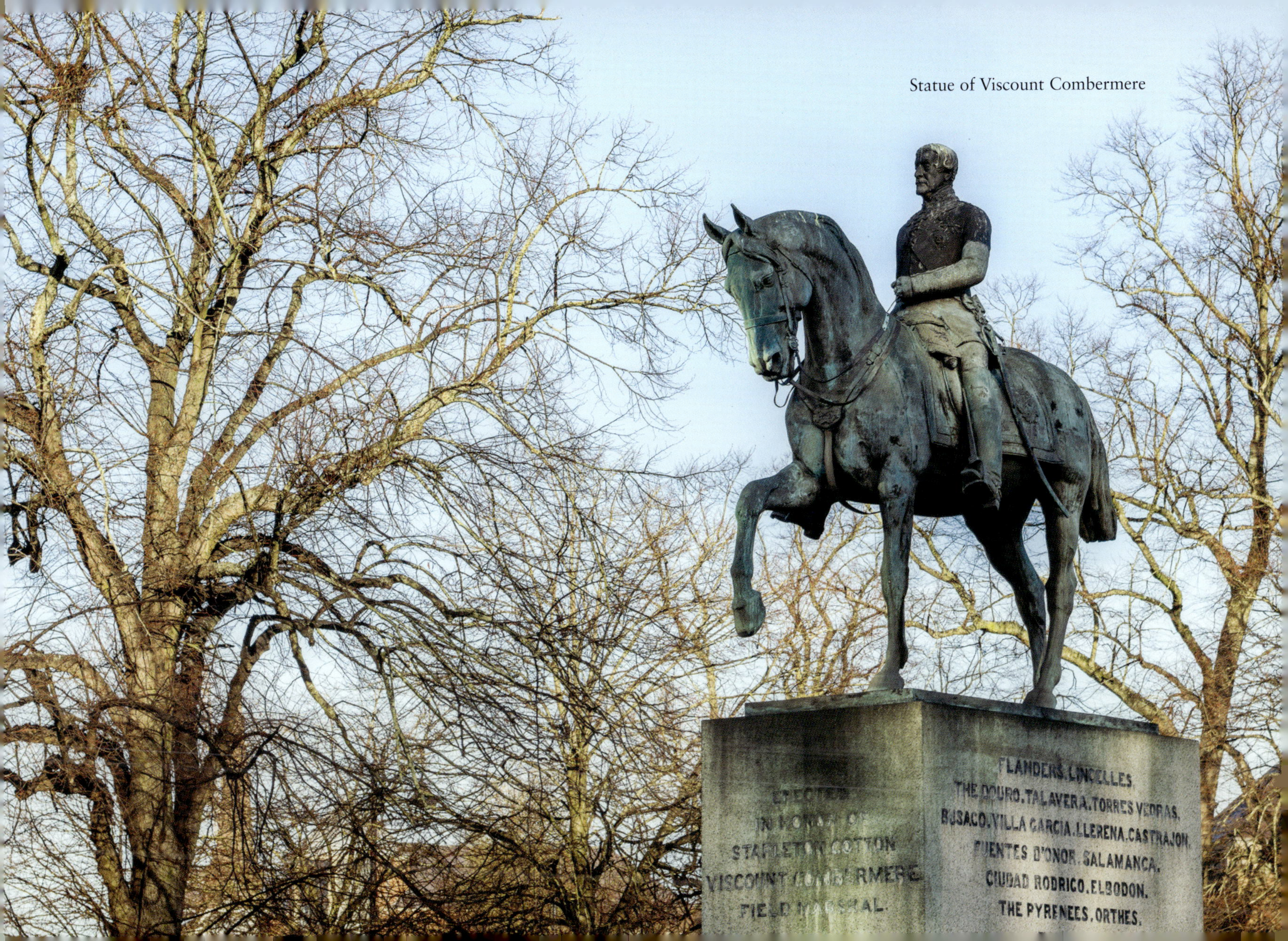

Statue of Viscount Combermere

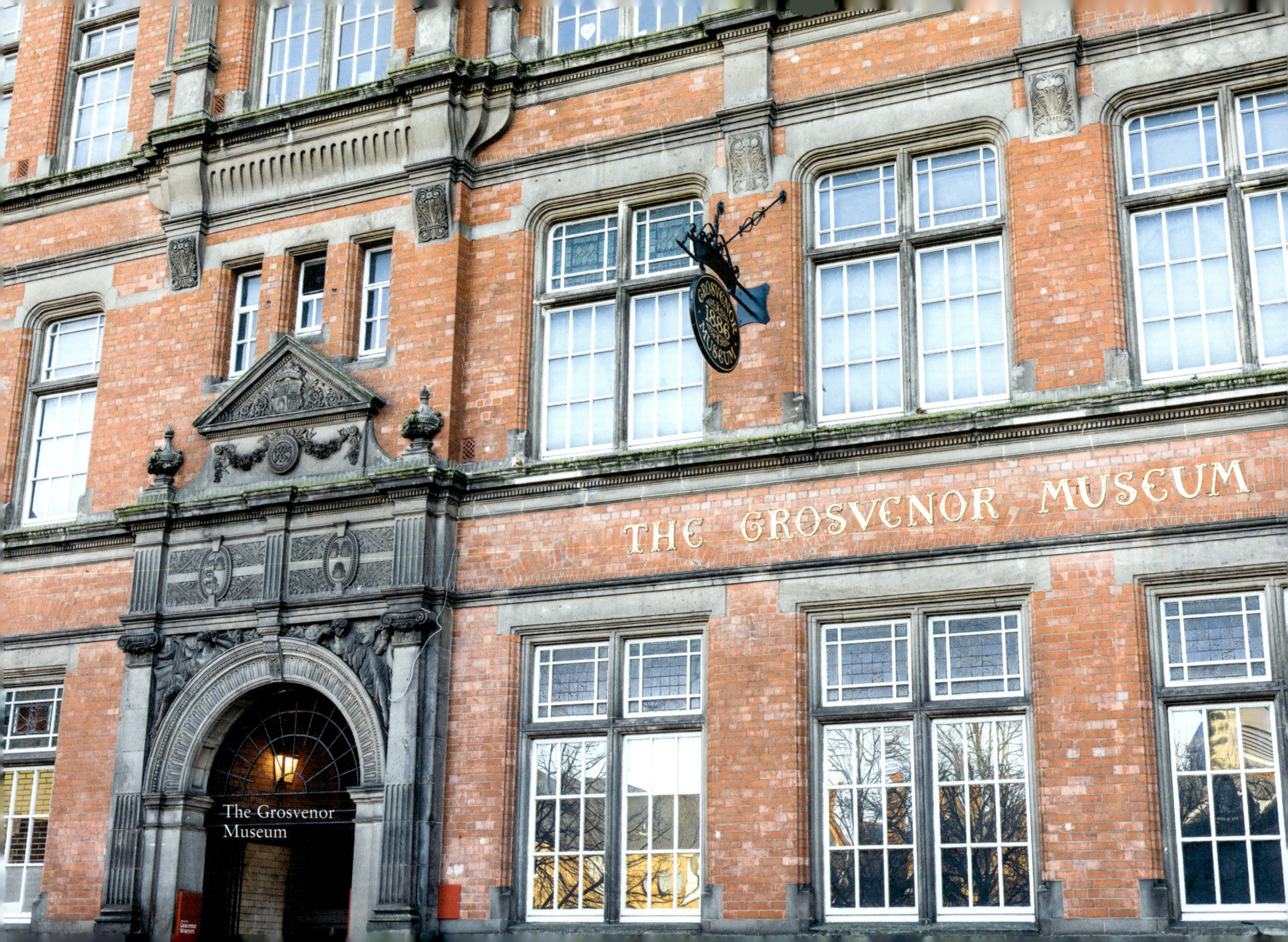
GROSVENOR
1886
MUSEUM
THE GROSVENOR MUSEUM
The Grosvenor
Museum

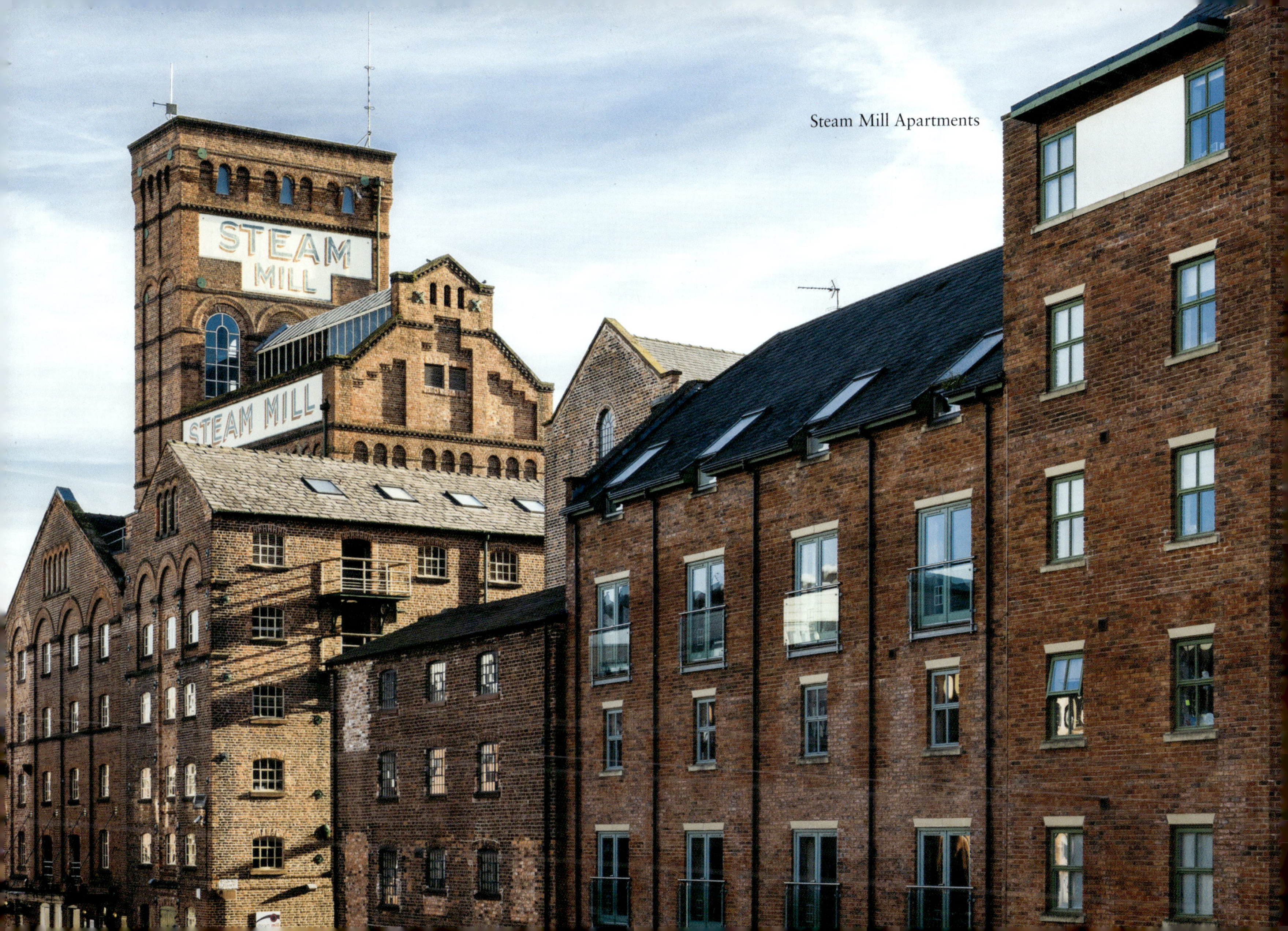

Steam Mill Apartments

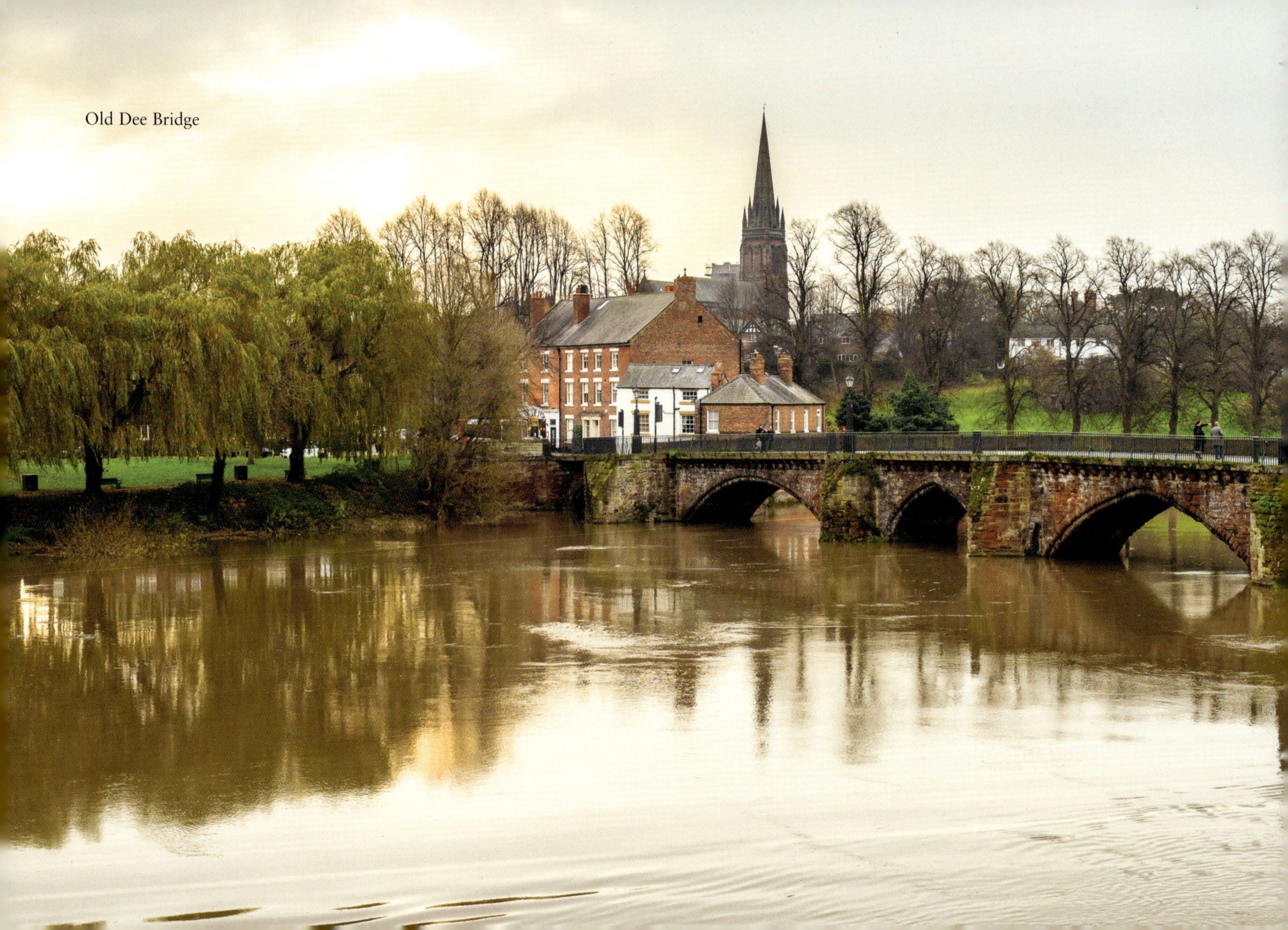
Old Dee Bridge

CHESHIRE TOWNS AND VILLAGES

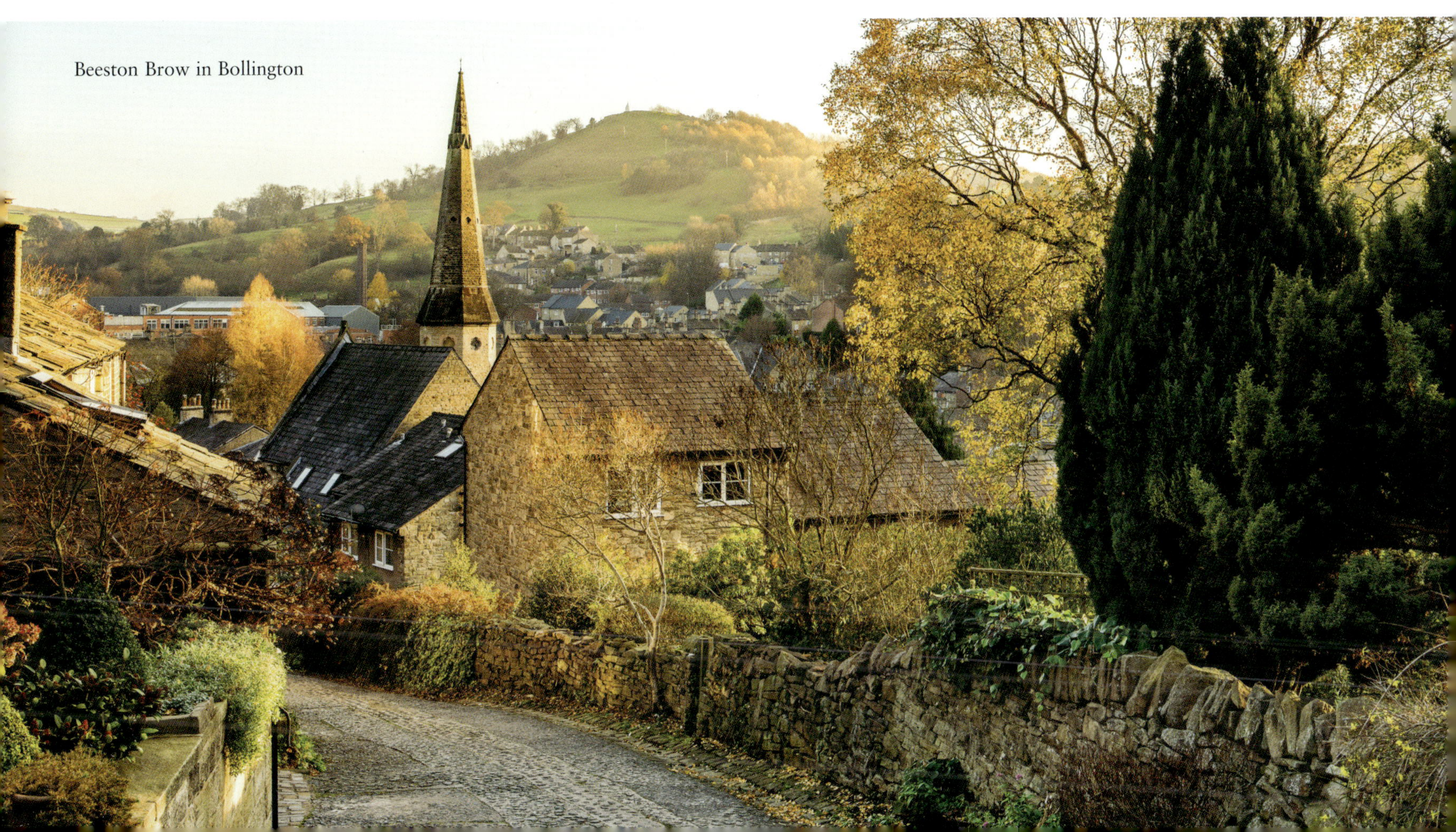

Beeston Brow in Bollington

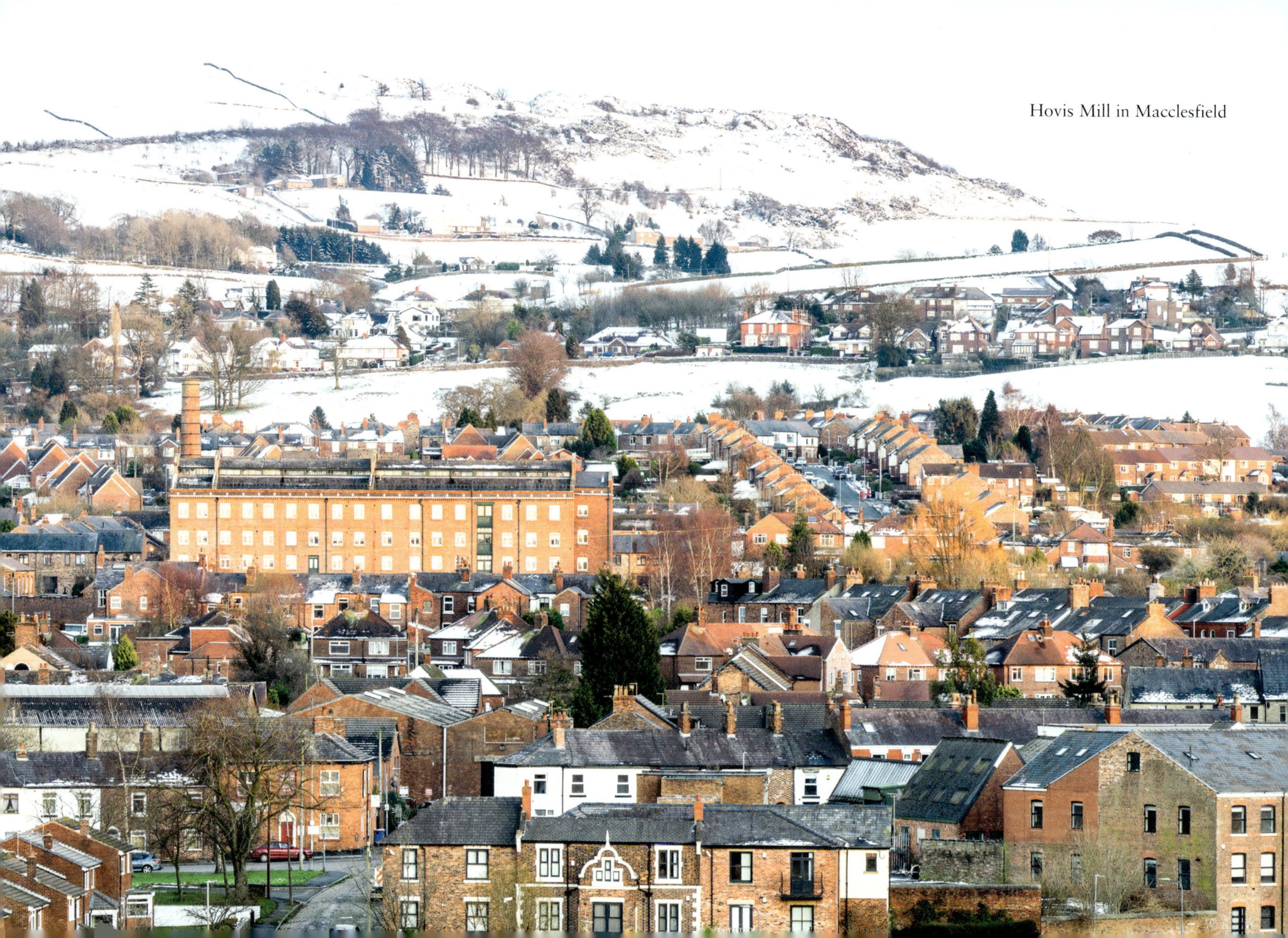

Hovis Mill in Macclesfield

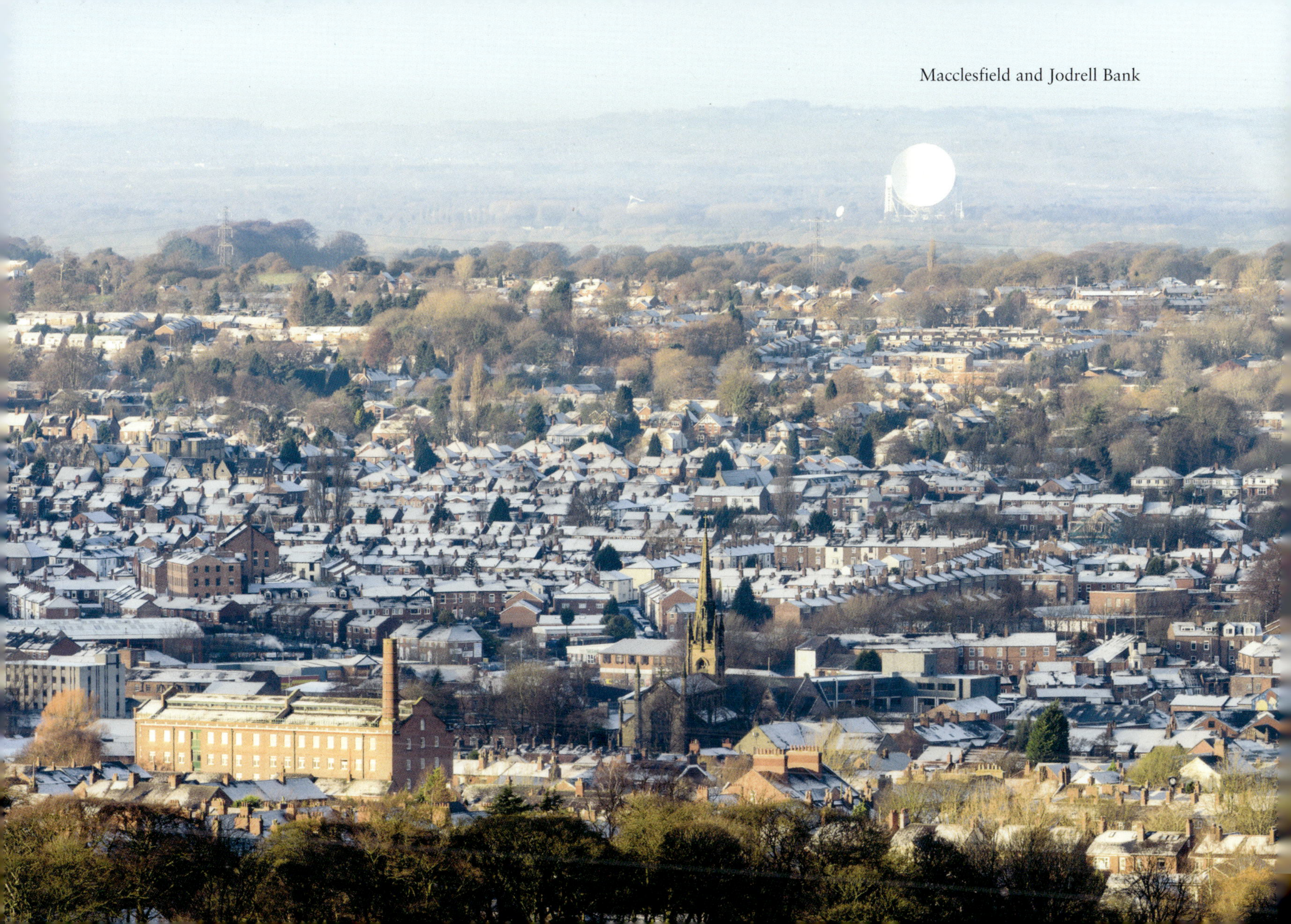

Macclesfield and Jodrell Bank

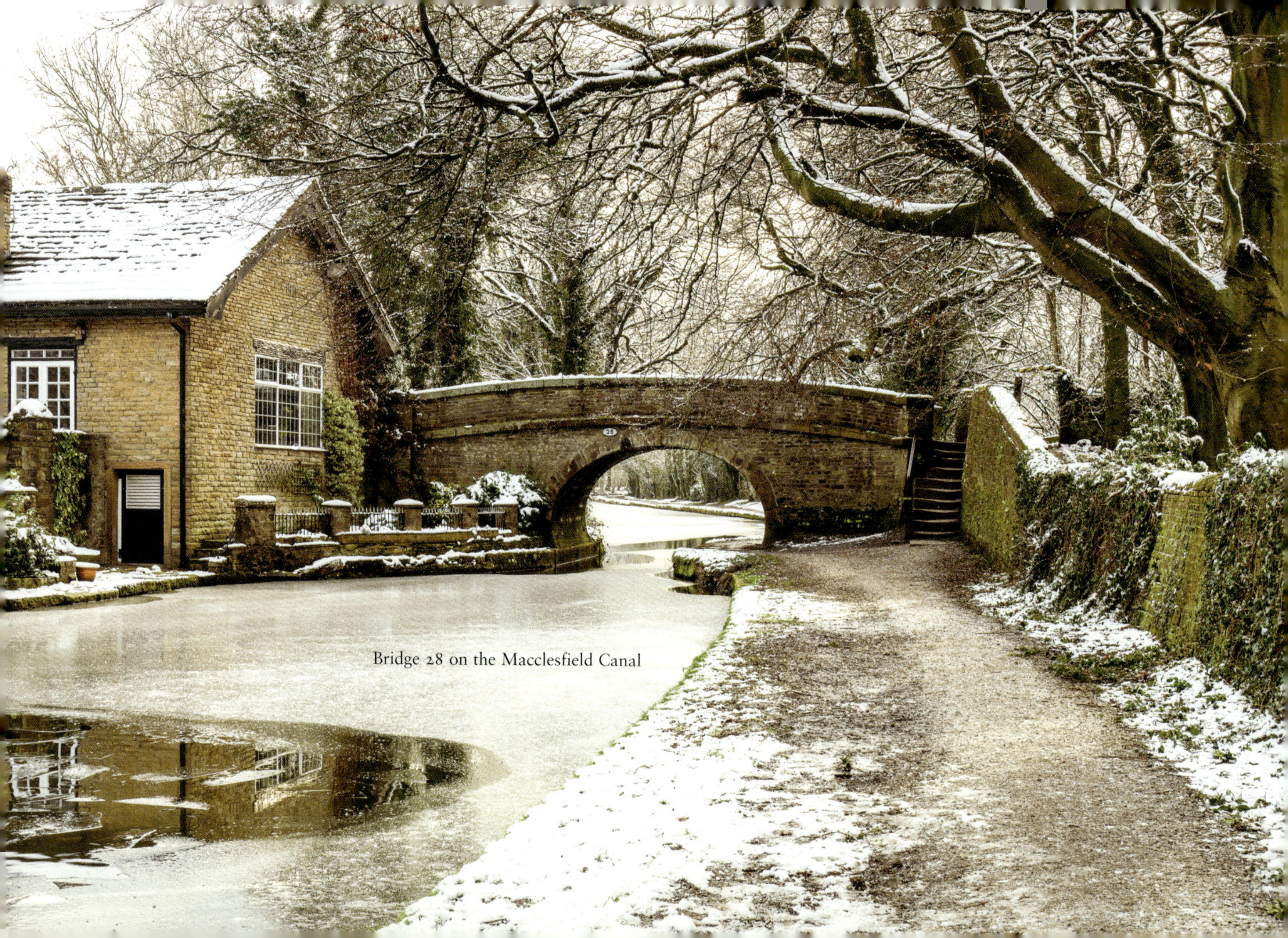

Bridge 28 on the Macclesfield Canal

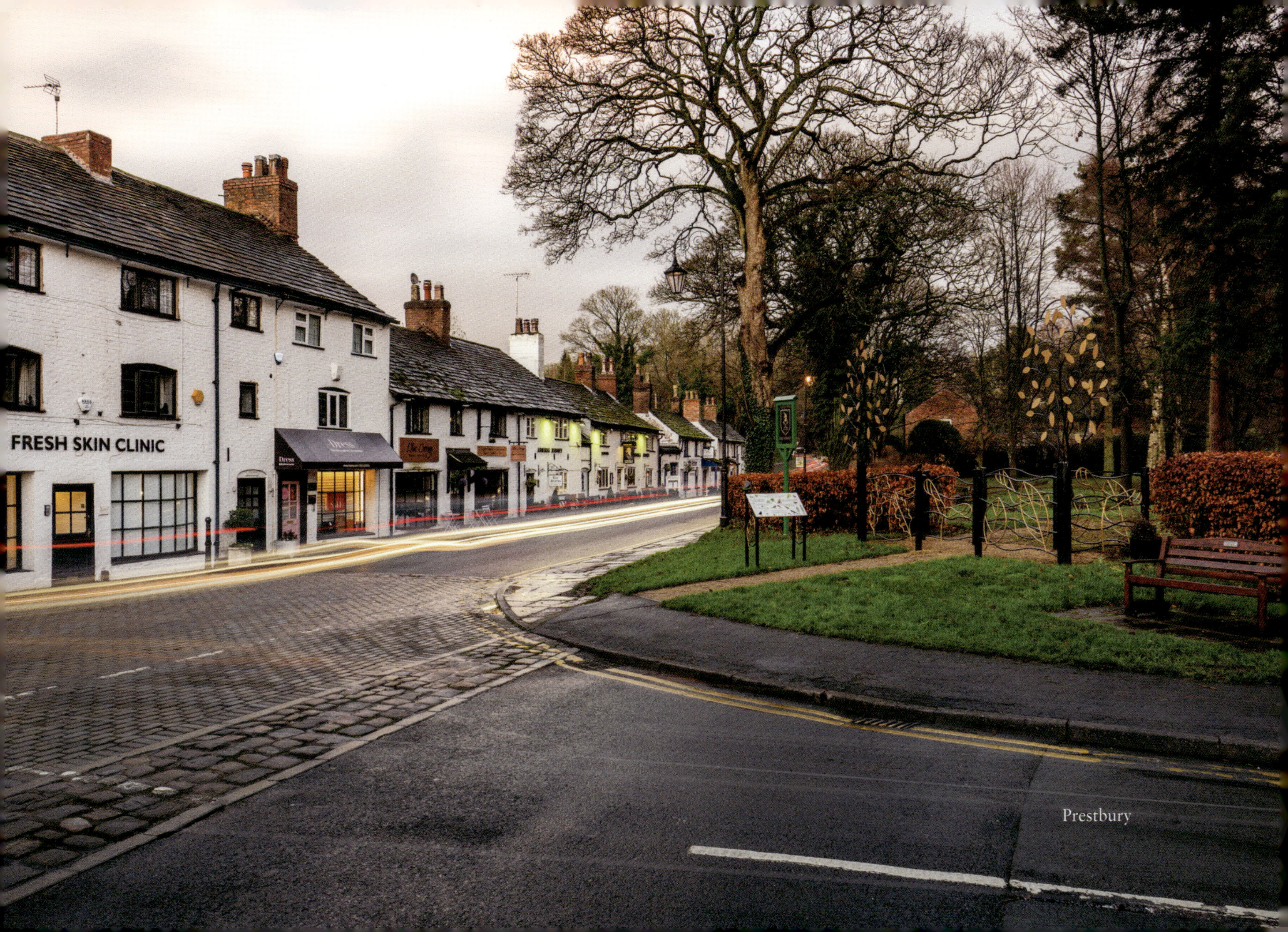

Prestbury

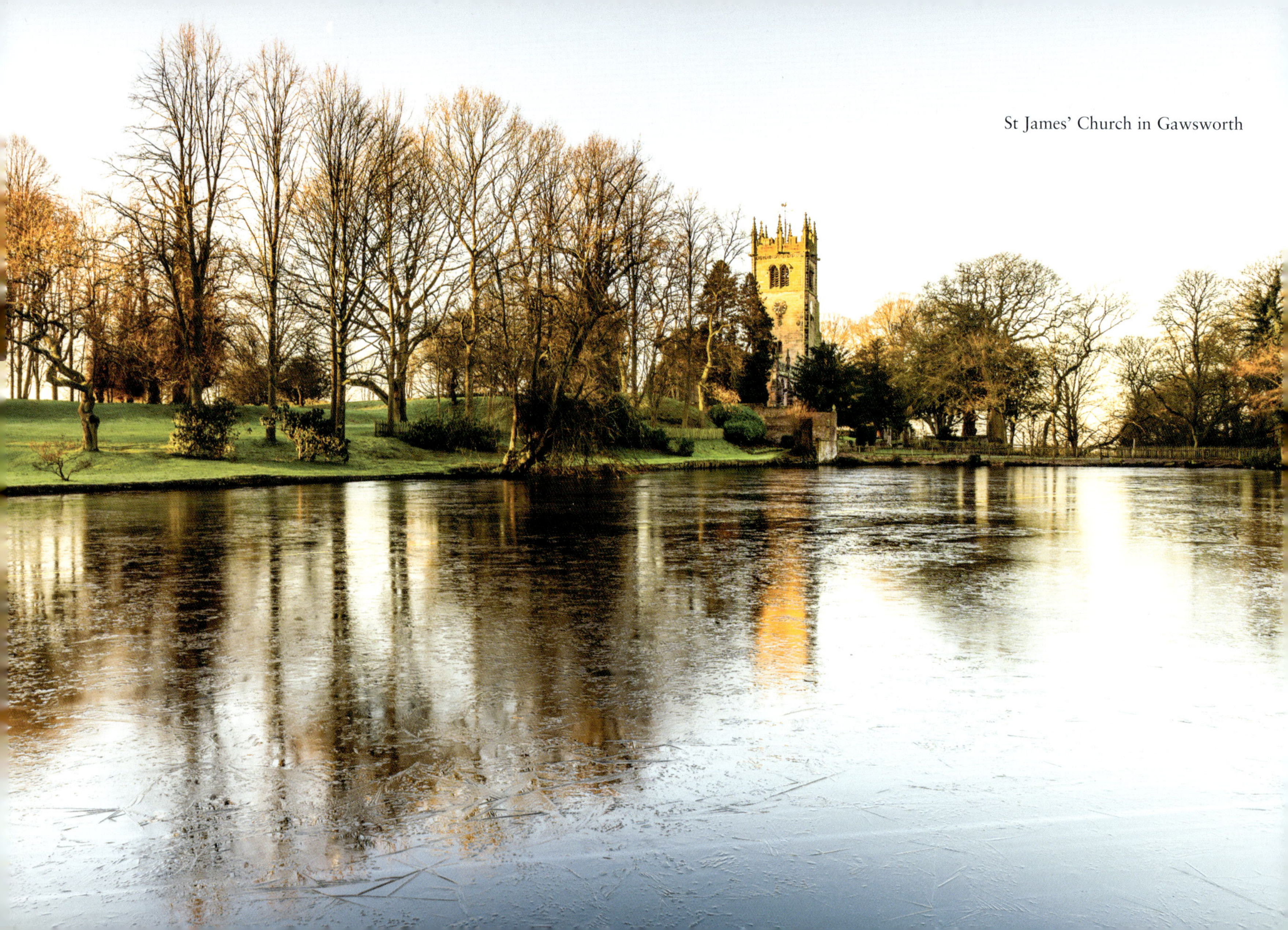

St James' Church in Gawsworth

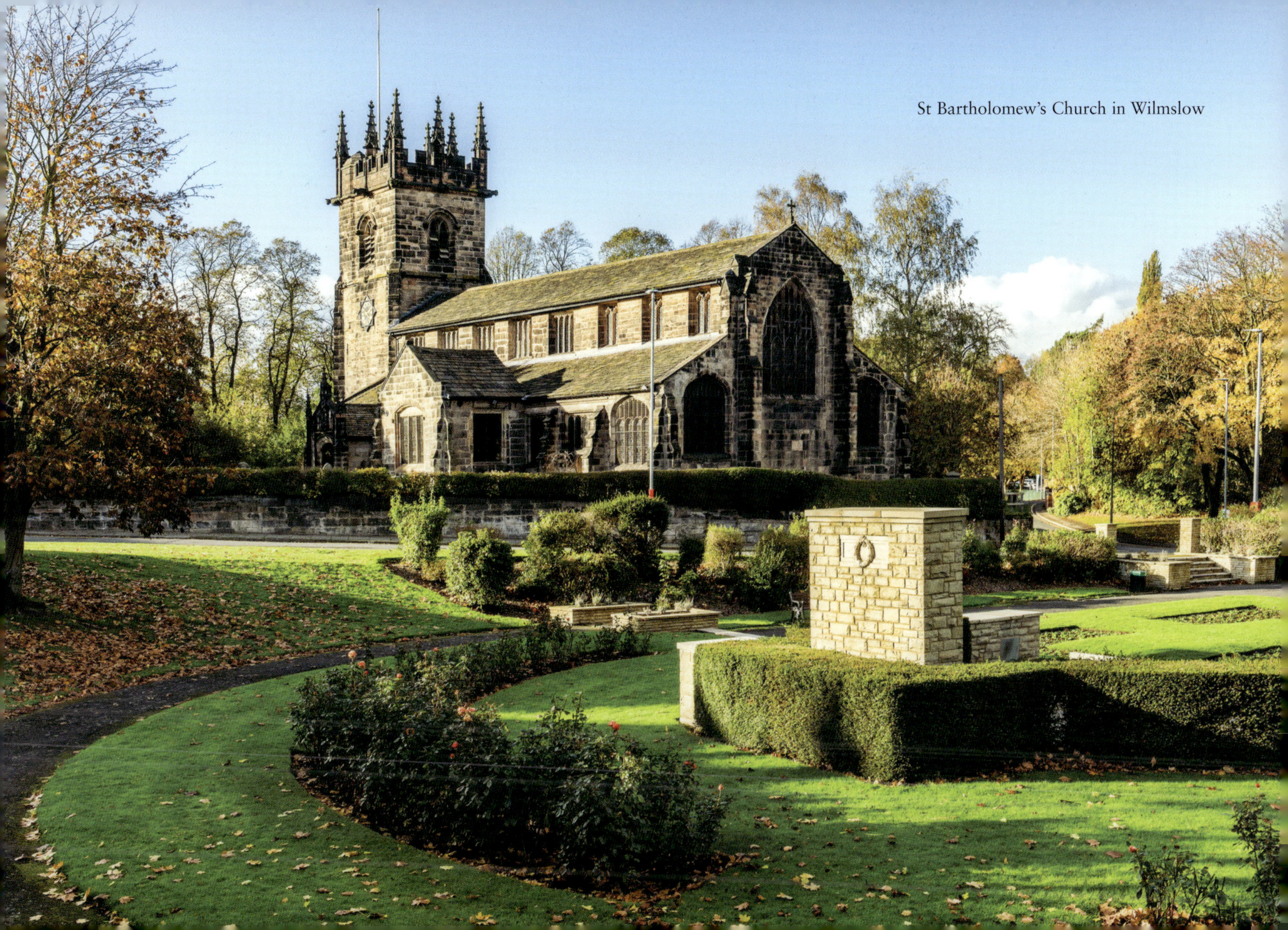

St Bartholomew's Church in Wilmslow

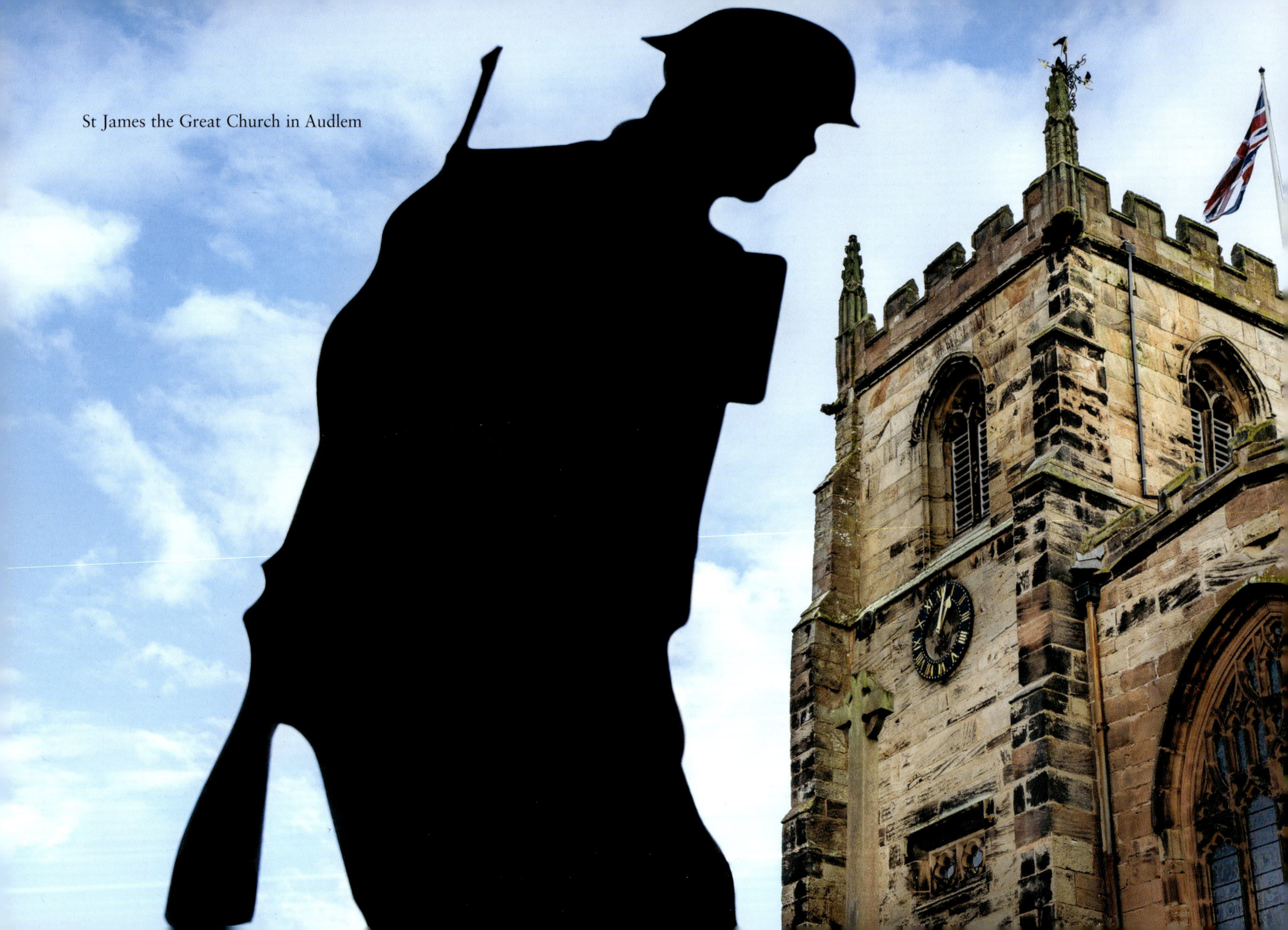

St James the Great Church in Audlem

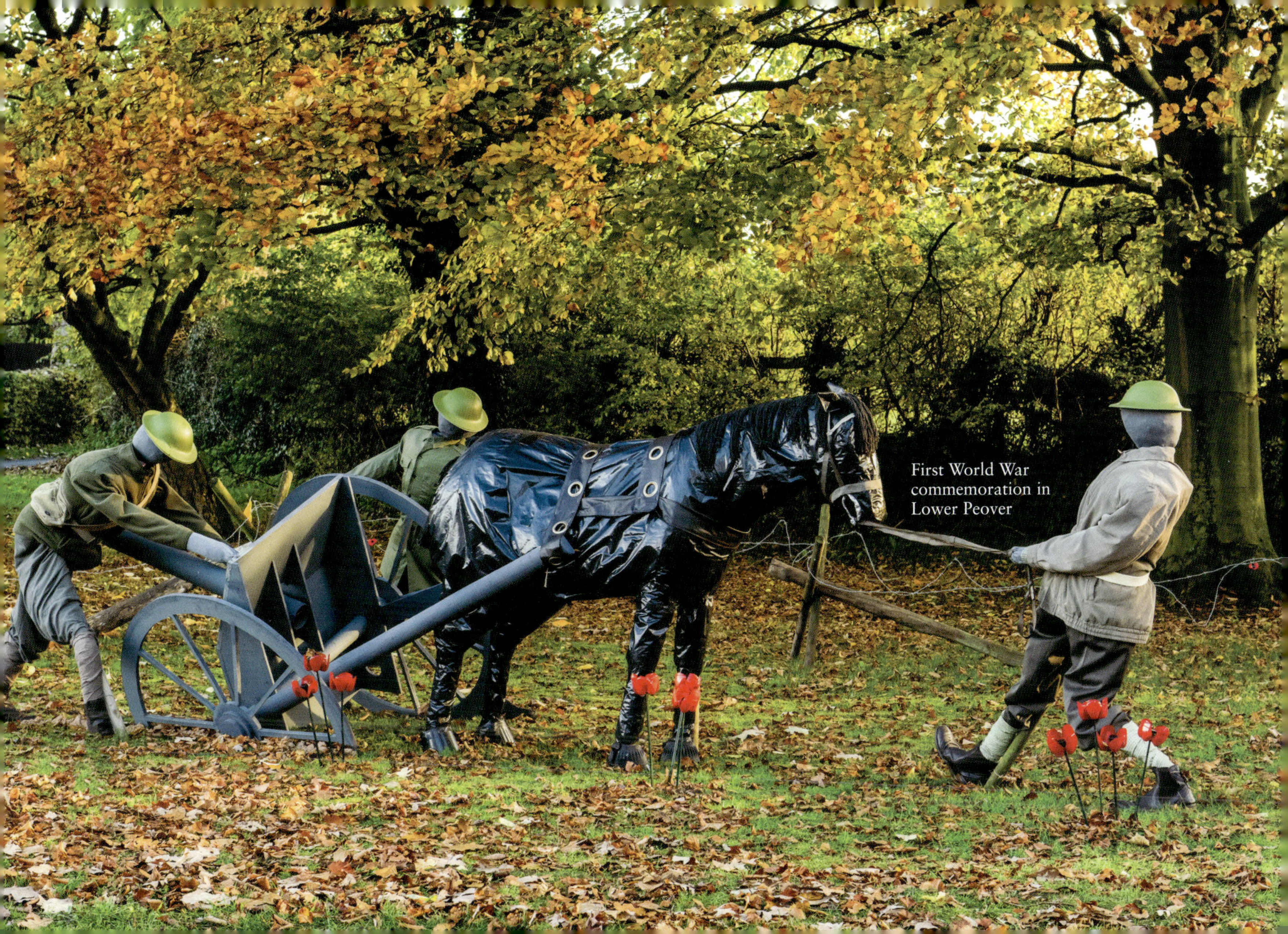

First World War commemoration in Lower Peover

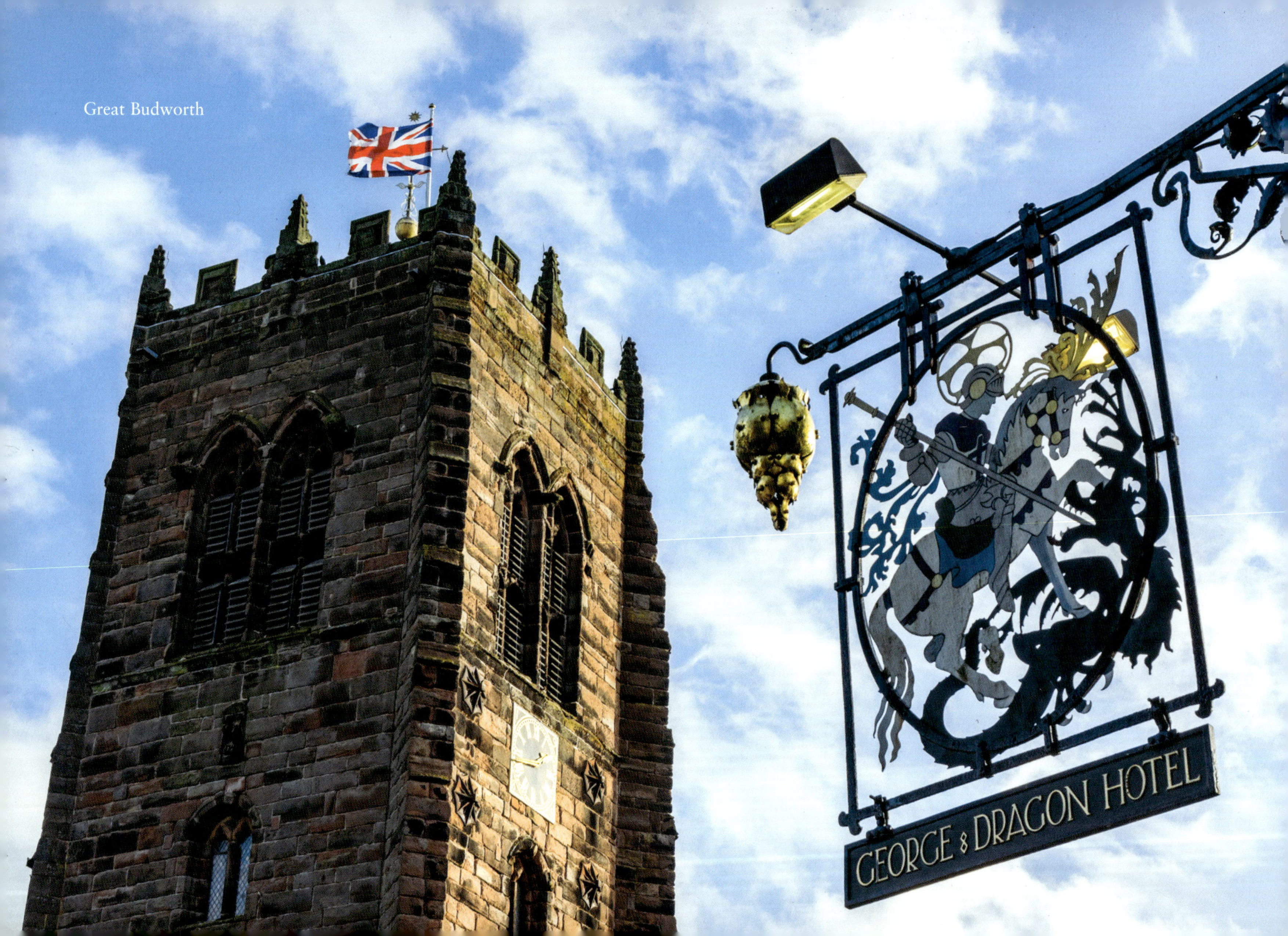

Great Budworth

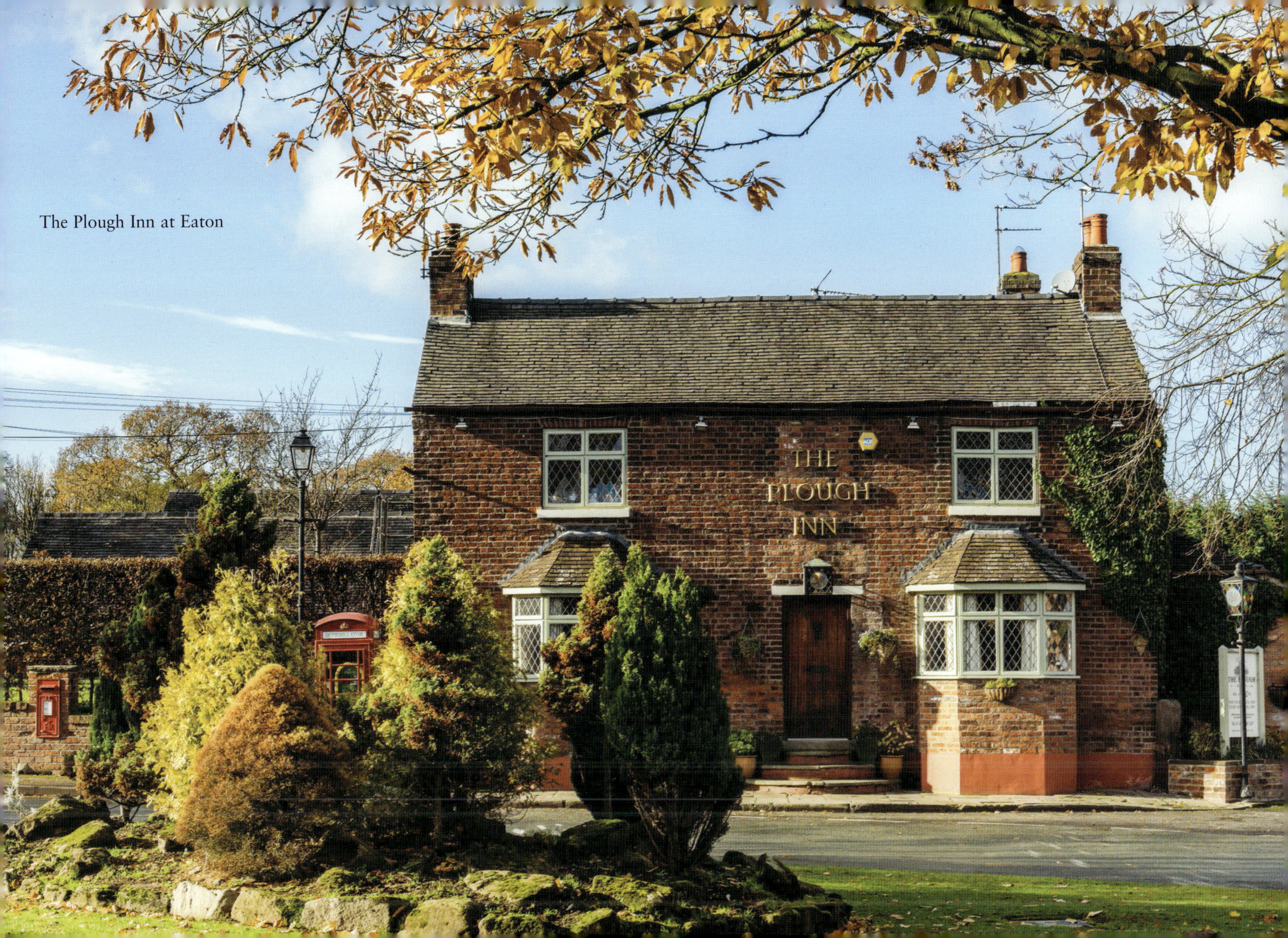

The Plough Inn at Eaton

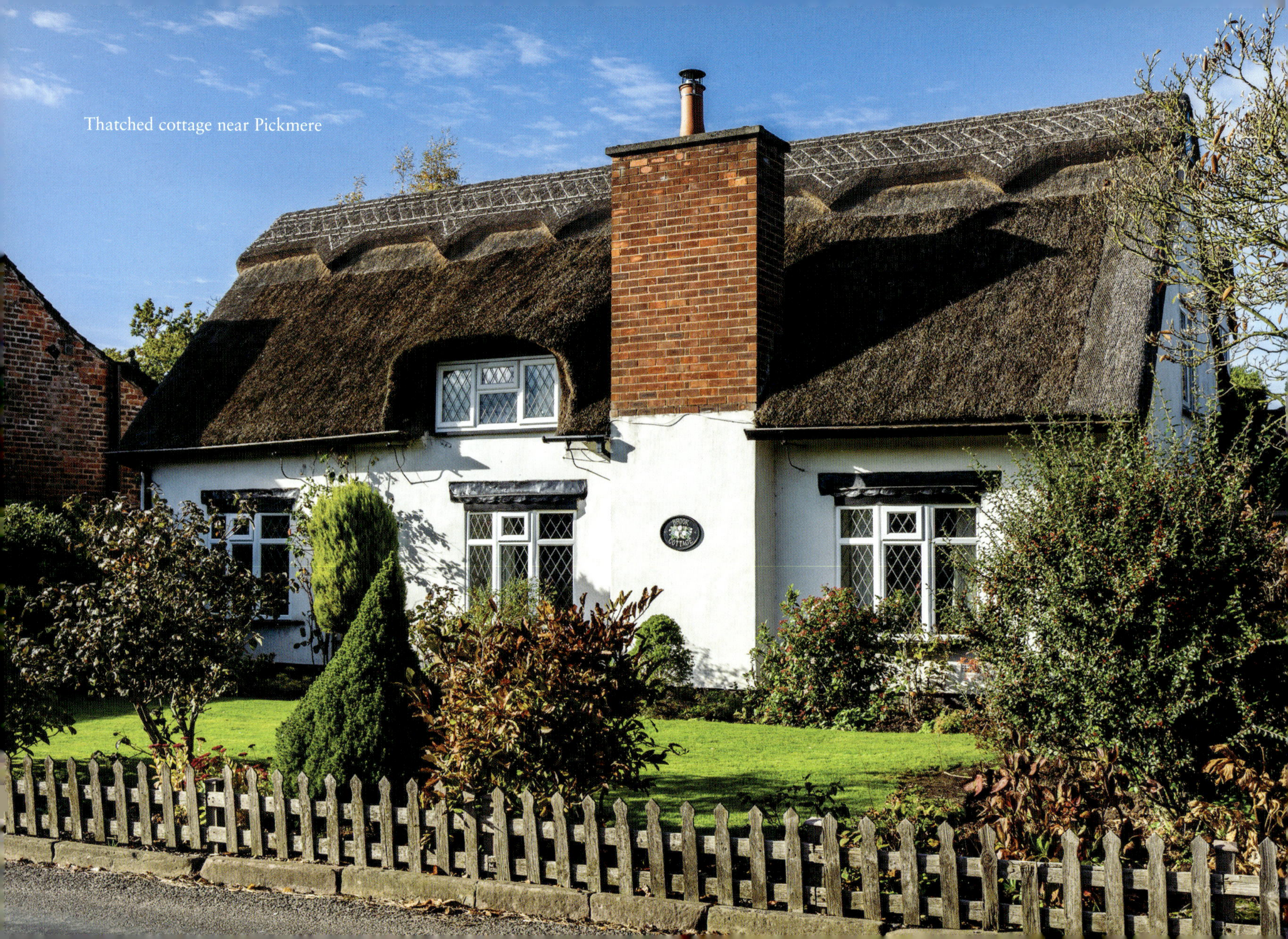

Thatched cottage near Pickmere

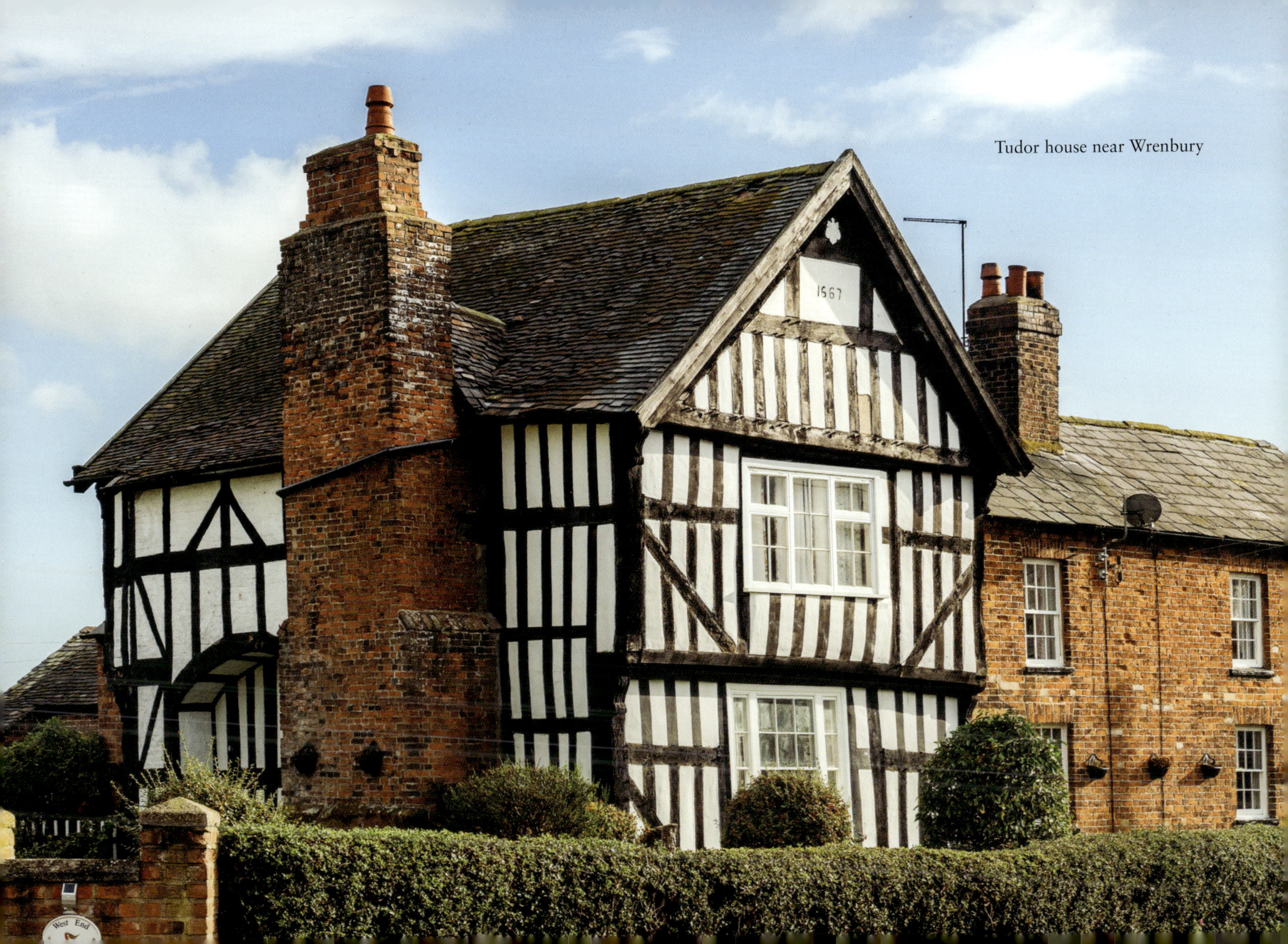

Tudor house near Wrenbury

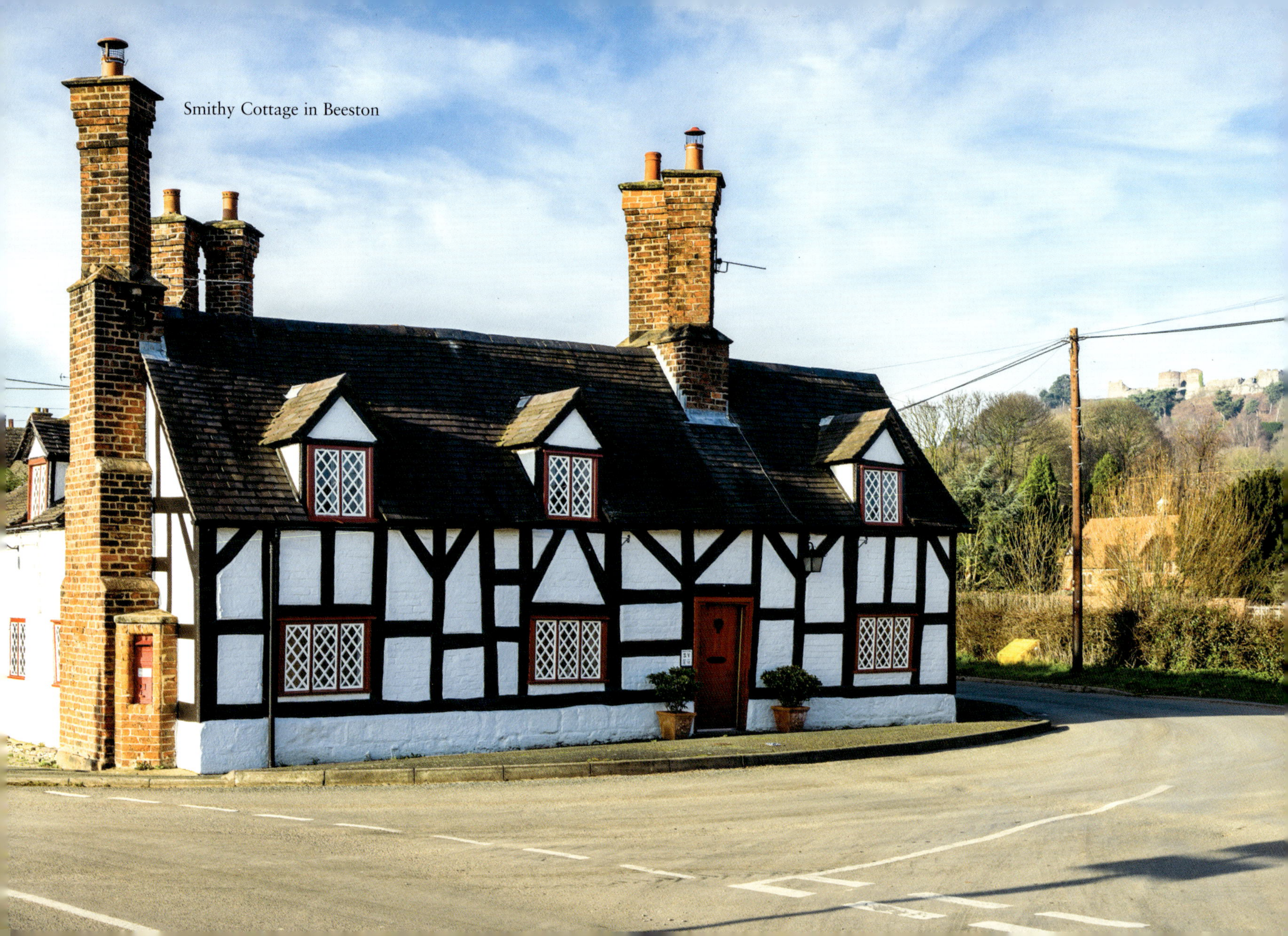

Smithy Cottage in Beeston

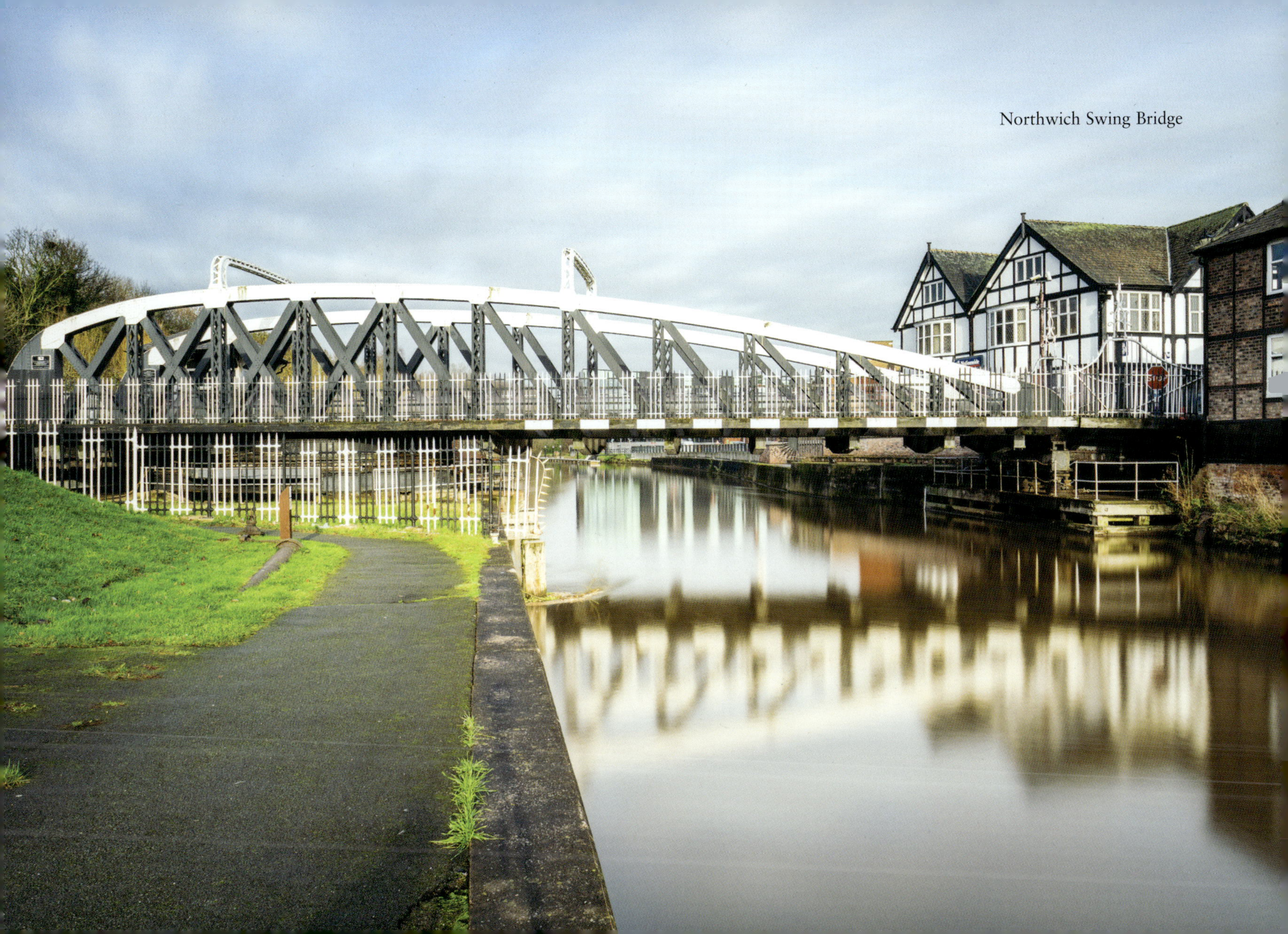

Northwich Swing Bridge

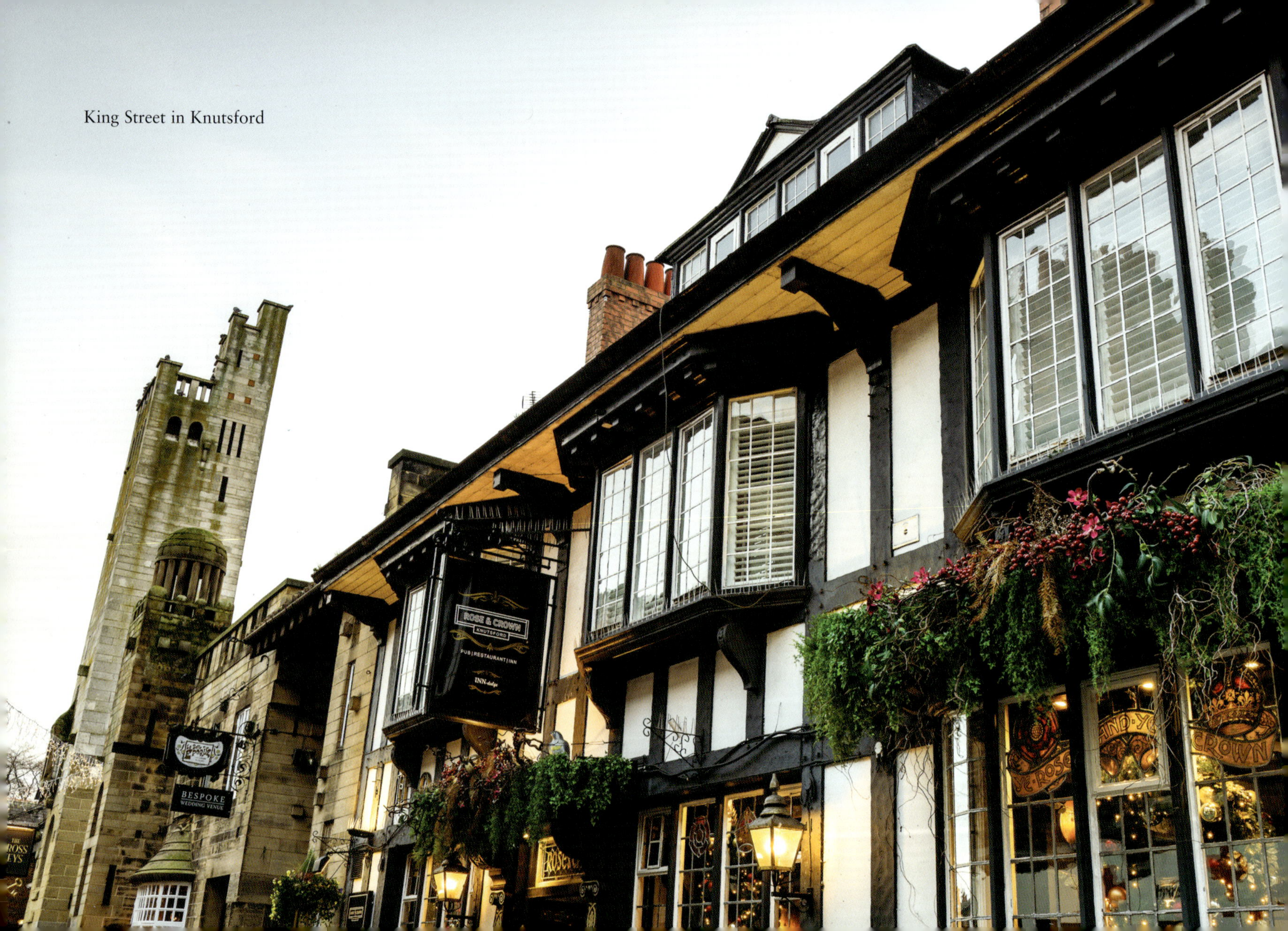

King Street in Knutsford

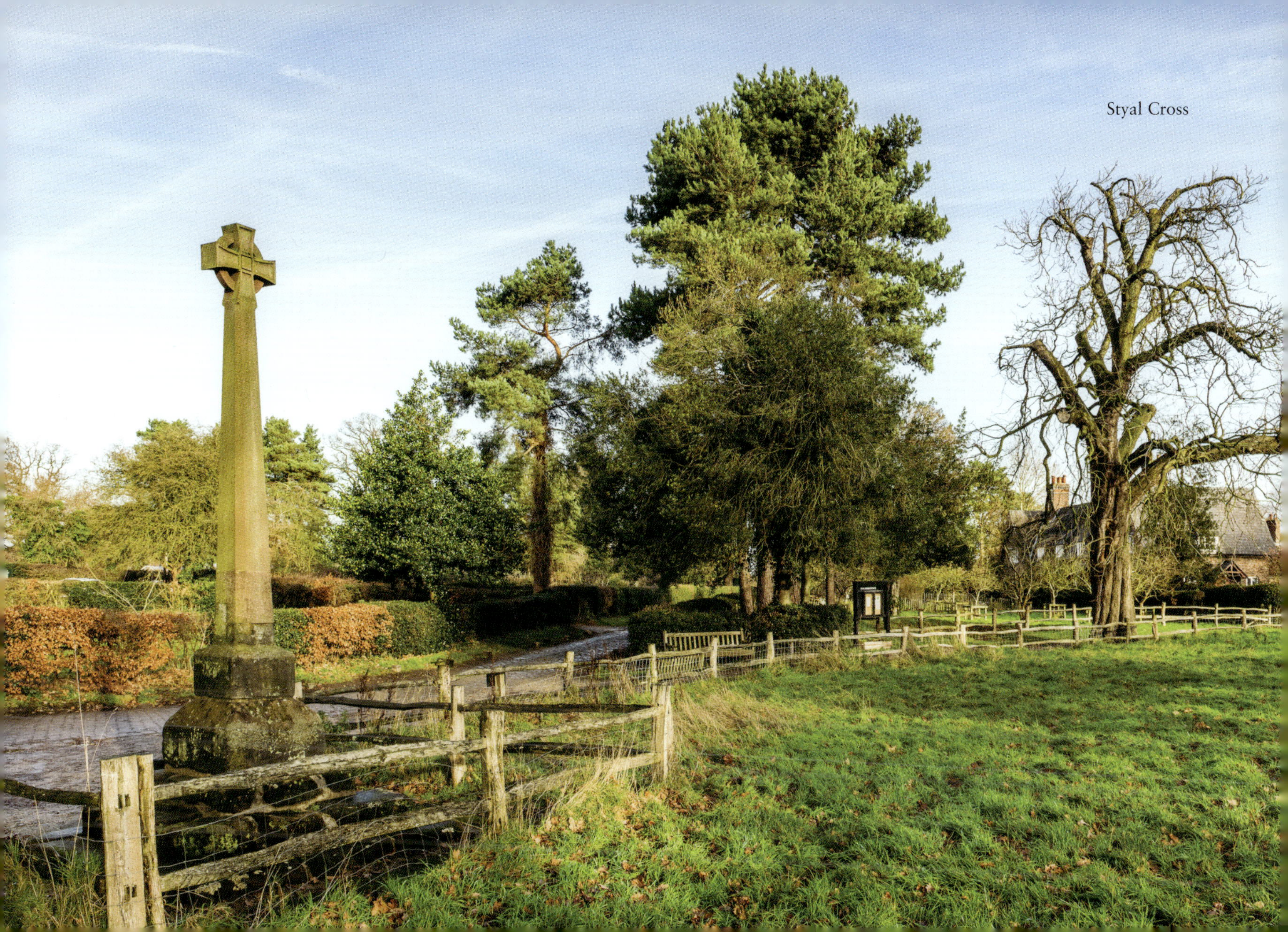

Styal Cross

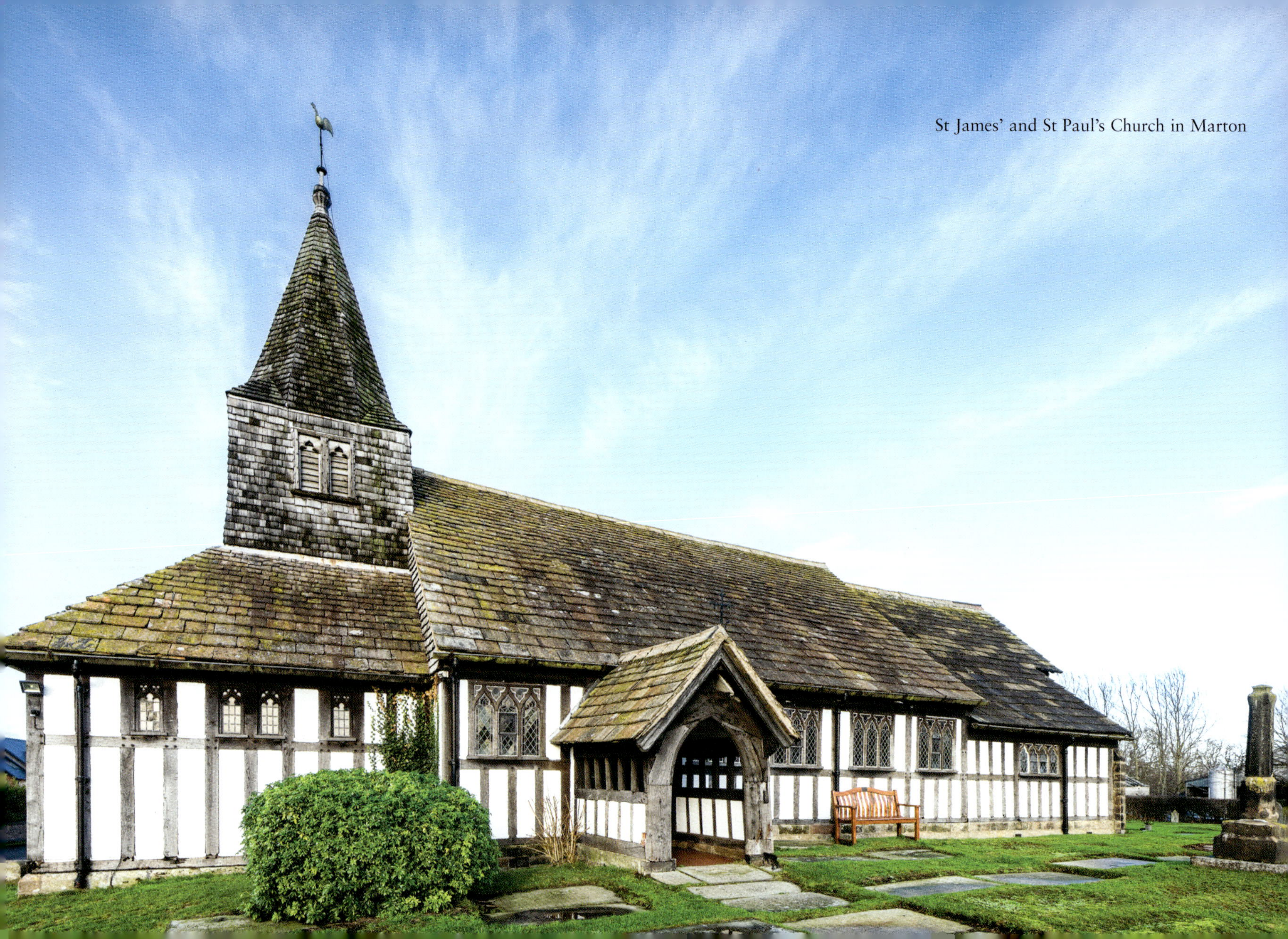

St James' and St Paul's Church in Marton

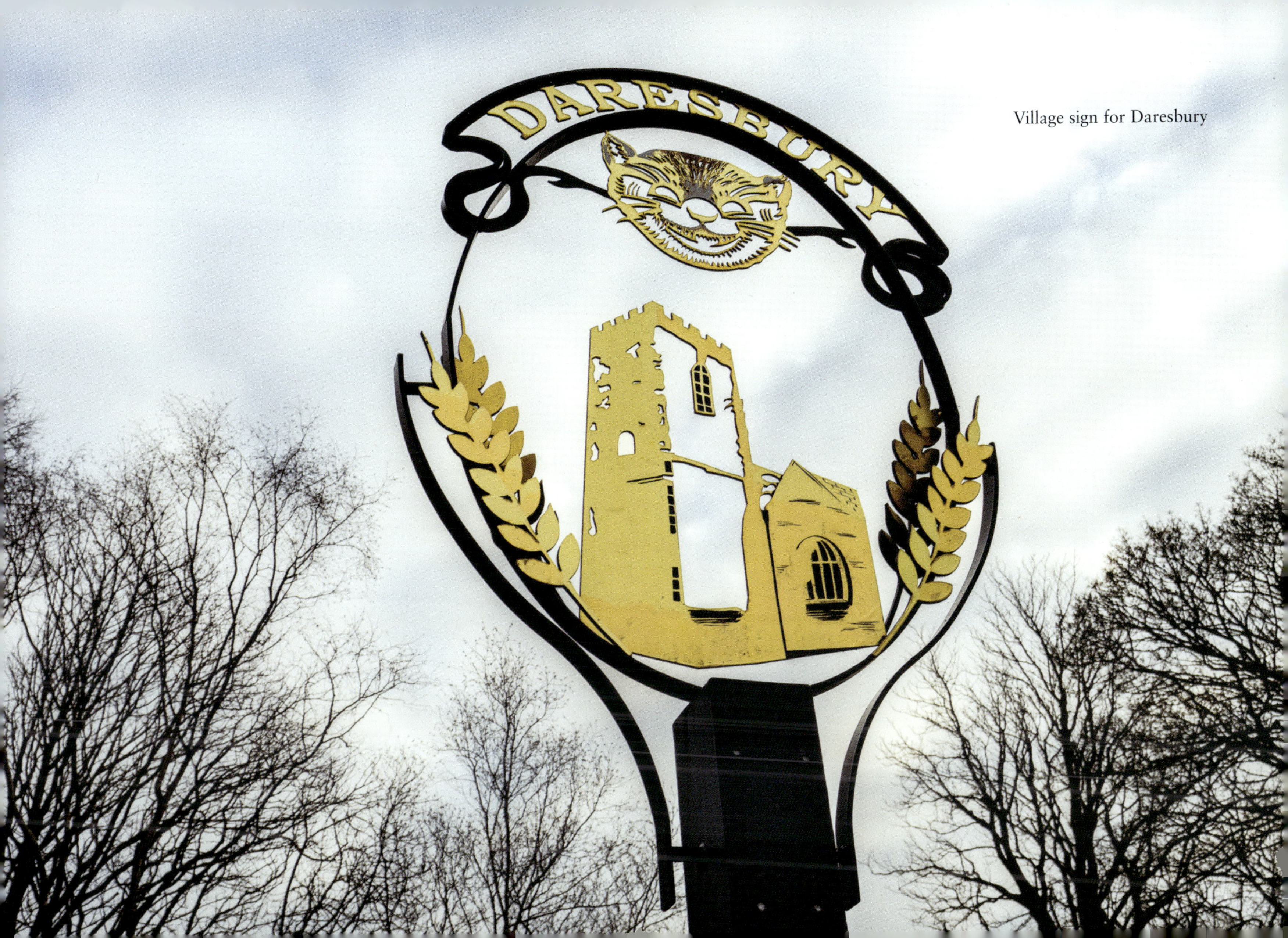

Village sign for Daresbury

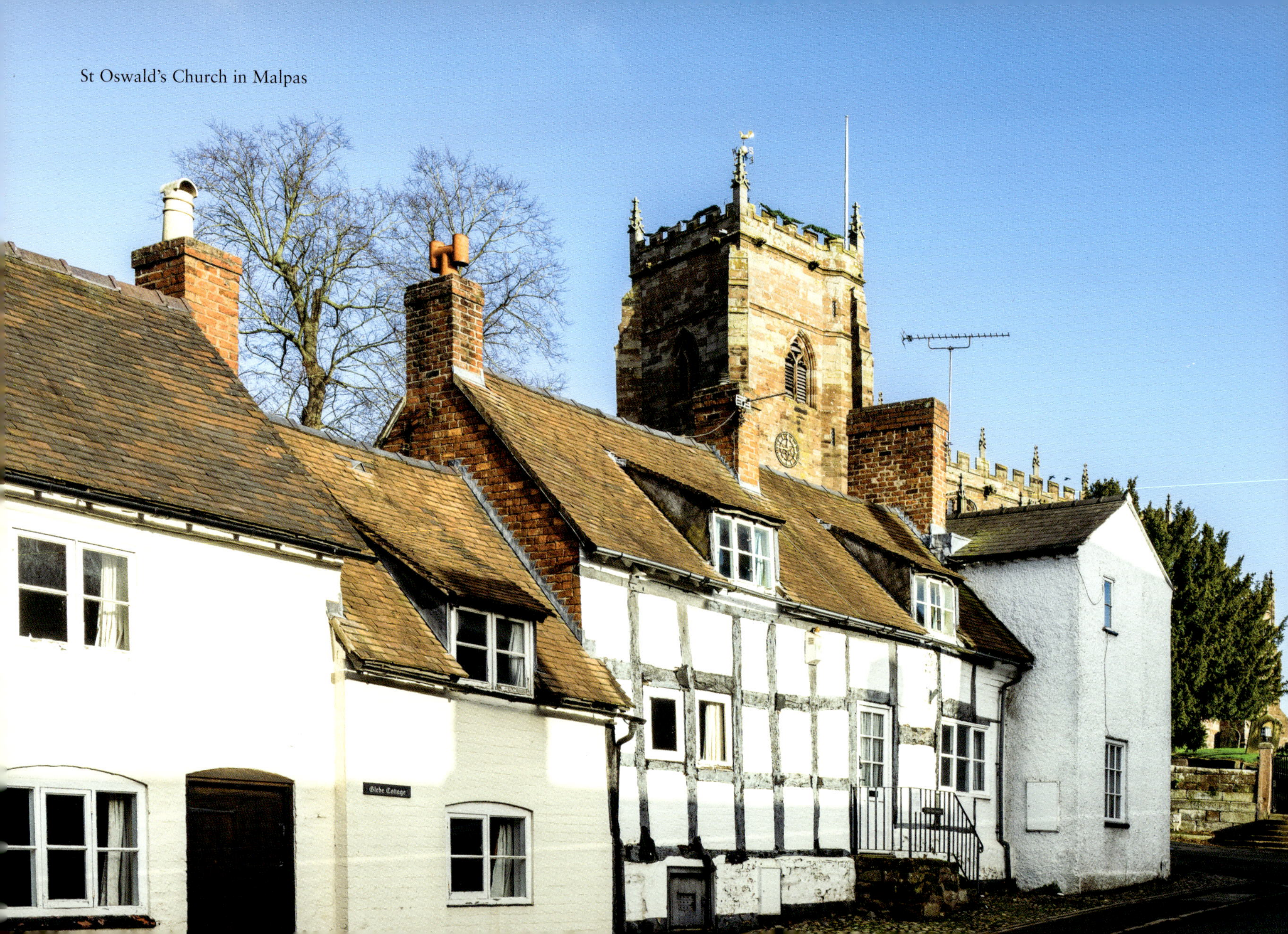

St Oswald's Church in Malpas

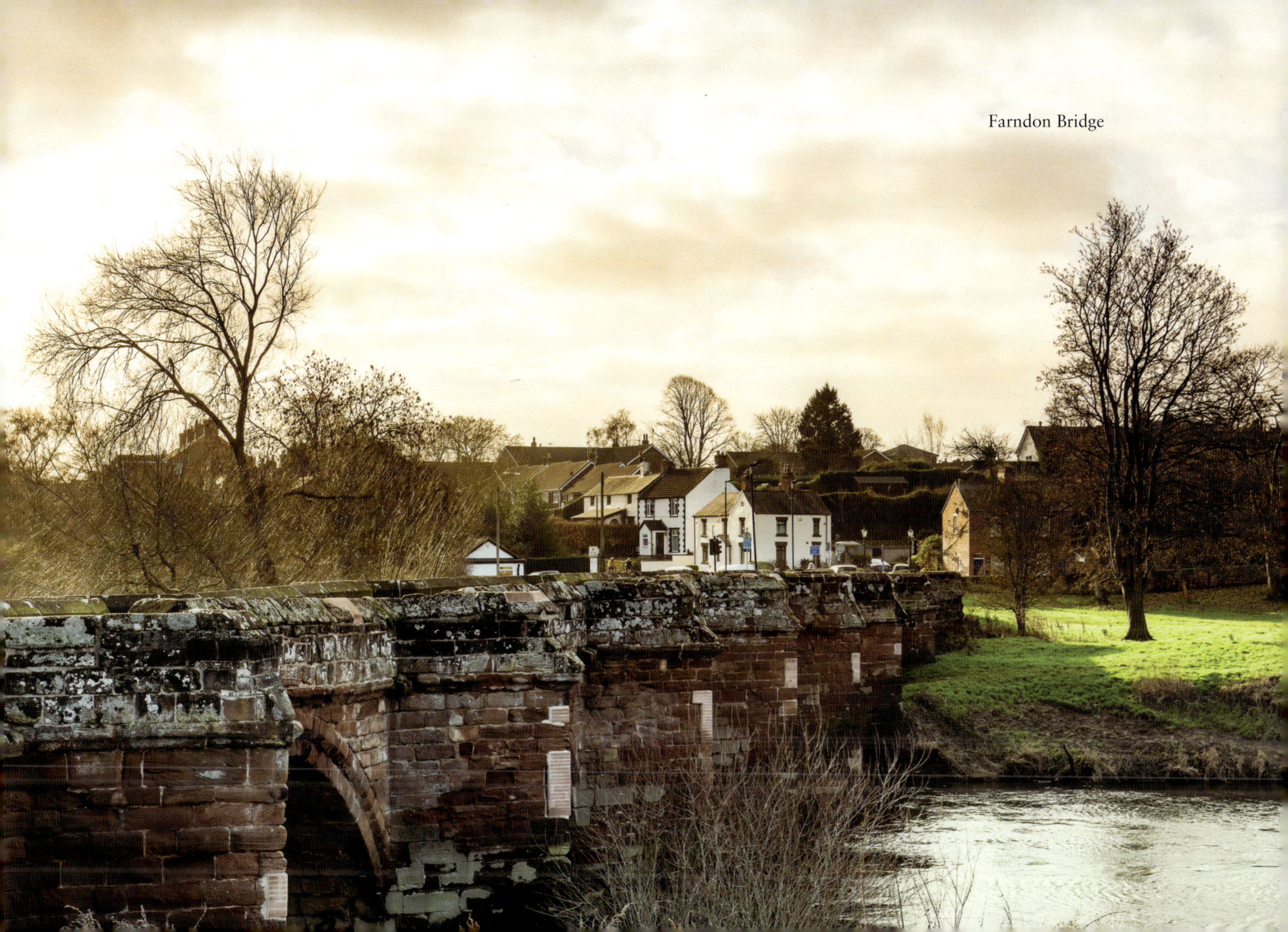

Farndon Bridge

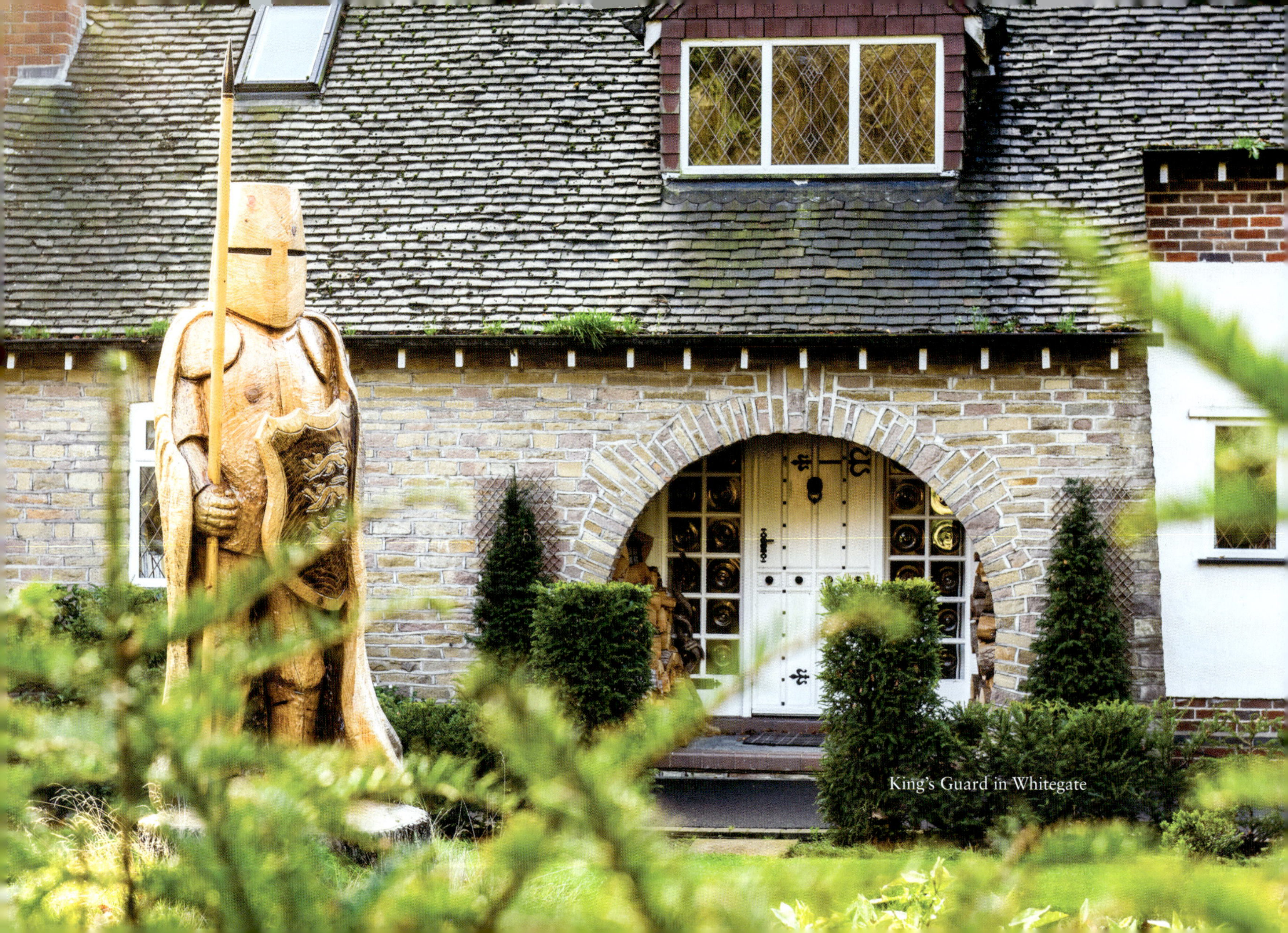

King's Guard in Whitegate

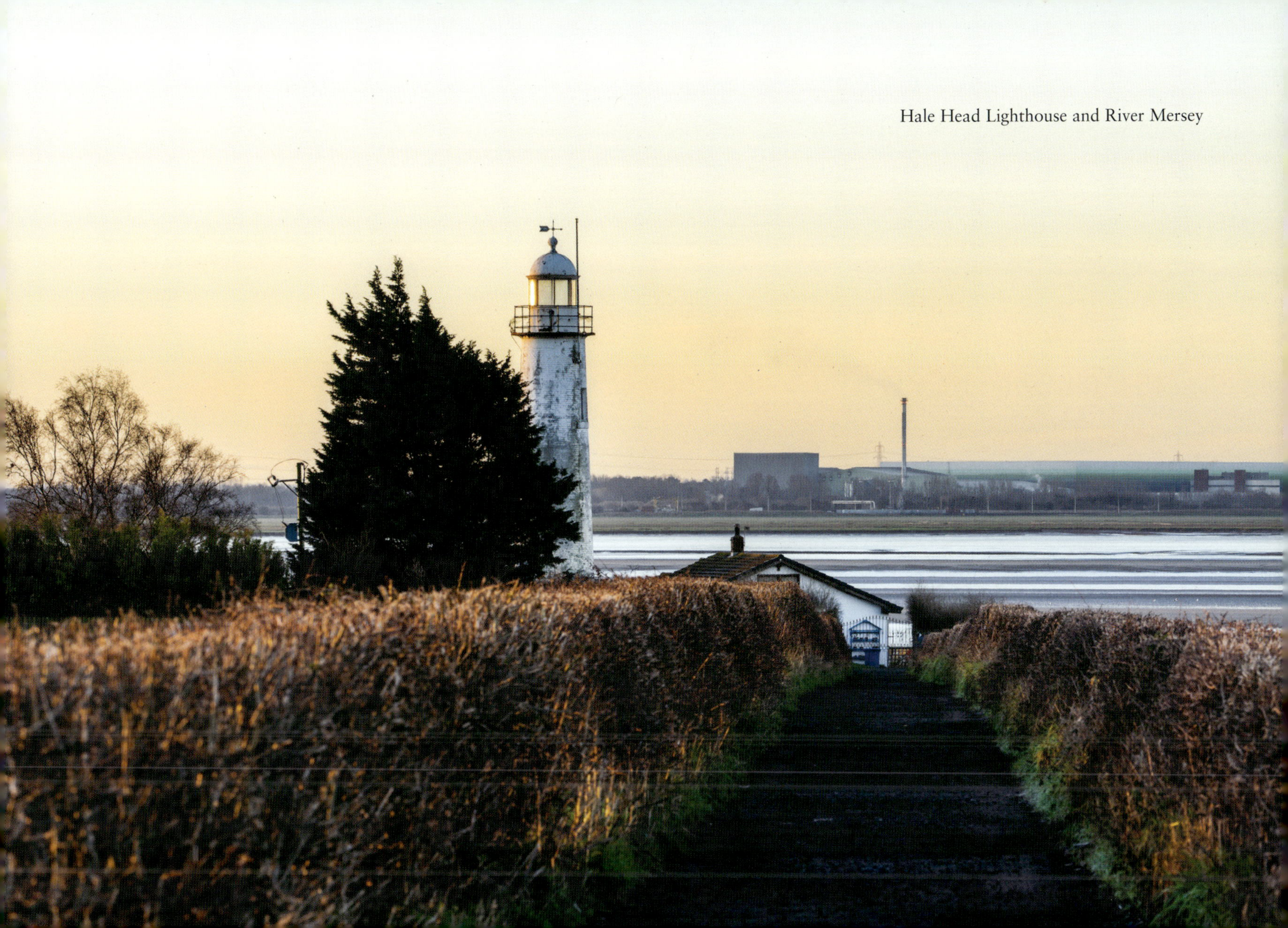

Hale Head Lighthouse and River Mersey

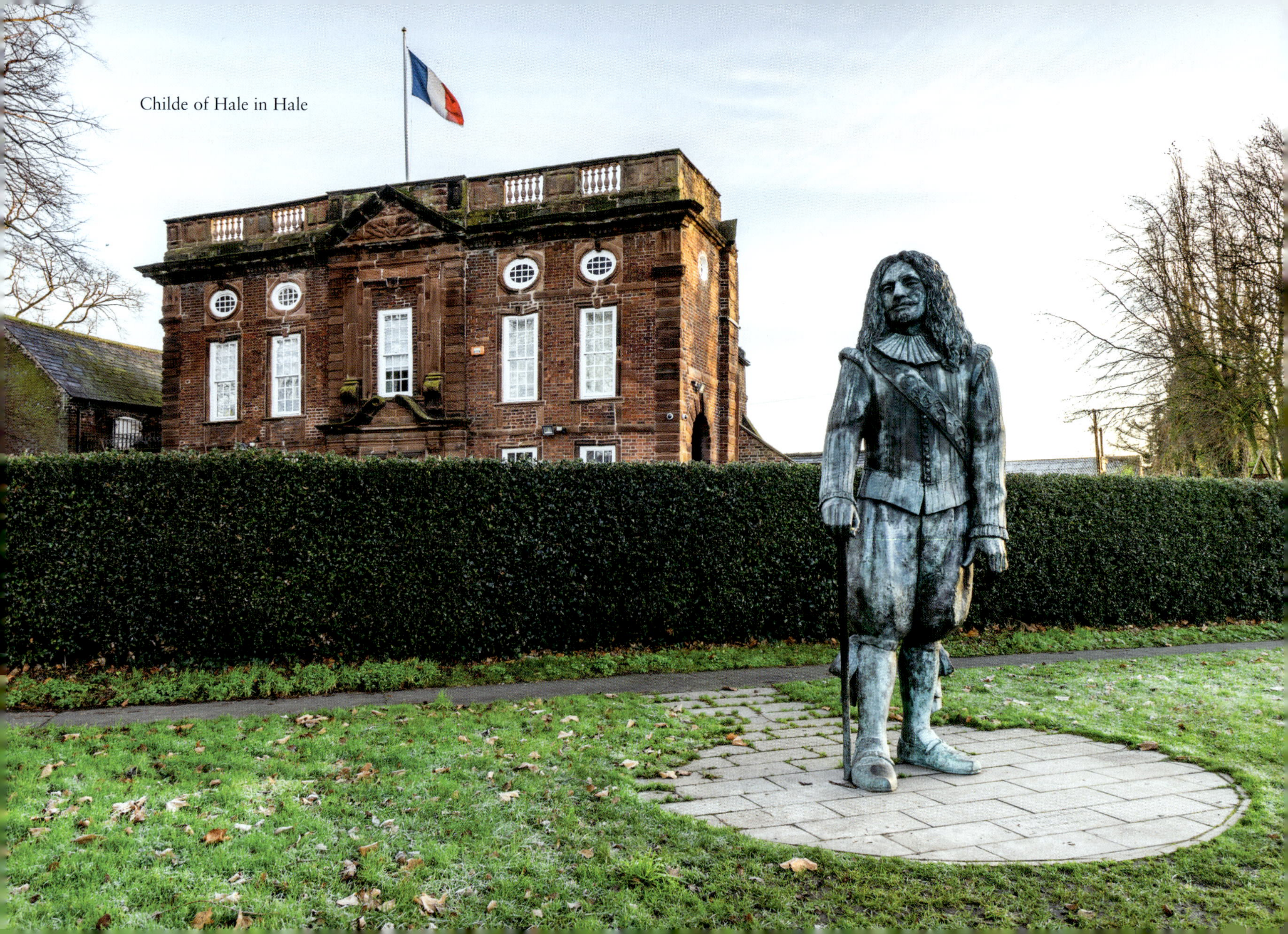

Childe of Hale in Hale

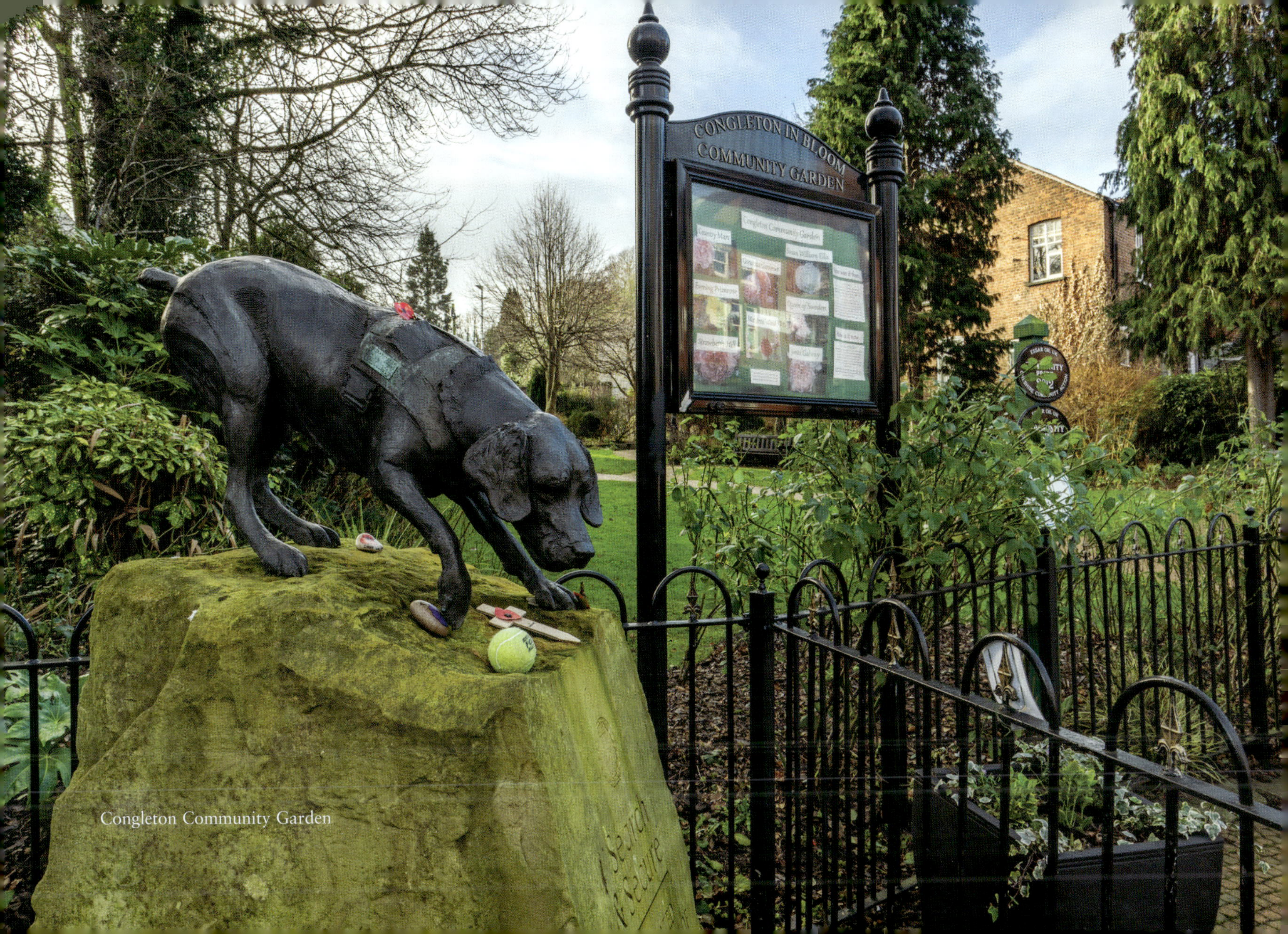

Congleton Community Garden

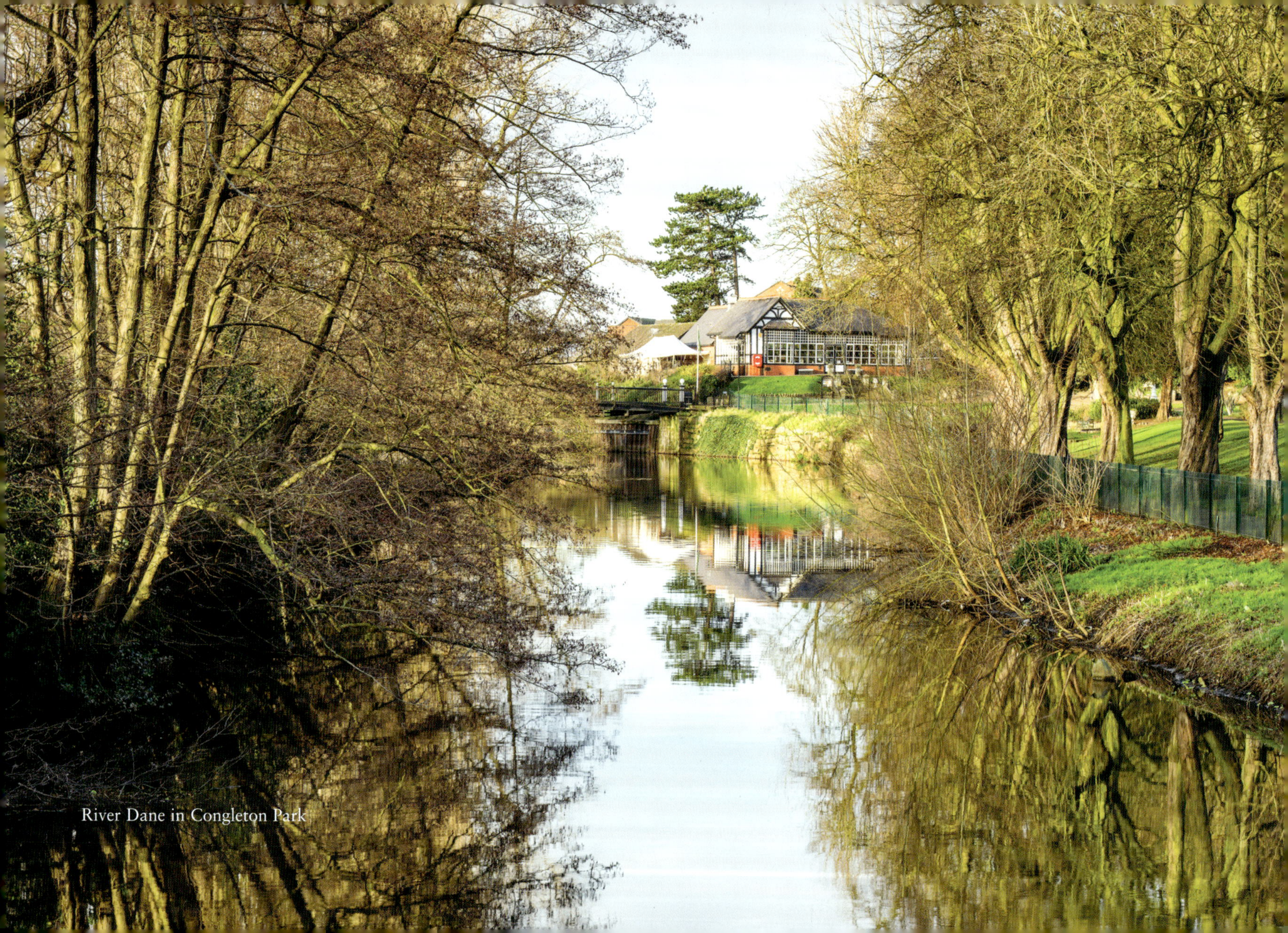

River Dane in Congleton Park

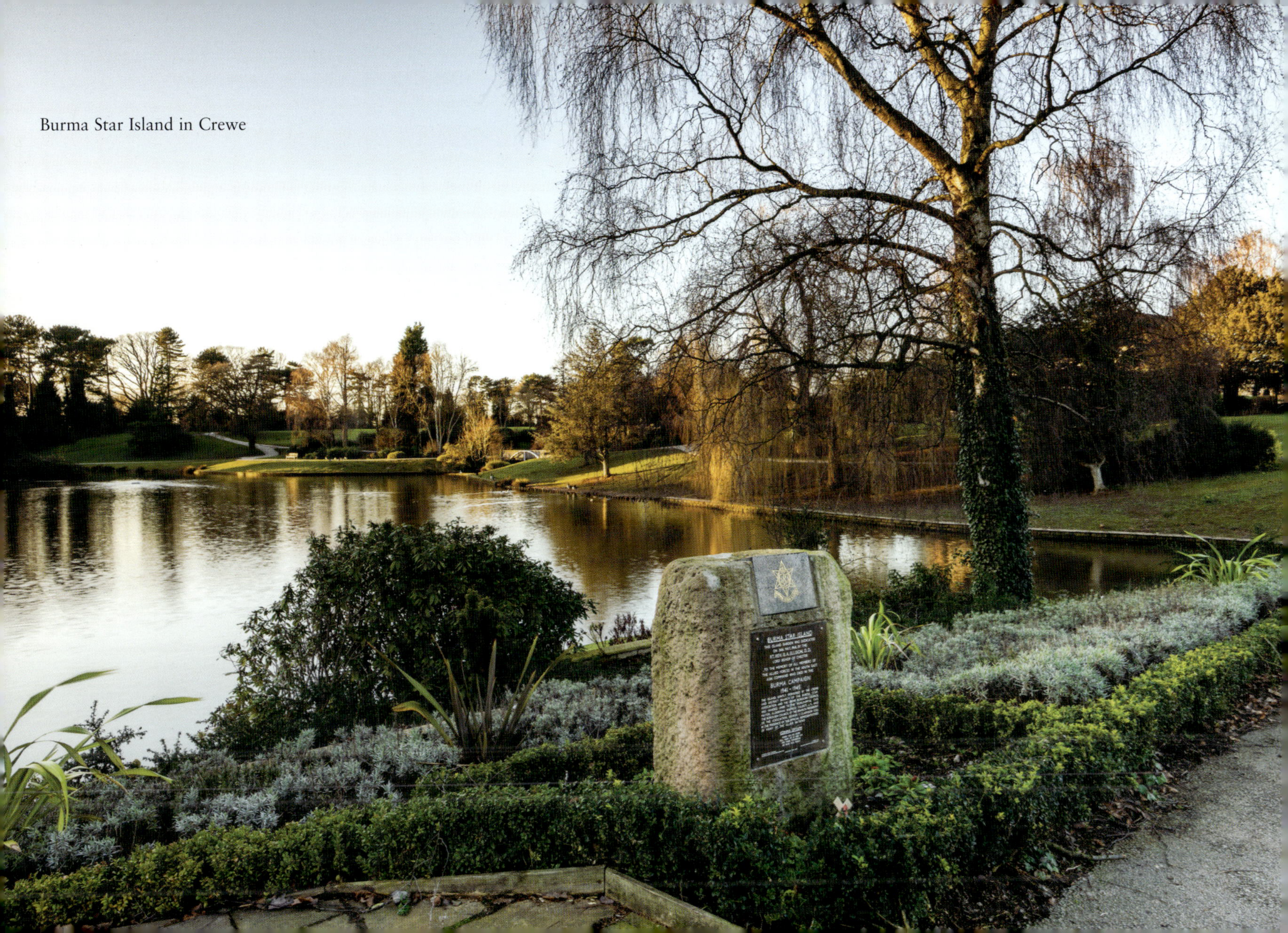

Burma Star Island in Crewe

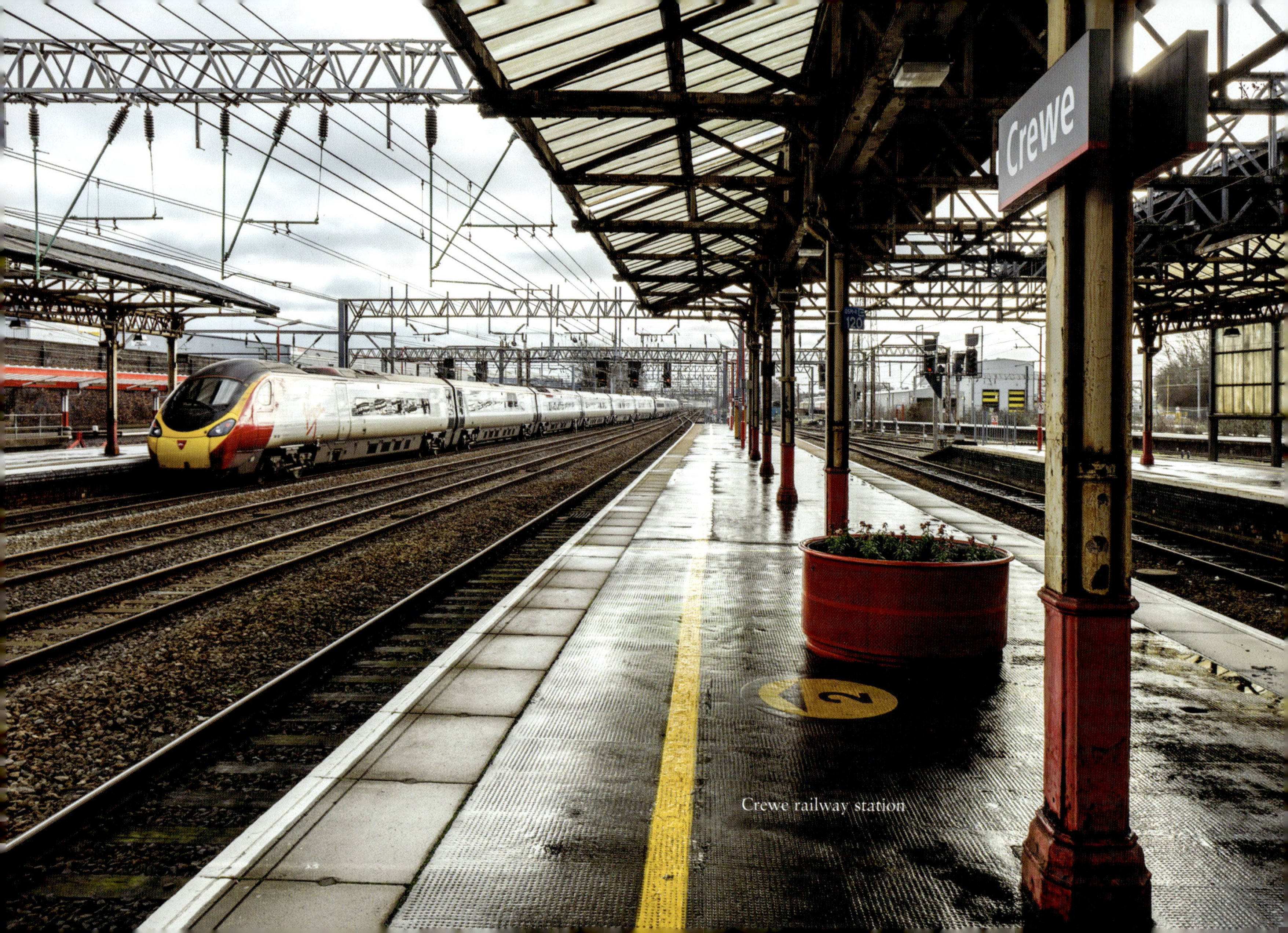

Crewe railway station

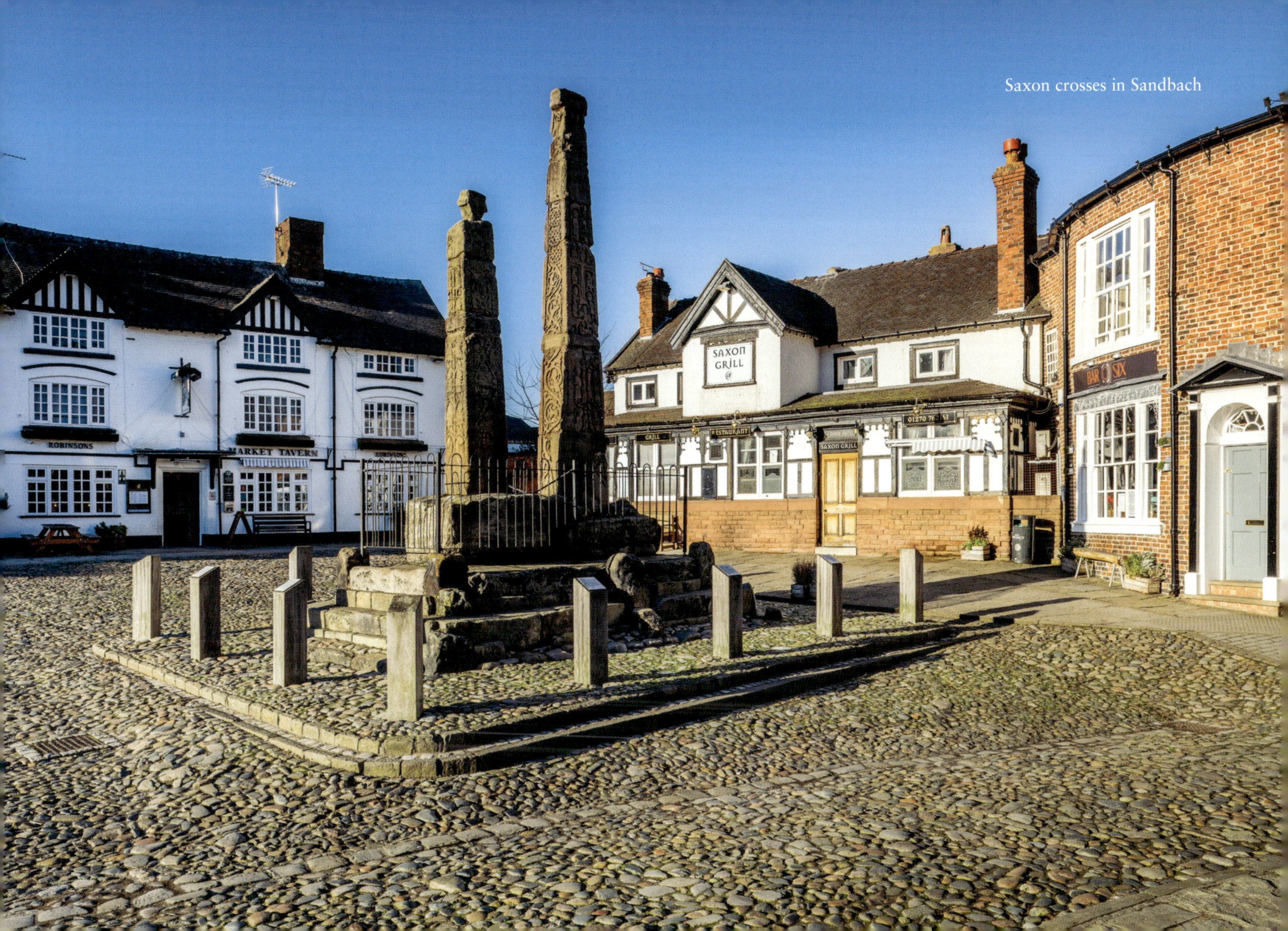

Saxon crosses in Sandbach

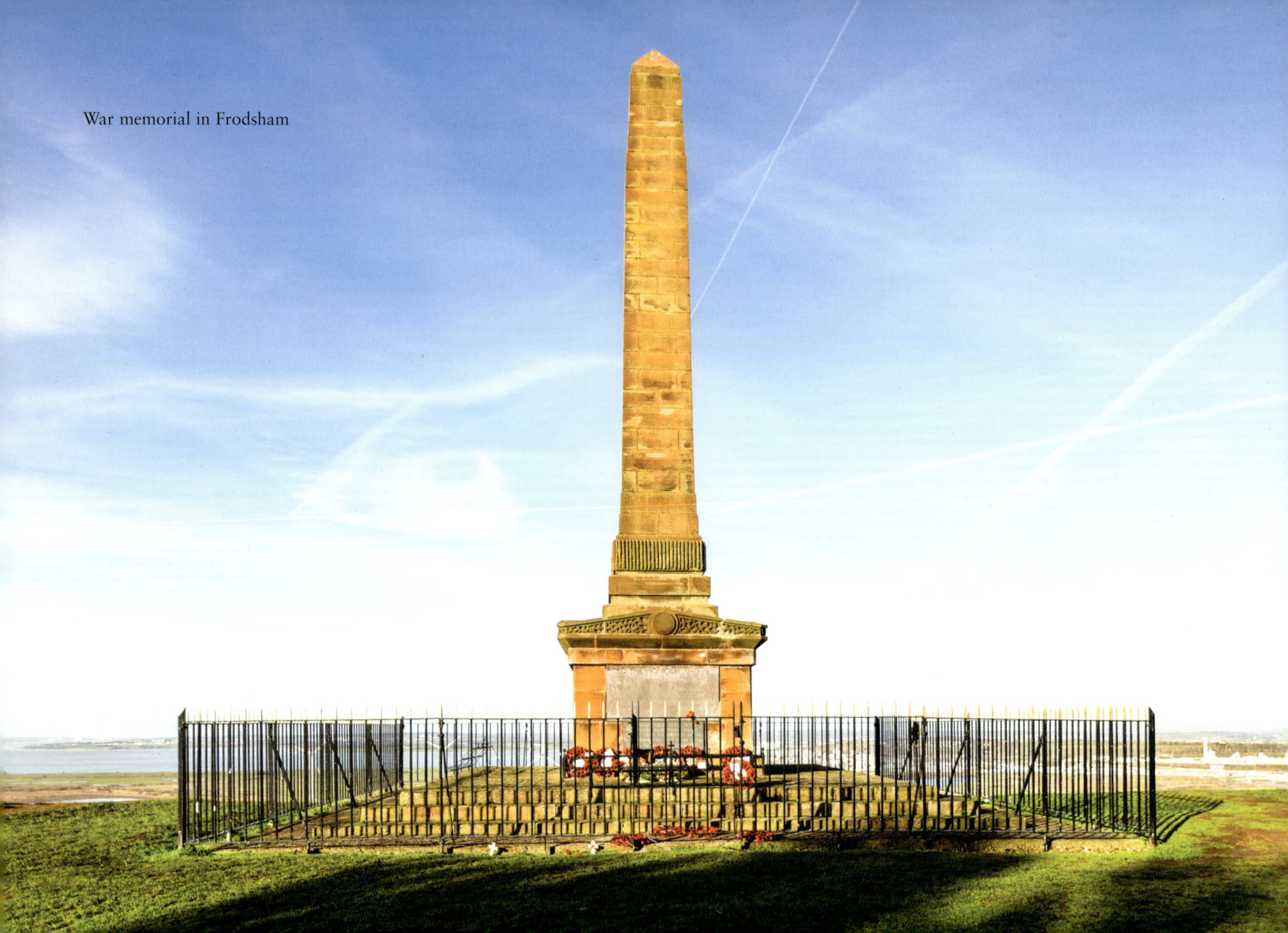

War memorial in Frodsham

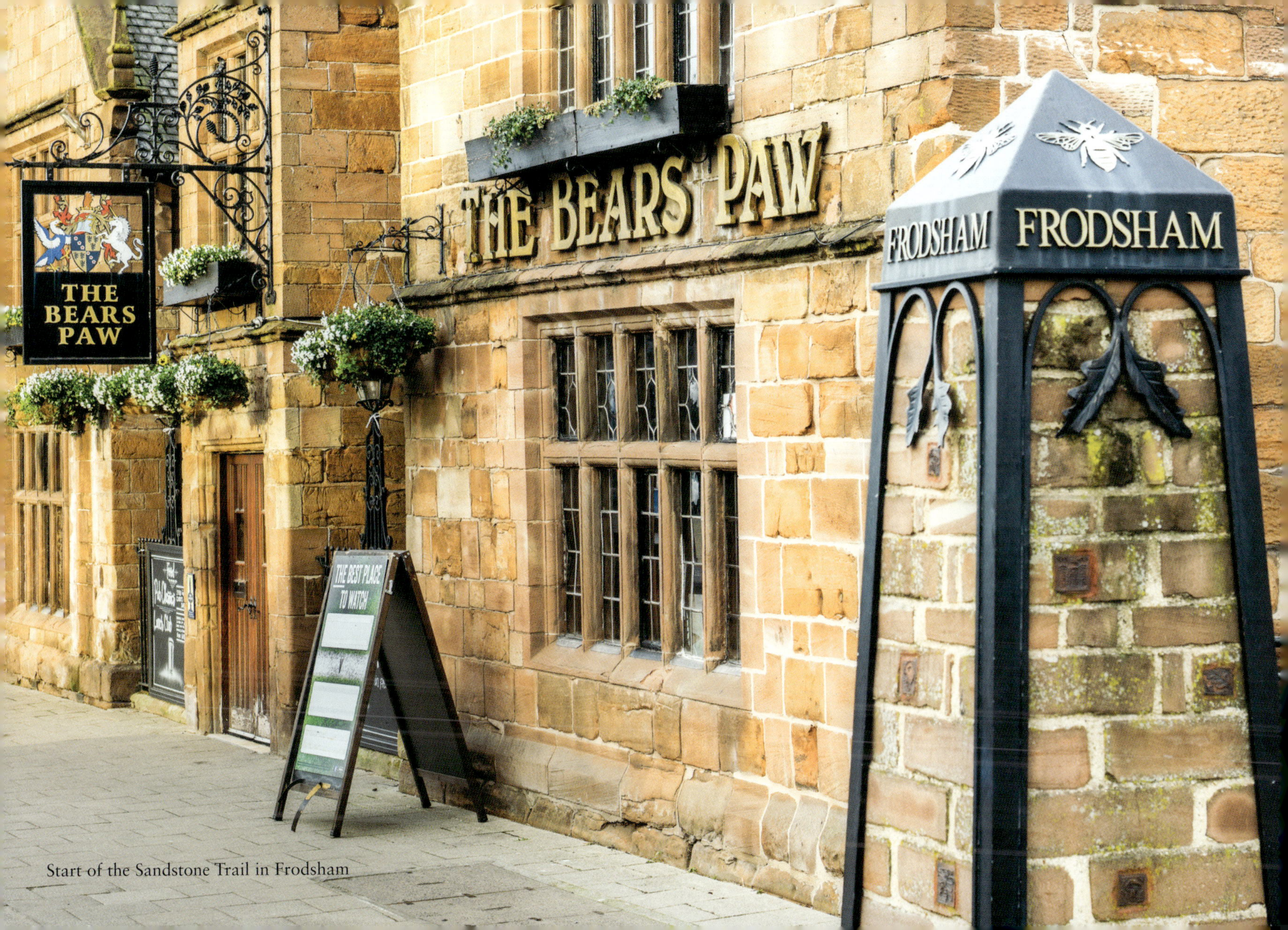

Start of the Sandstone Trail in Frodsham

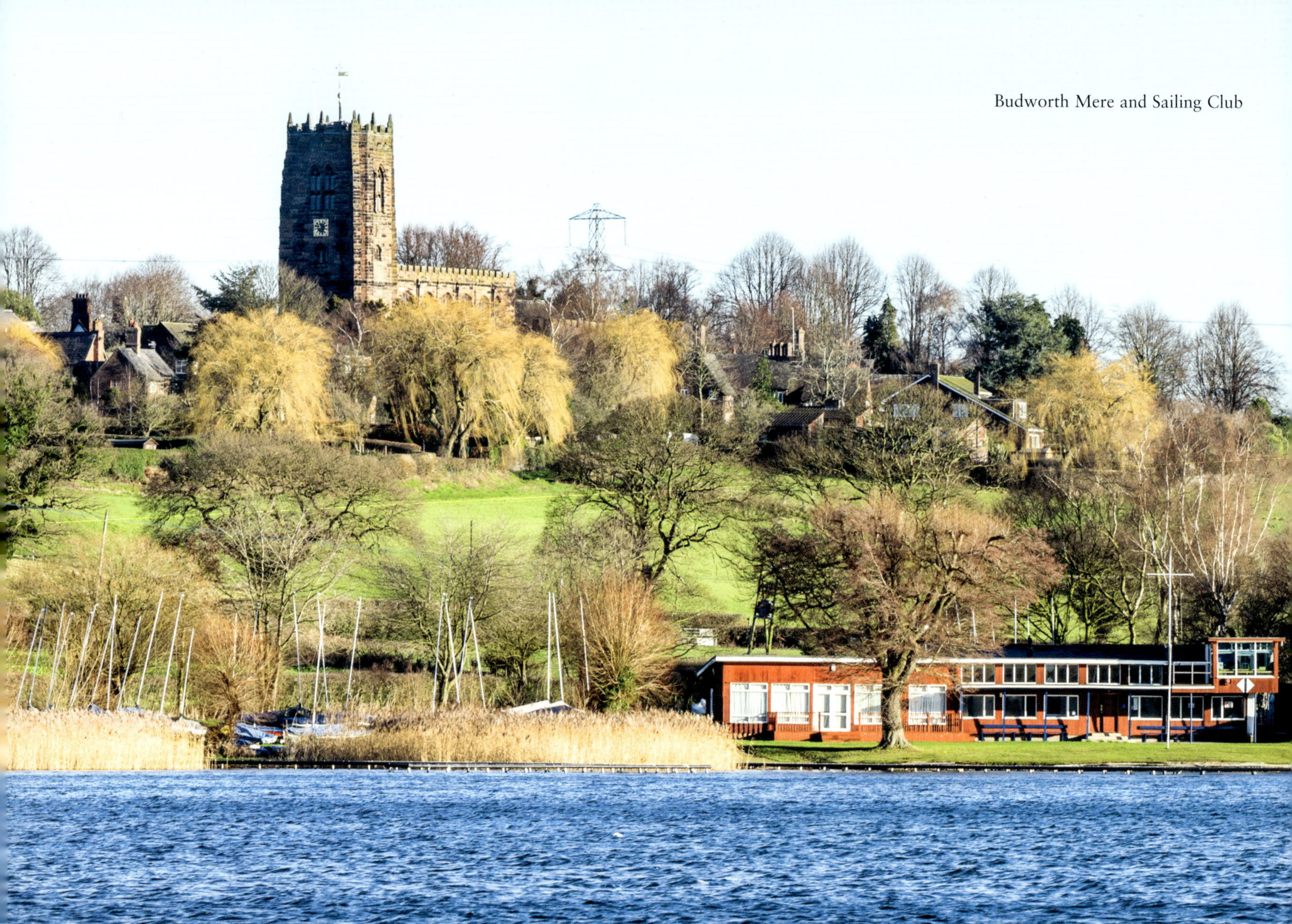

Budworth Mere and Sailing Club

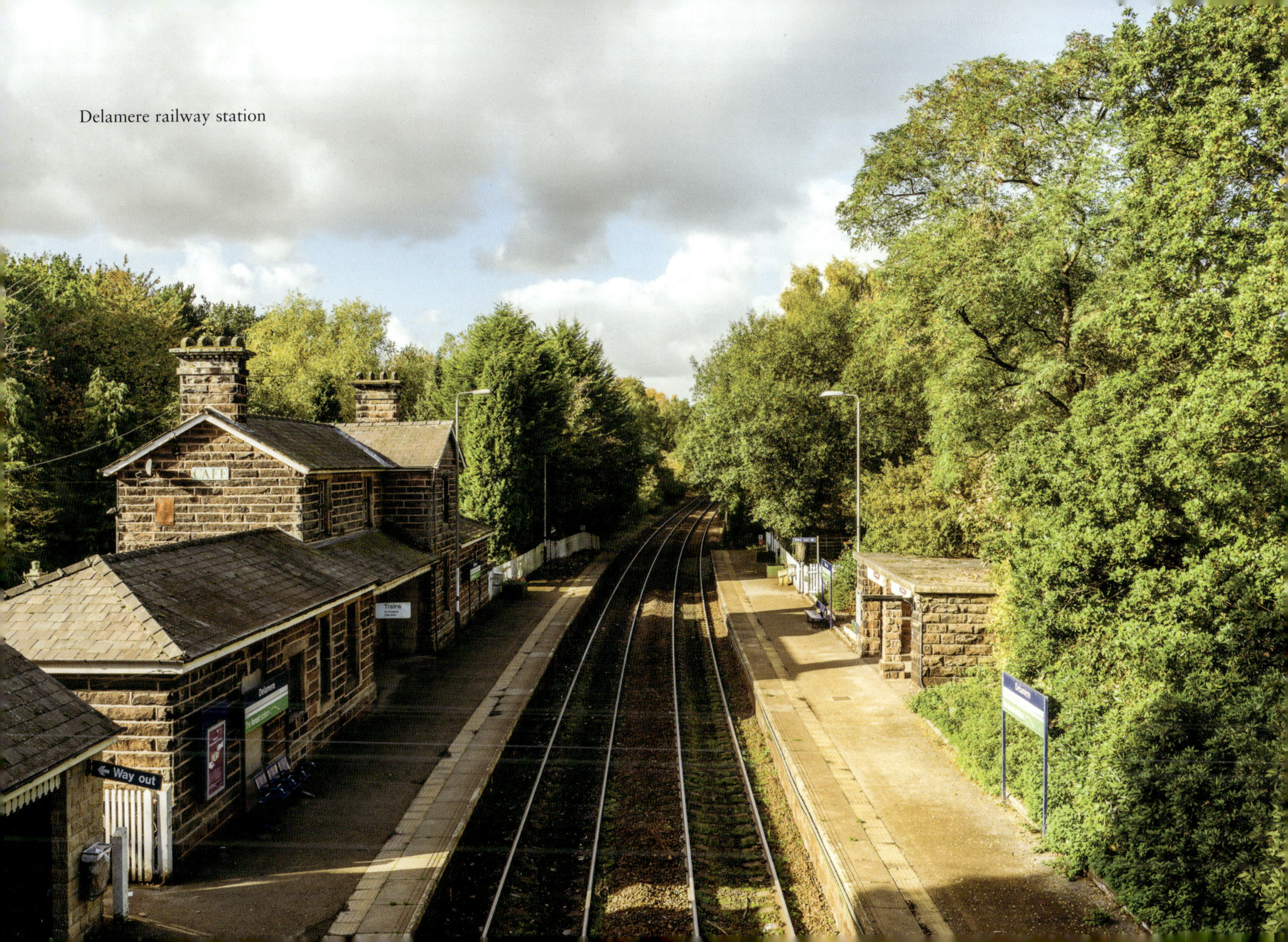

Delamere railway station

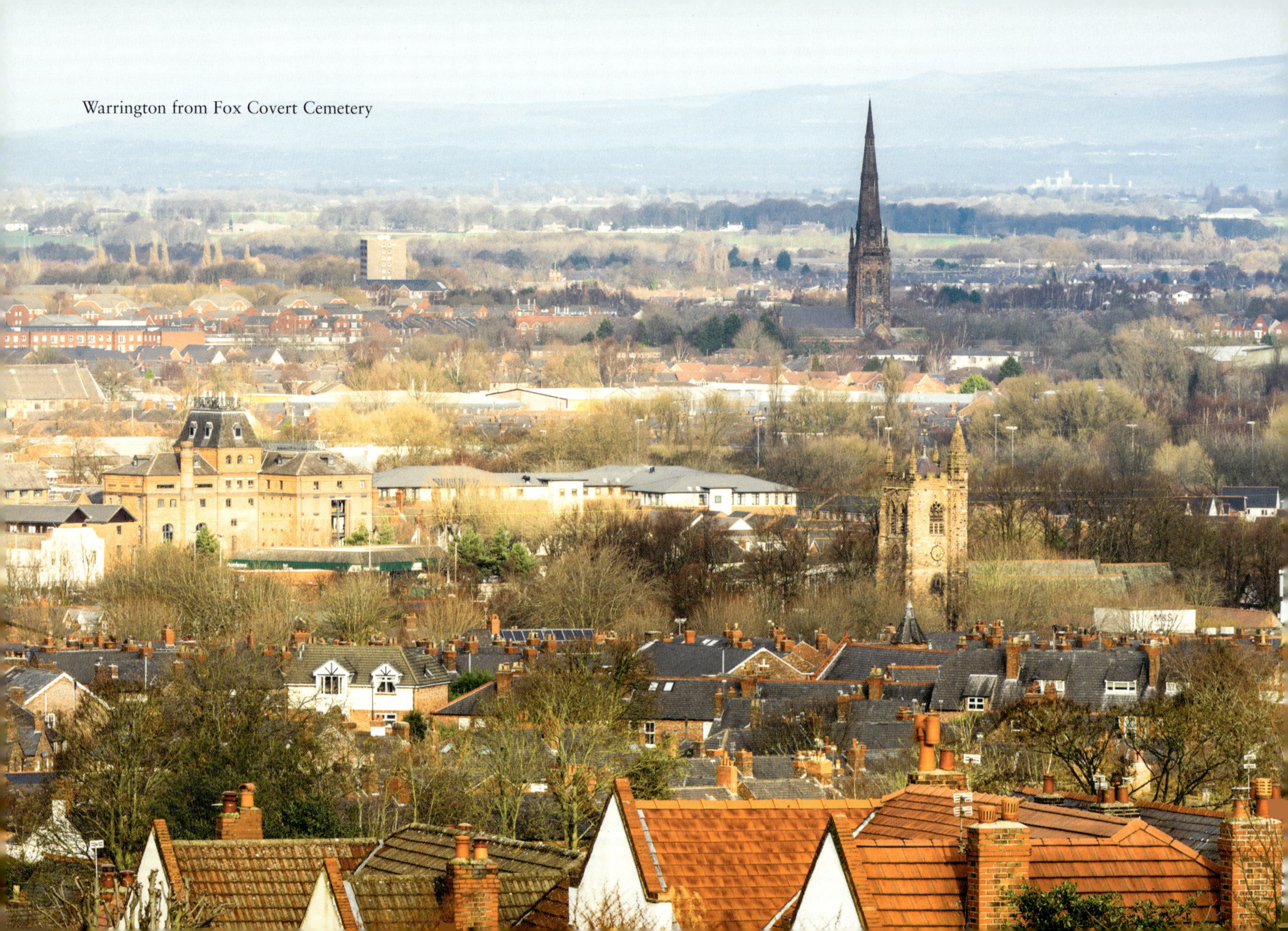

Warrington from Fox Covert Cemetery

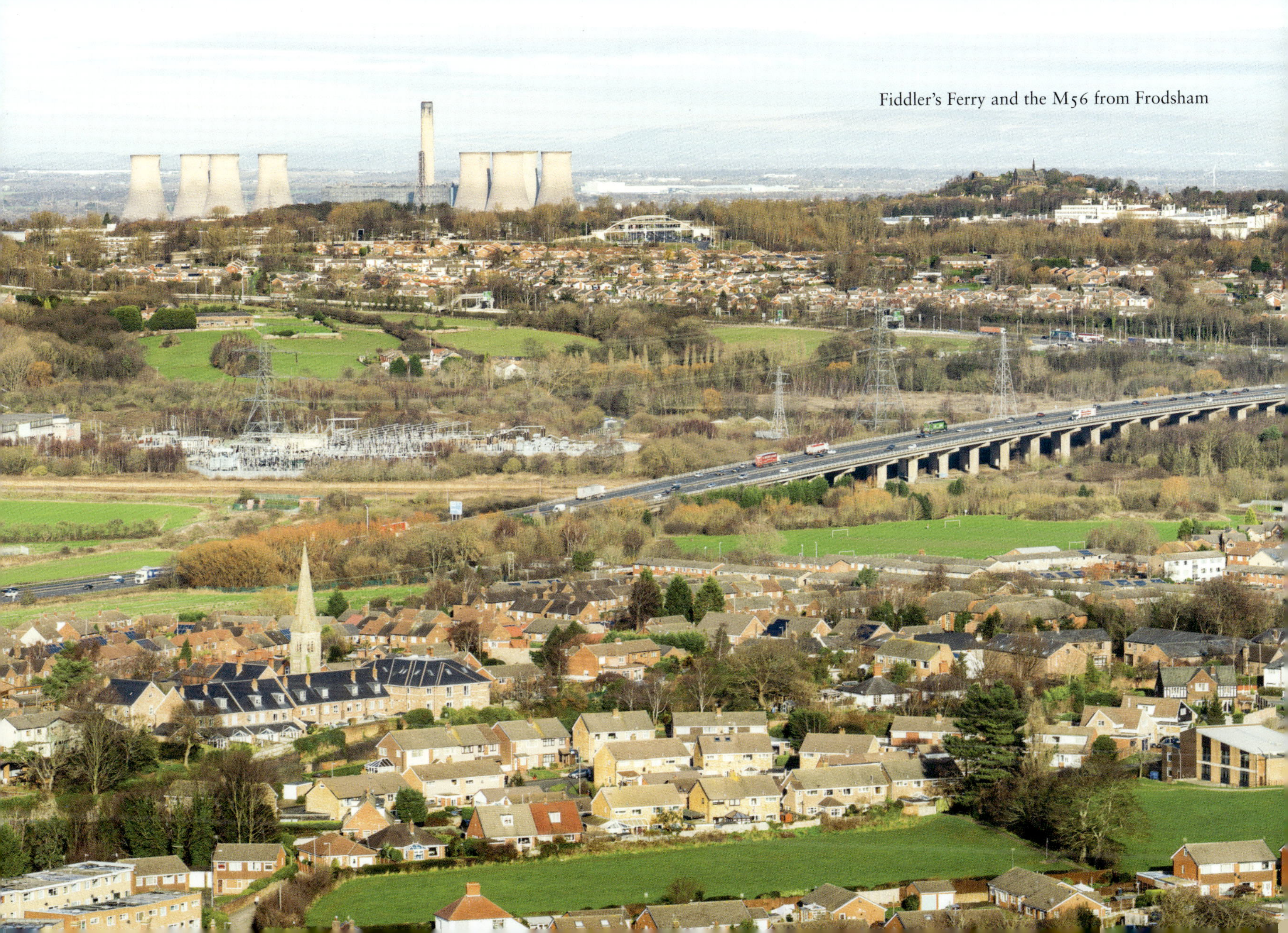

Fiddler's Ferry and the M56 from Frodsham

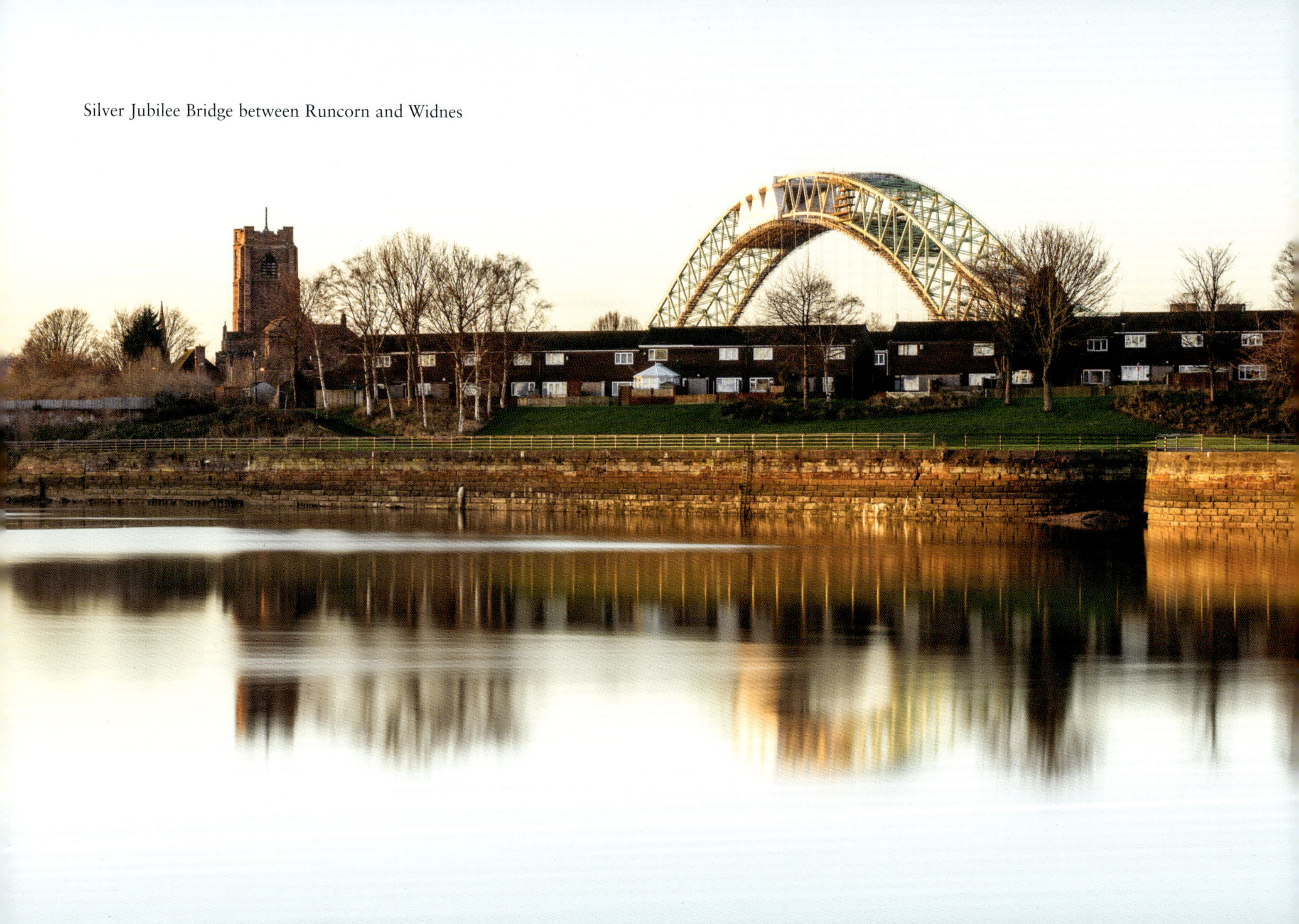

Silver Jubilee Bridge between Runcorn and Widnes

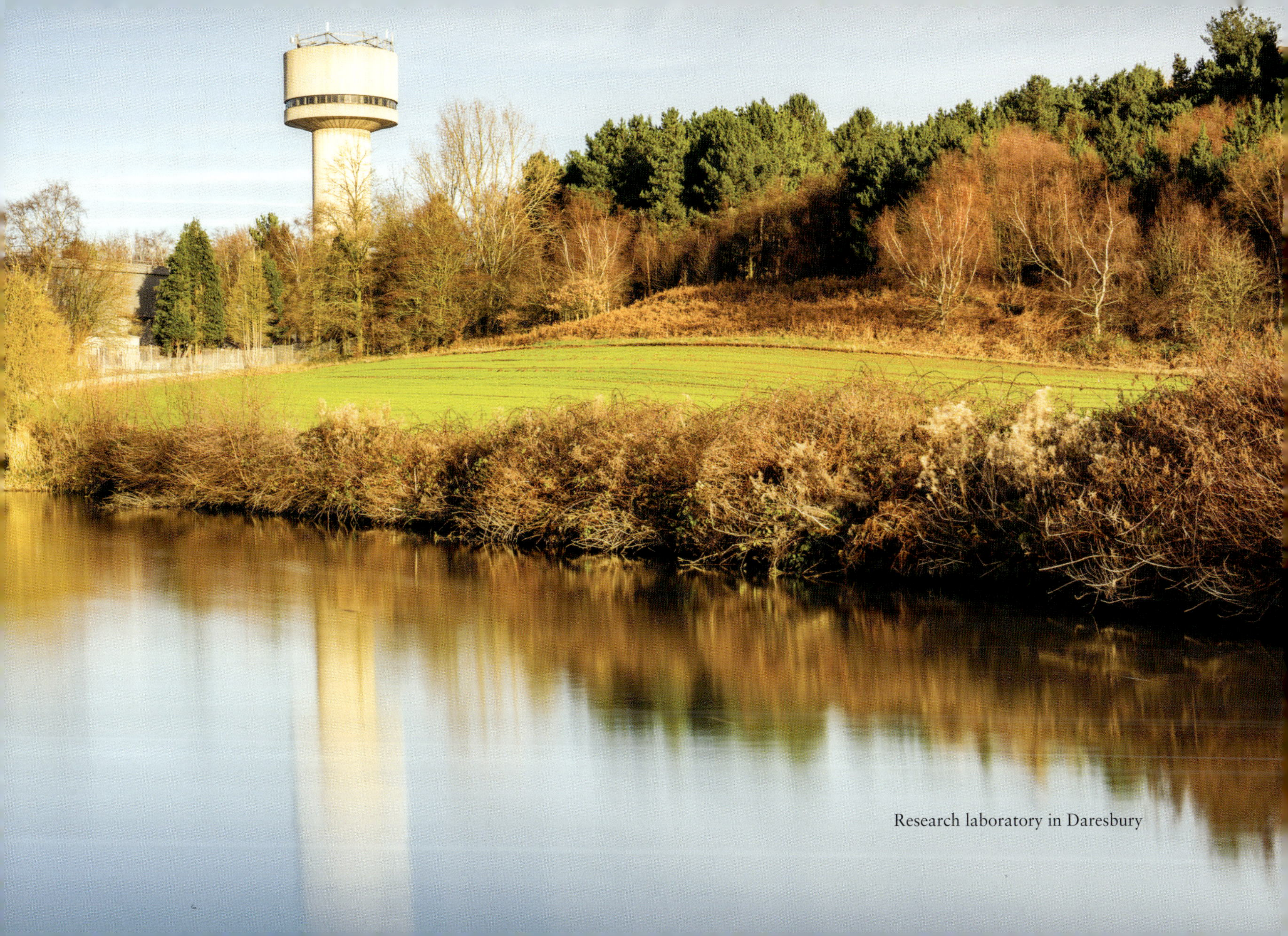

Research laboratory in Daresbury

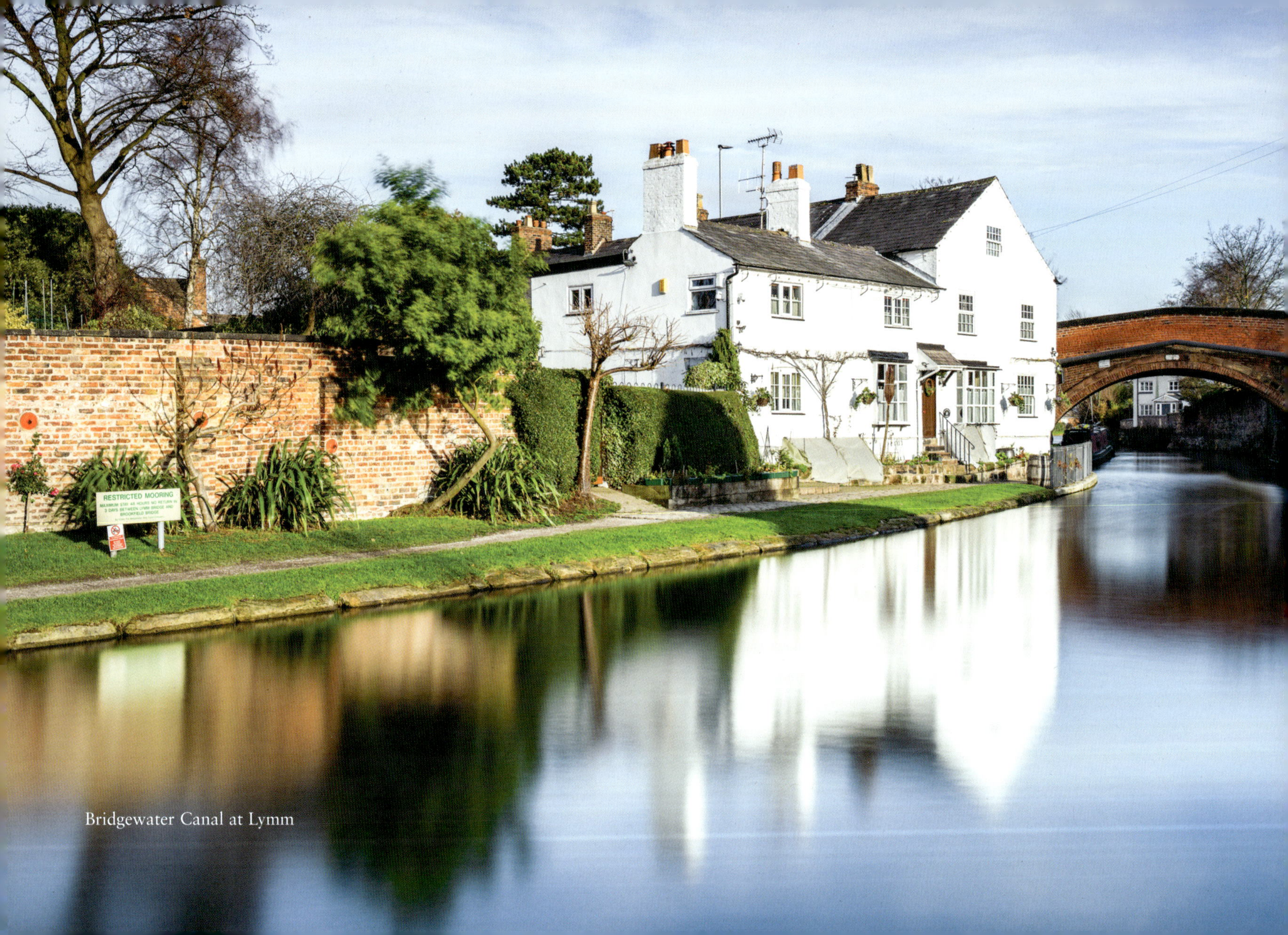

Bridgewater Canal at Lymm

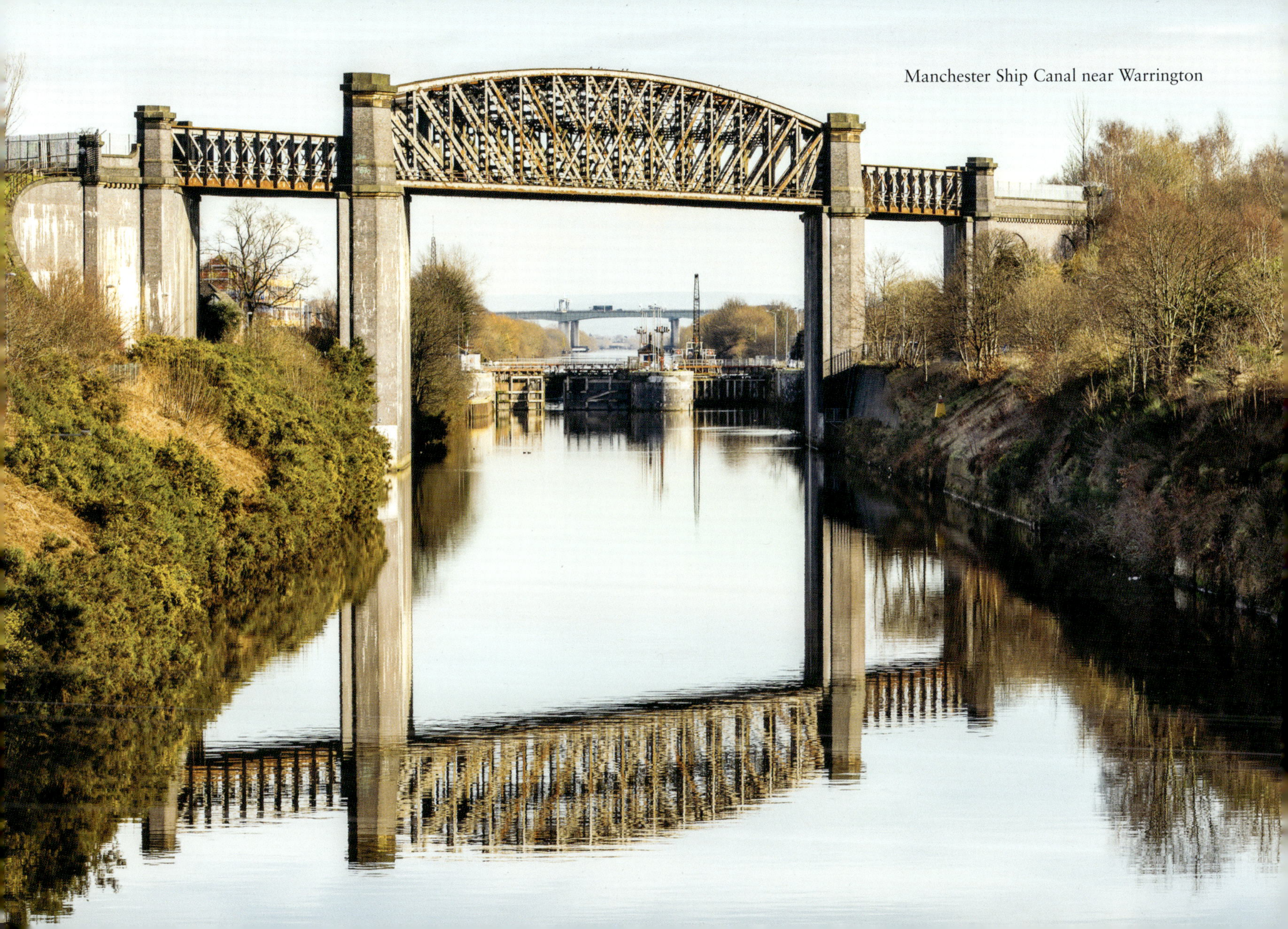

Manchester Ship Canal near Warrington

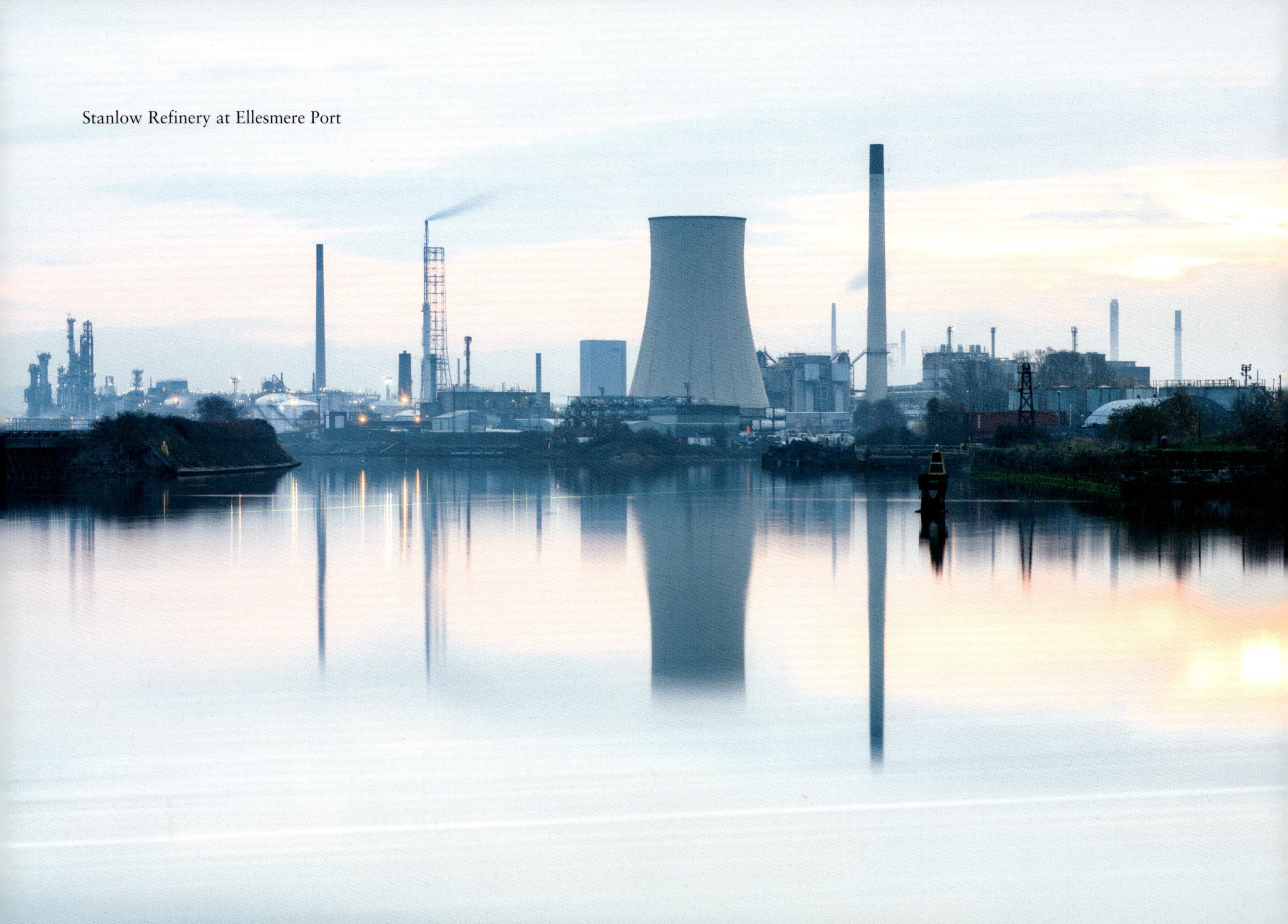

Stanlow Refinery at Ellesmere Port

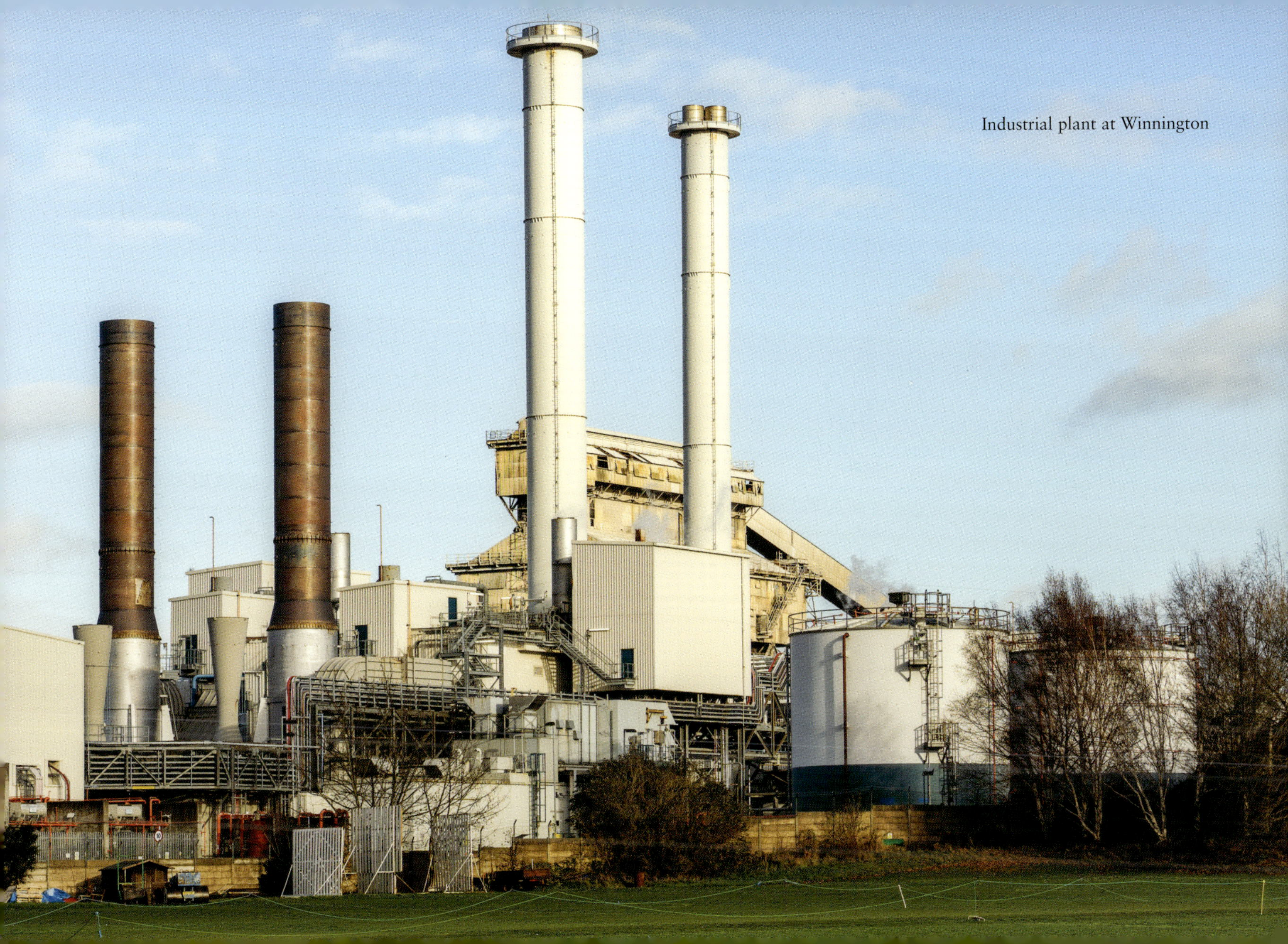

Industrial plant at Winnington

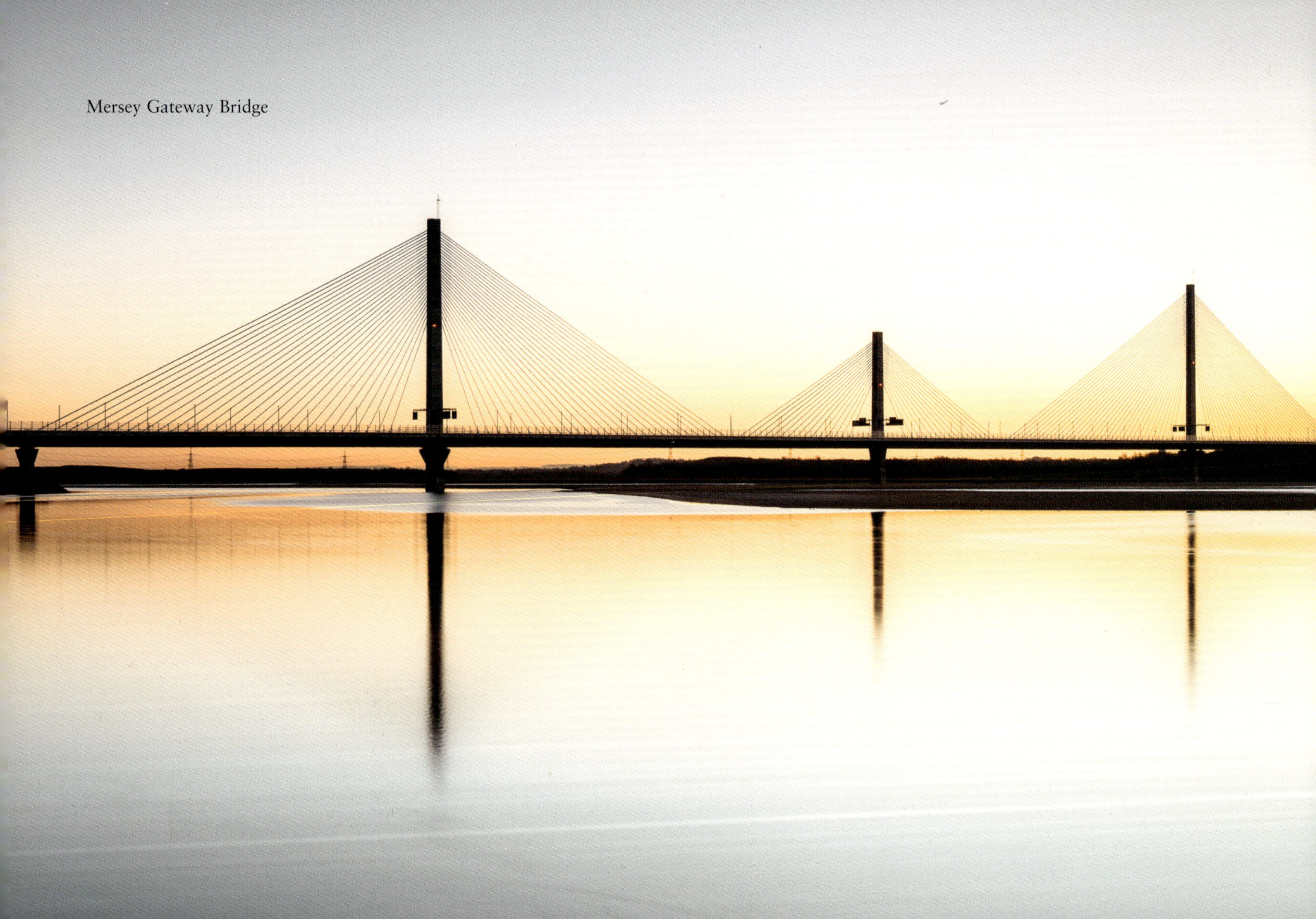
Mersey Gateway Bridge

CHESHIRE COUNTRYSIDE

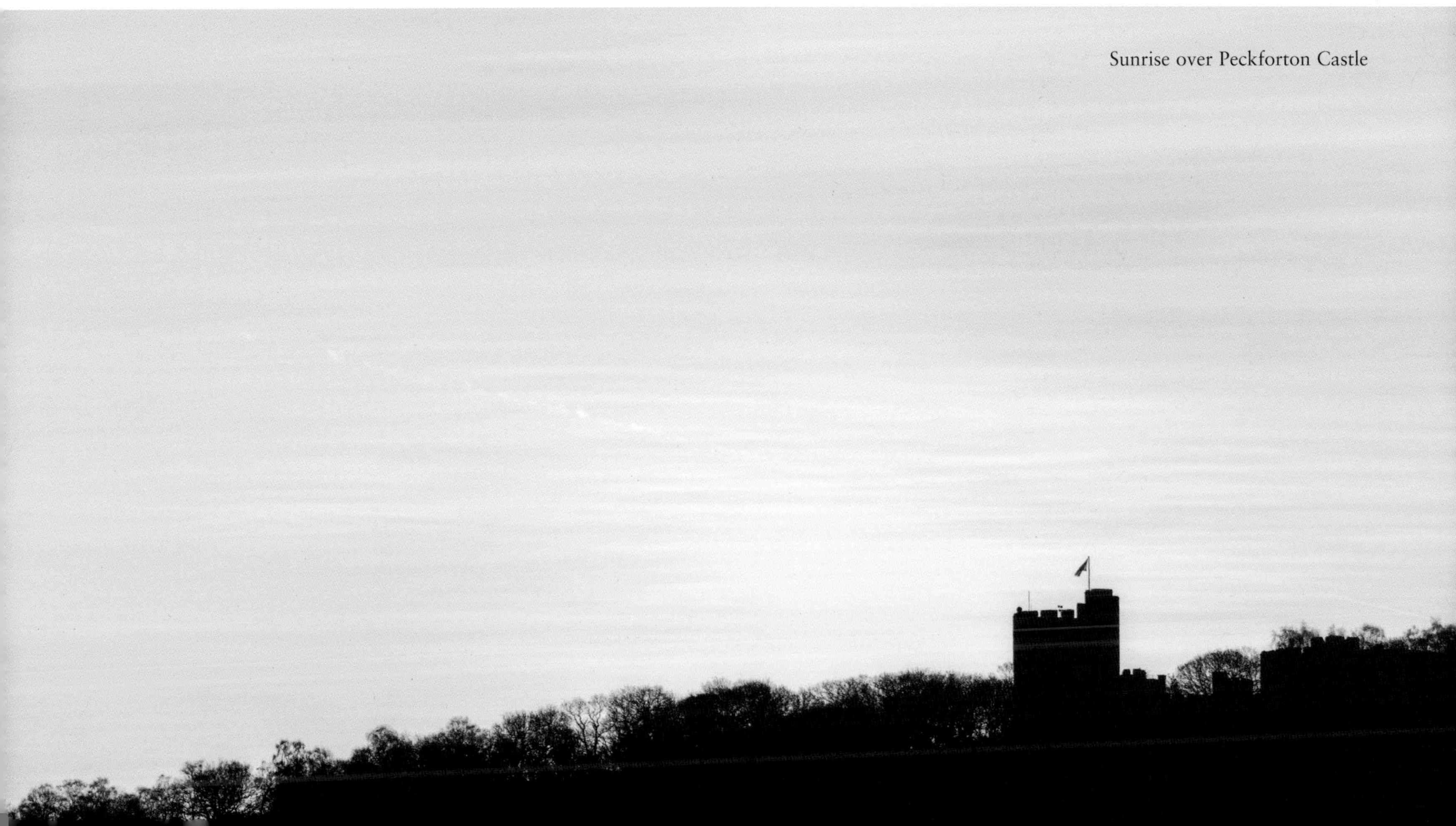
Sunrise over Peckforton Castle

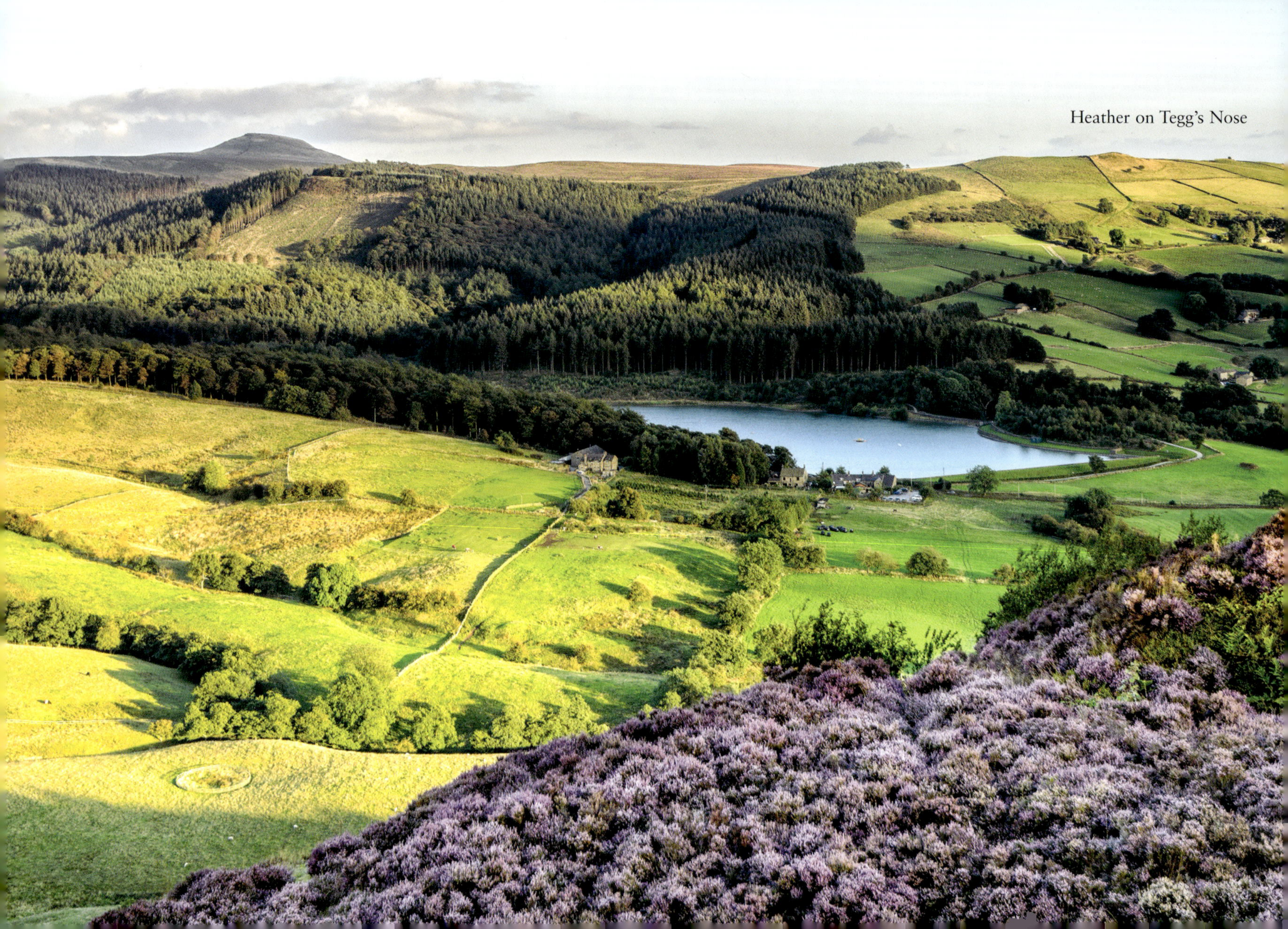

Heather on Tegg's Nose

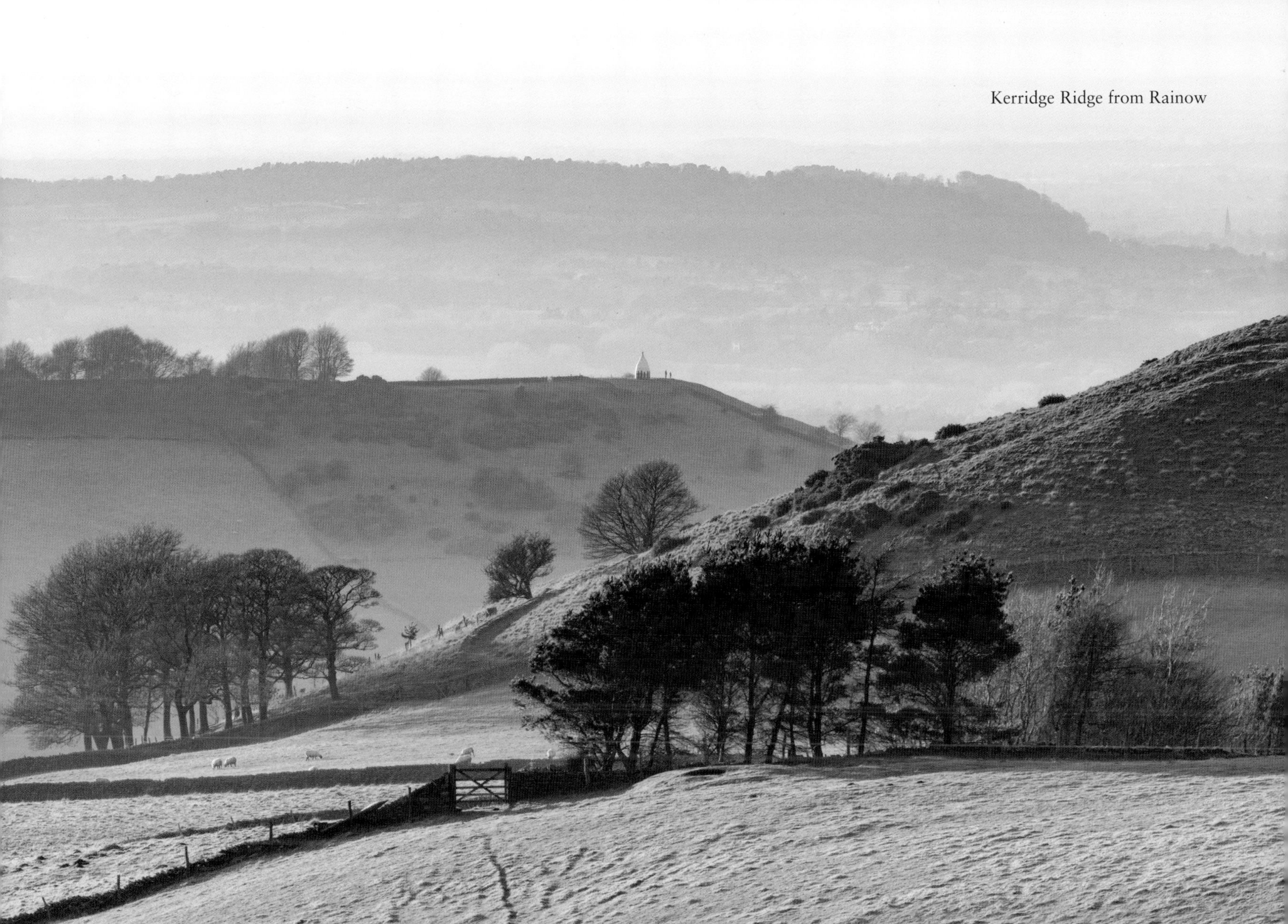

Kerridge Ridge from Rainow

Shutlingsloe in winter

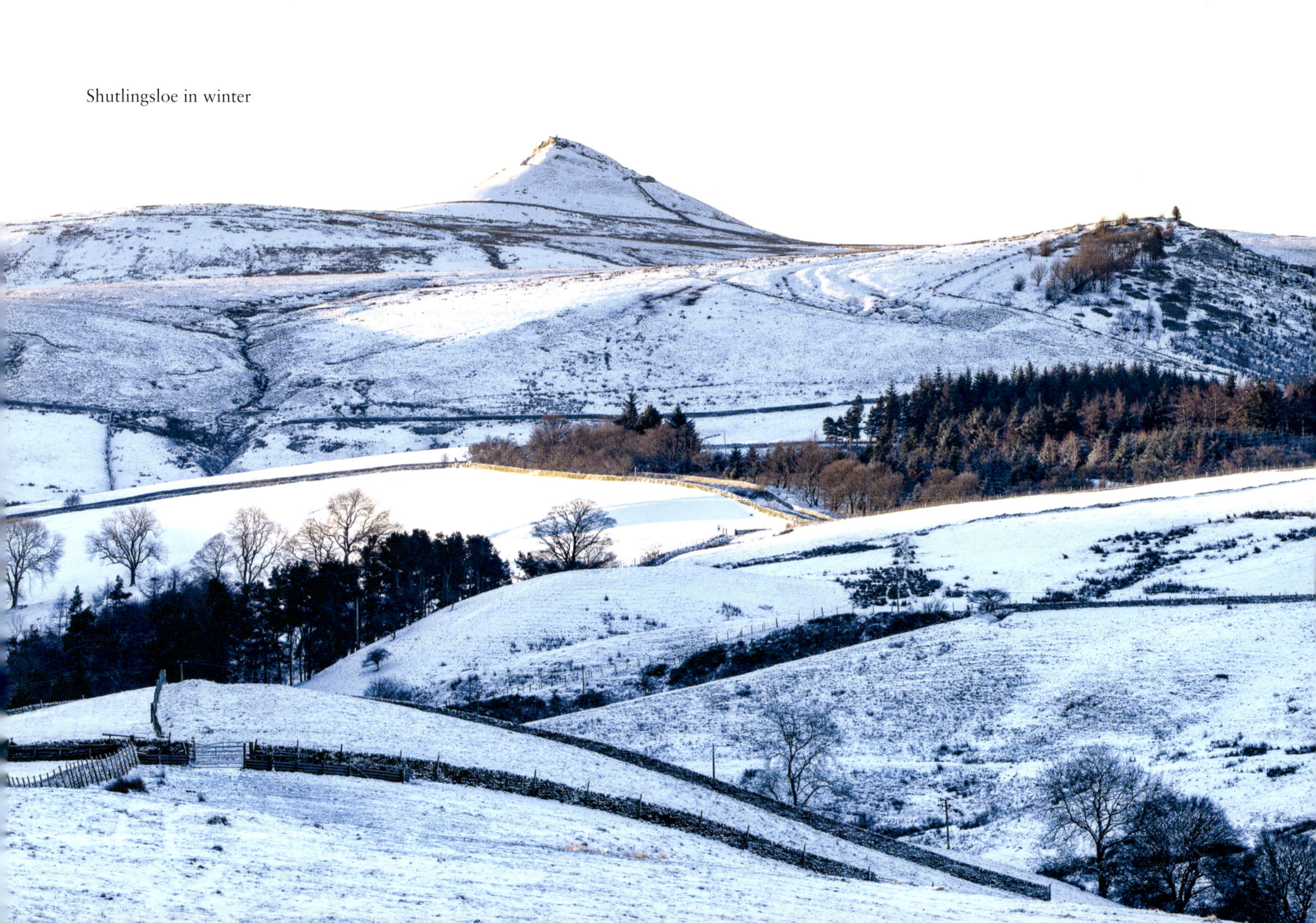

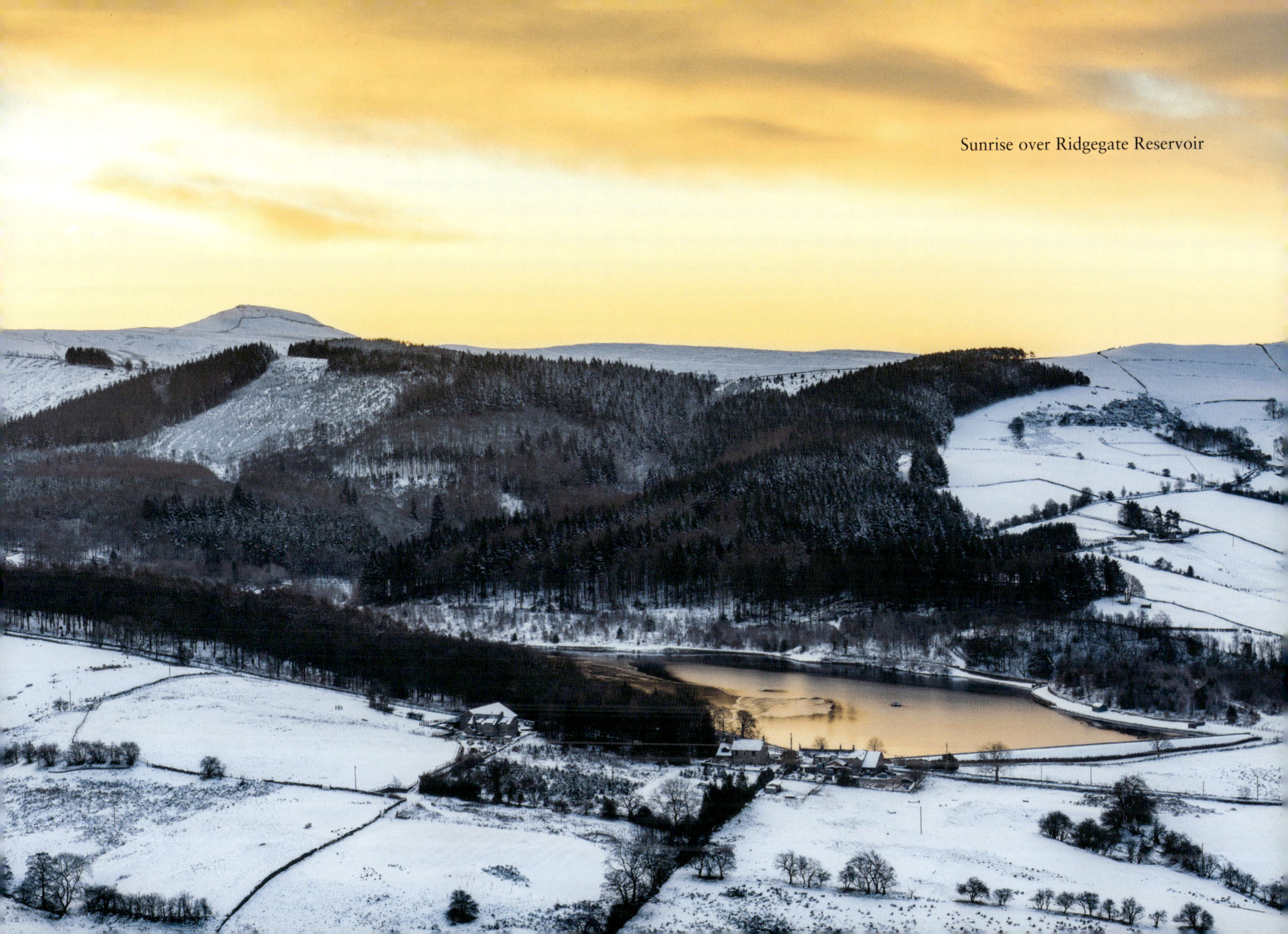

Sunrise over Ridgegate Reservoir

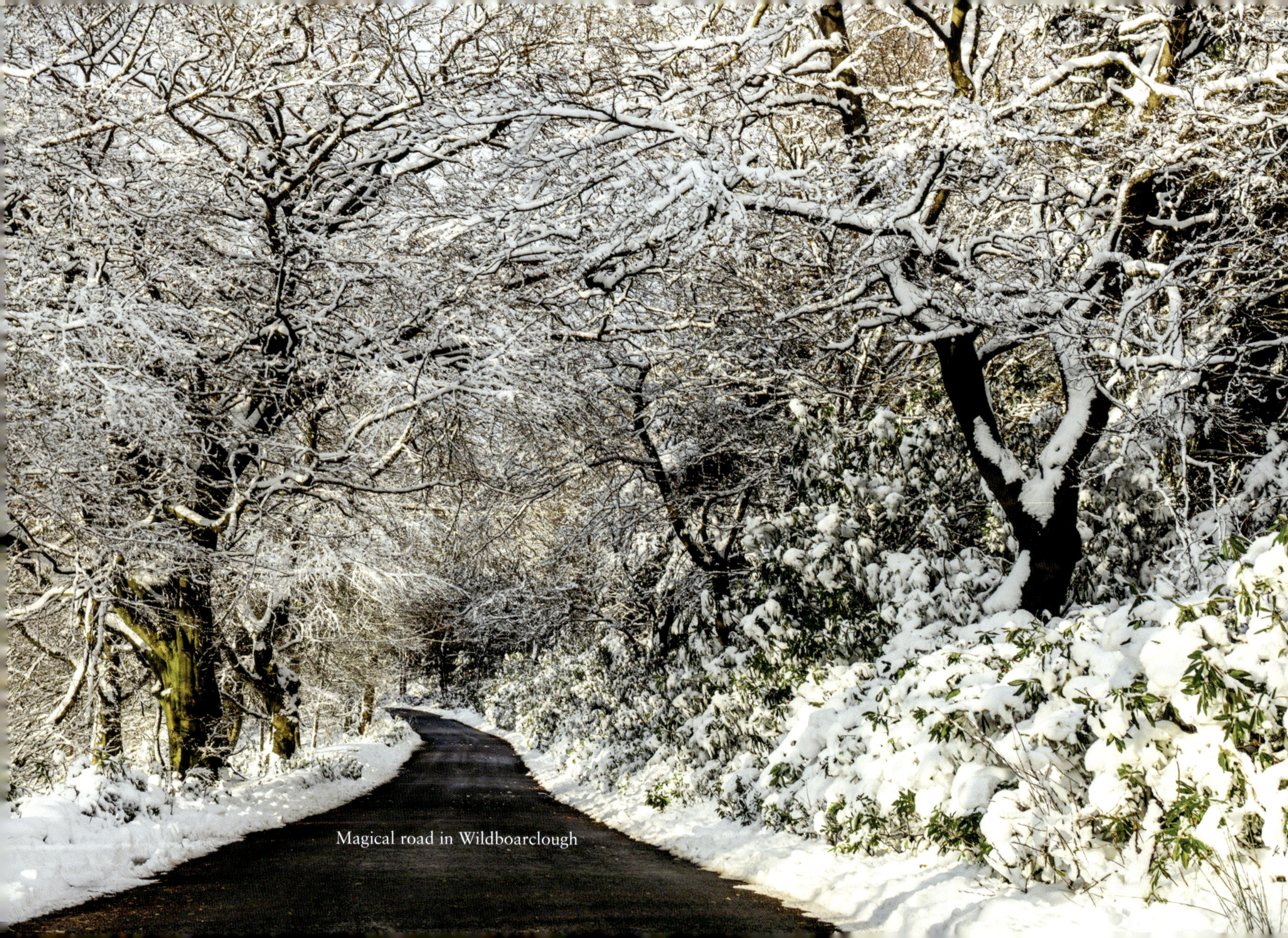

Magical road in Wildboarclough

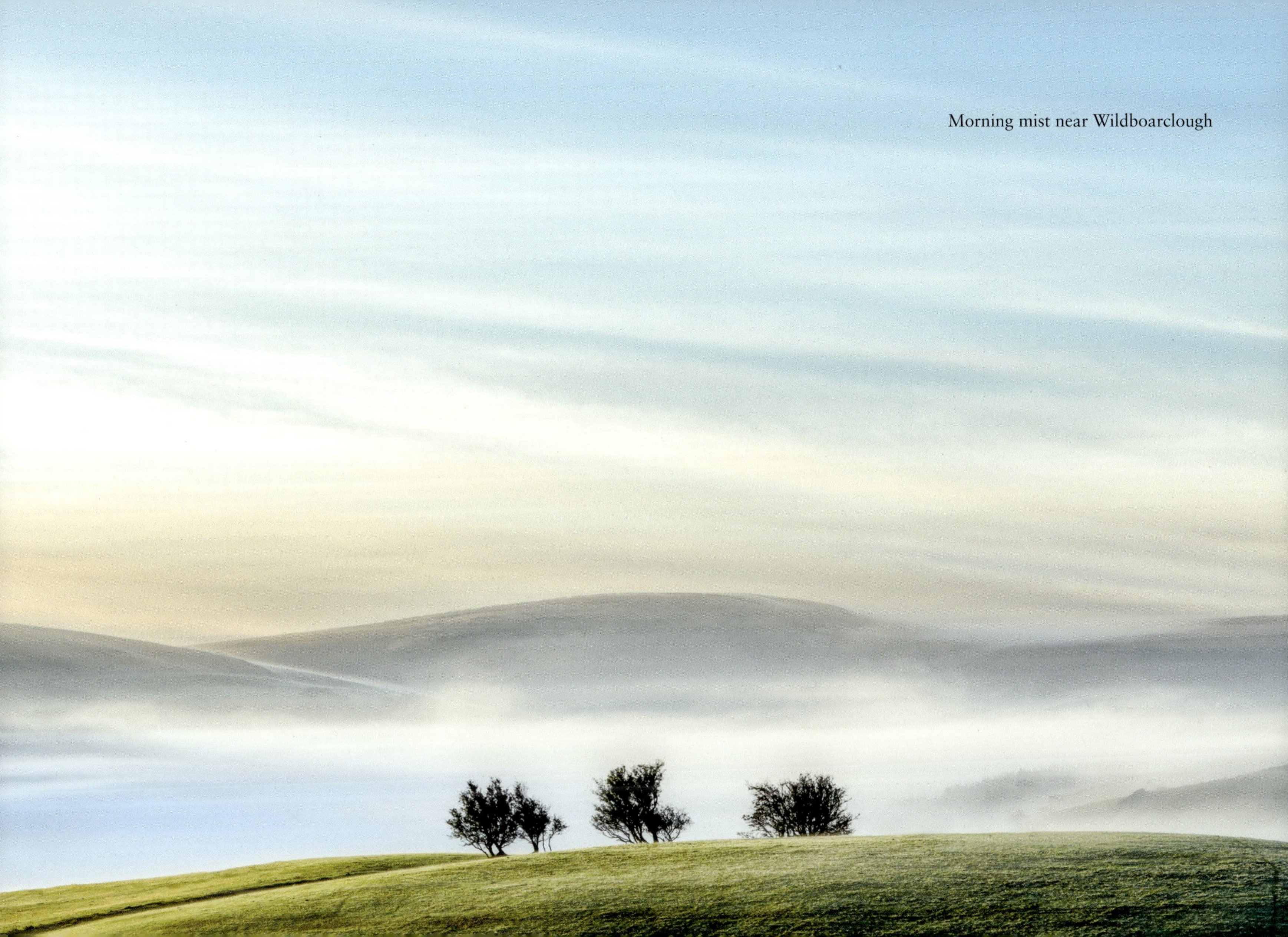

Morning mist near Wildboarclough

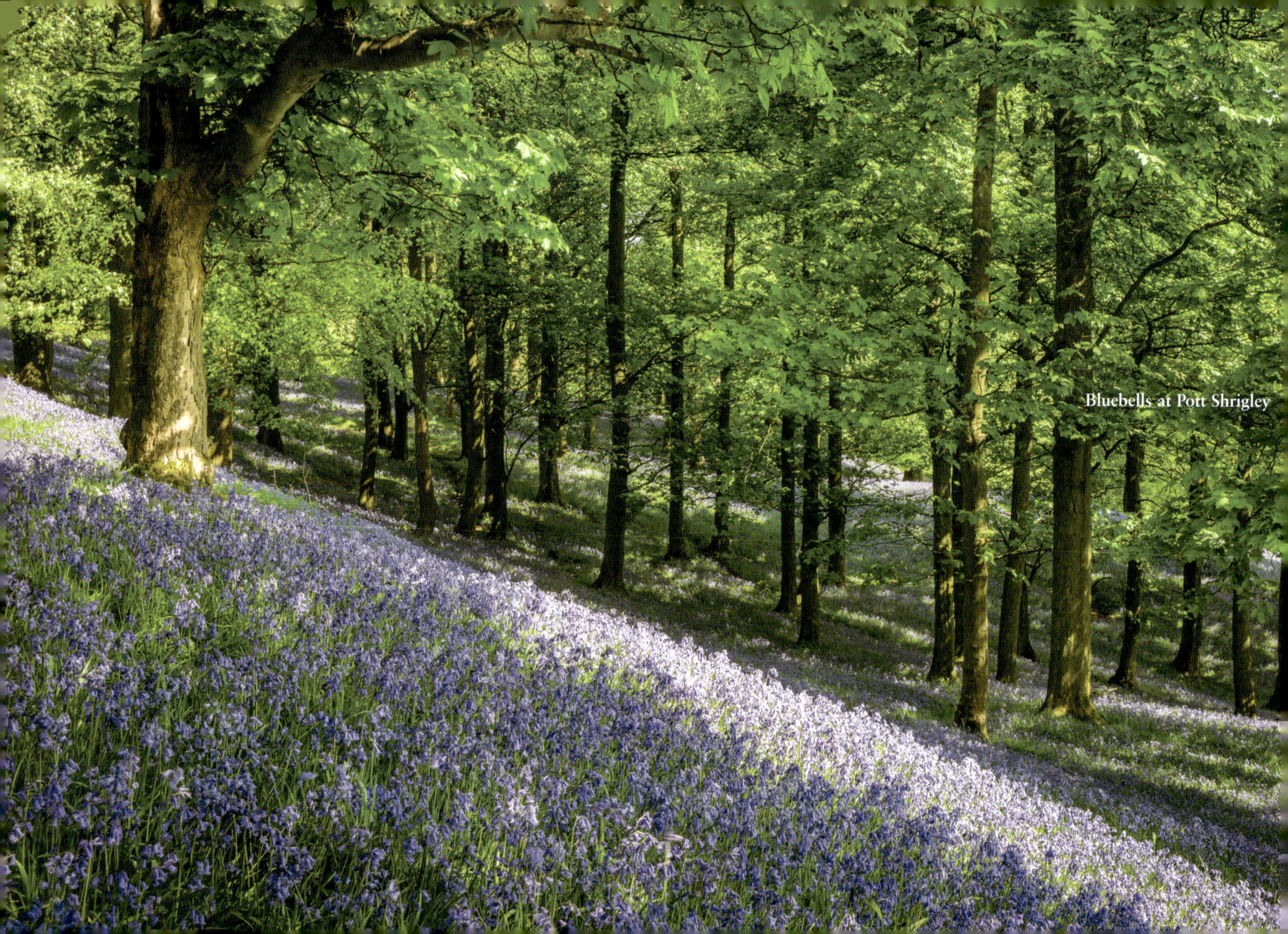

Bluebells at Pott Shrigley

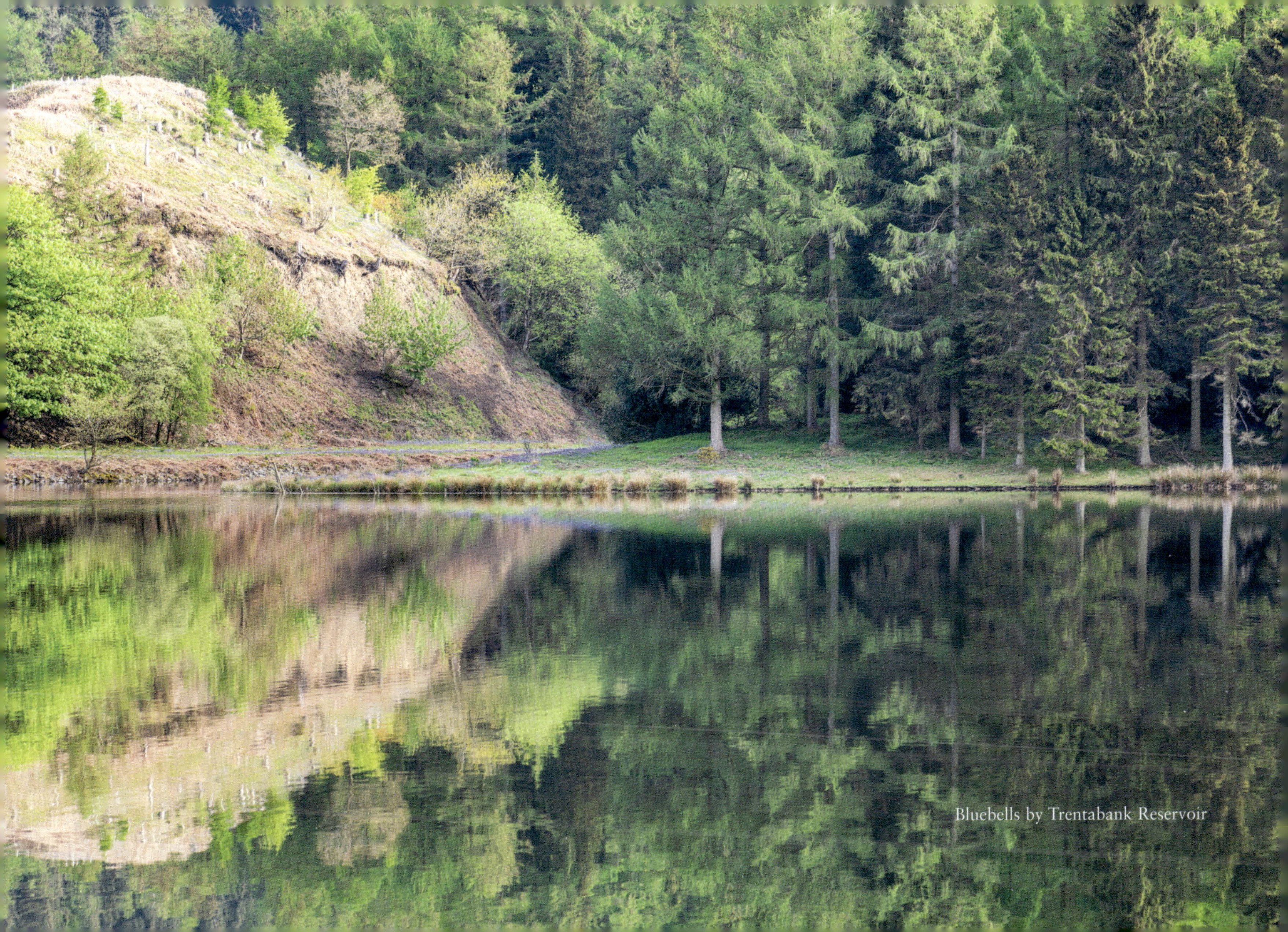

Bluebells by Trentabank Reservoir

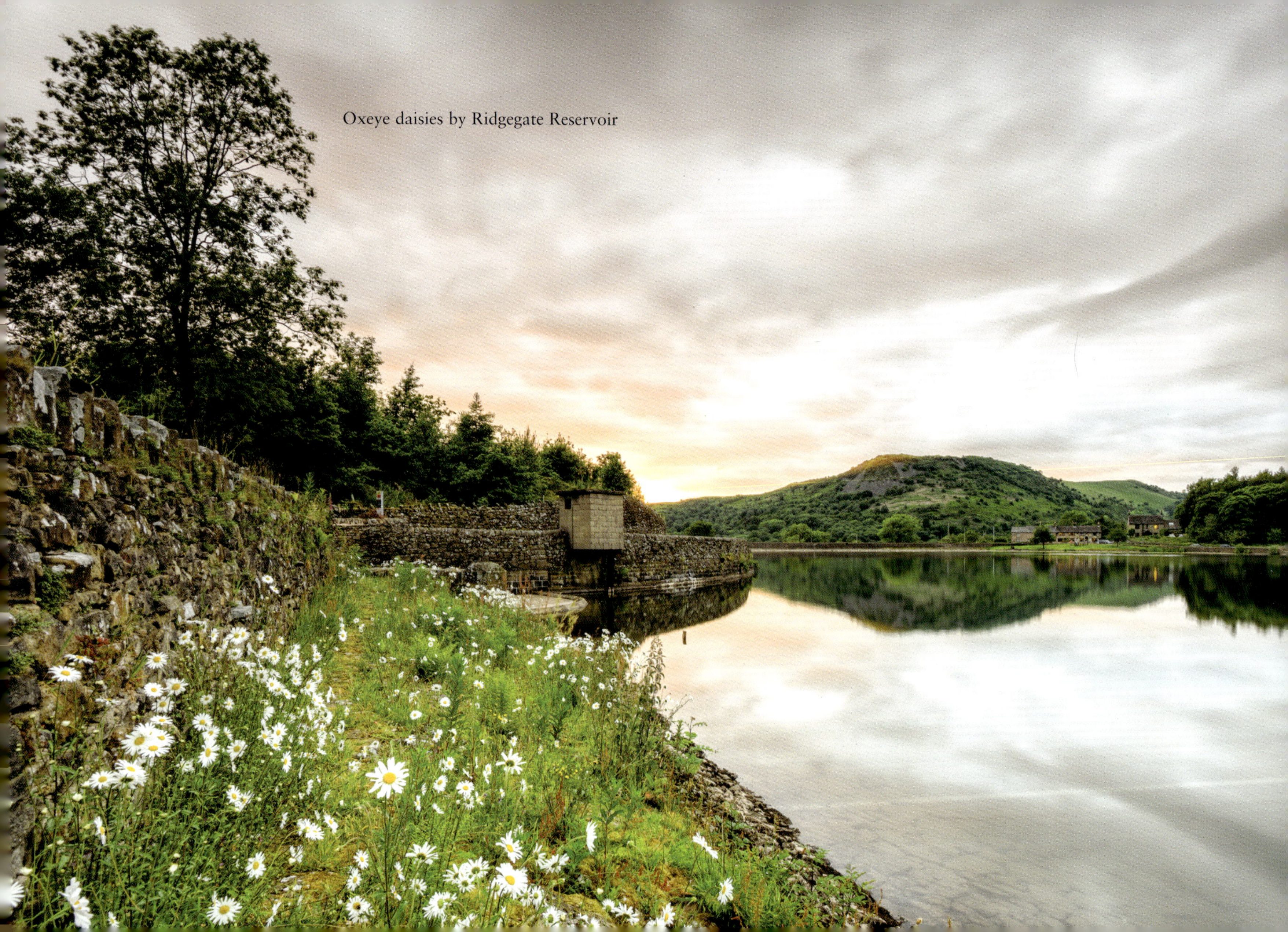

Oxeye daisies by Ridgegate Reservoir

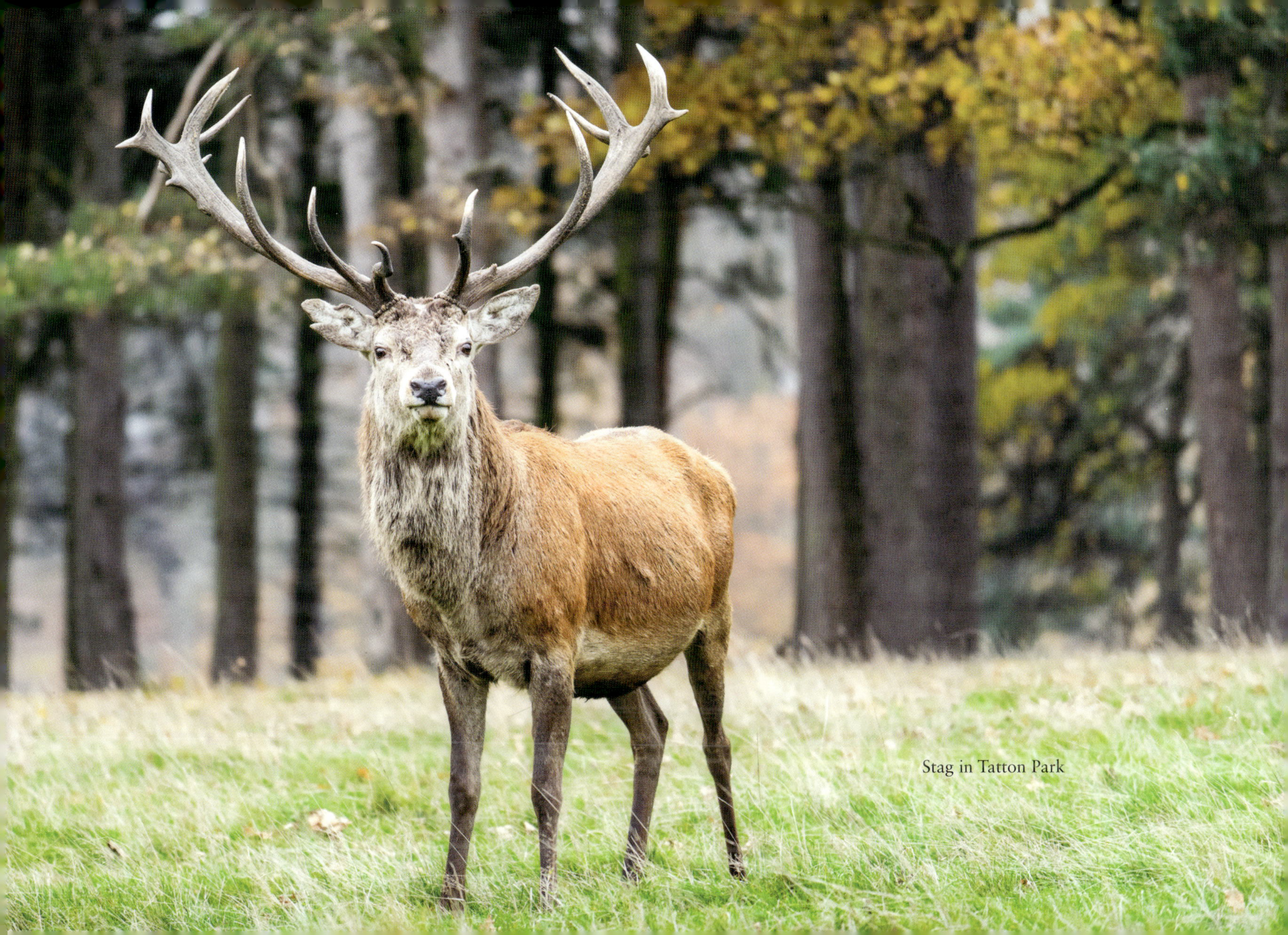

Stag in Tatton Park

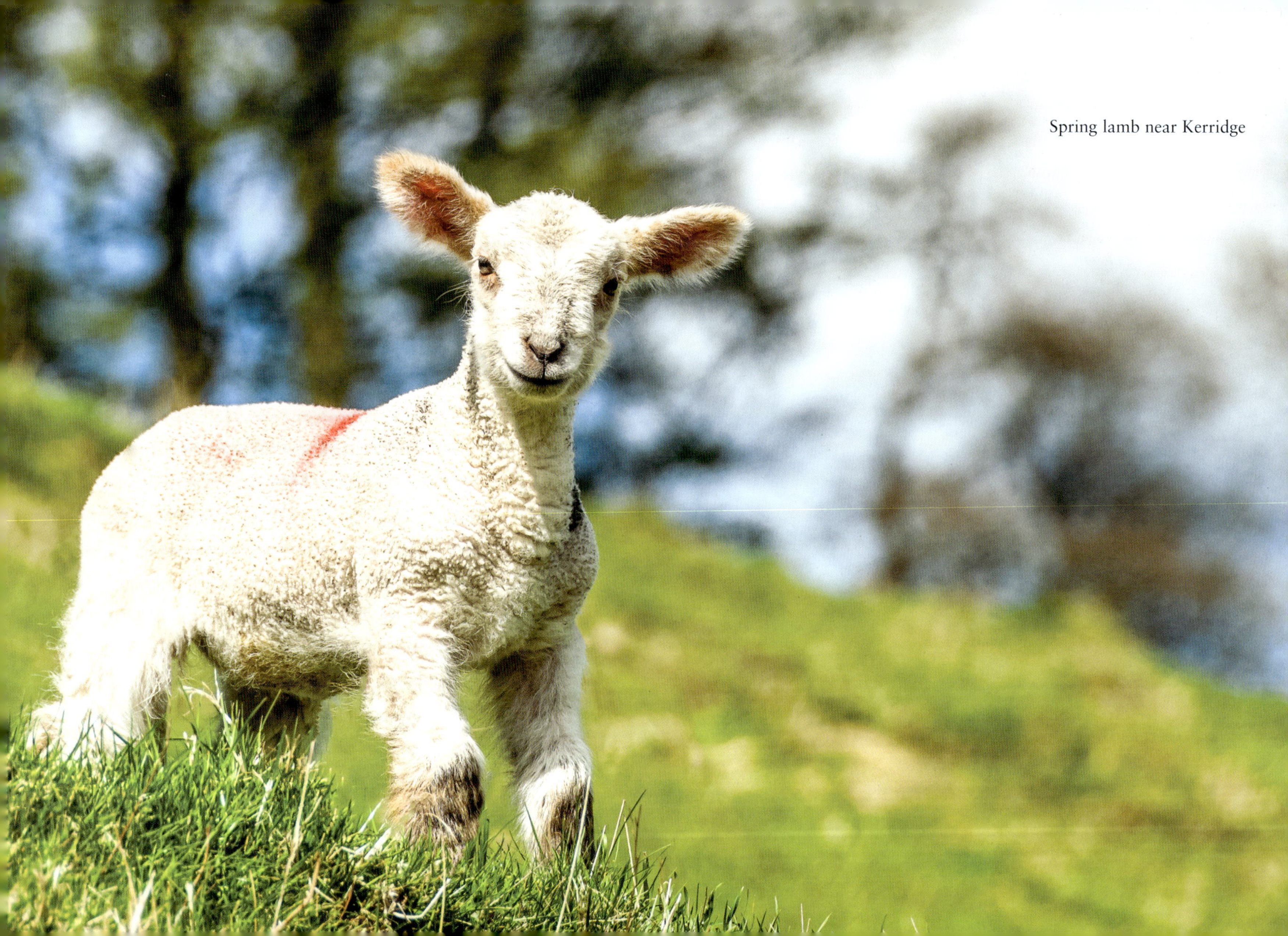

Spring lamb near Kerridge

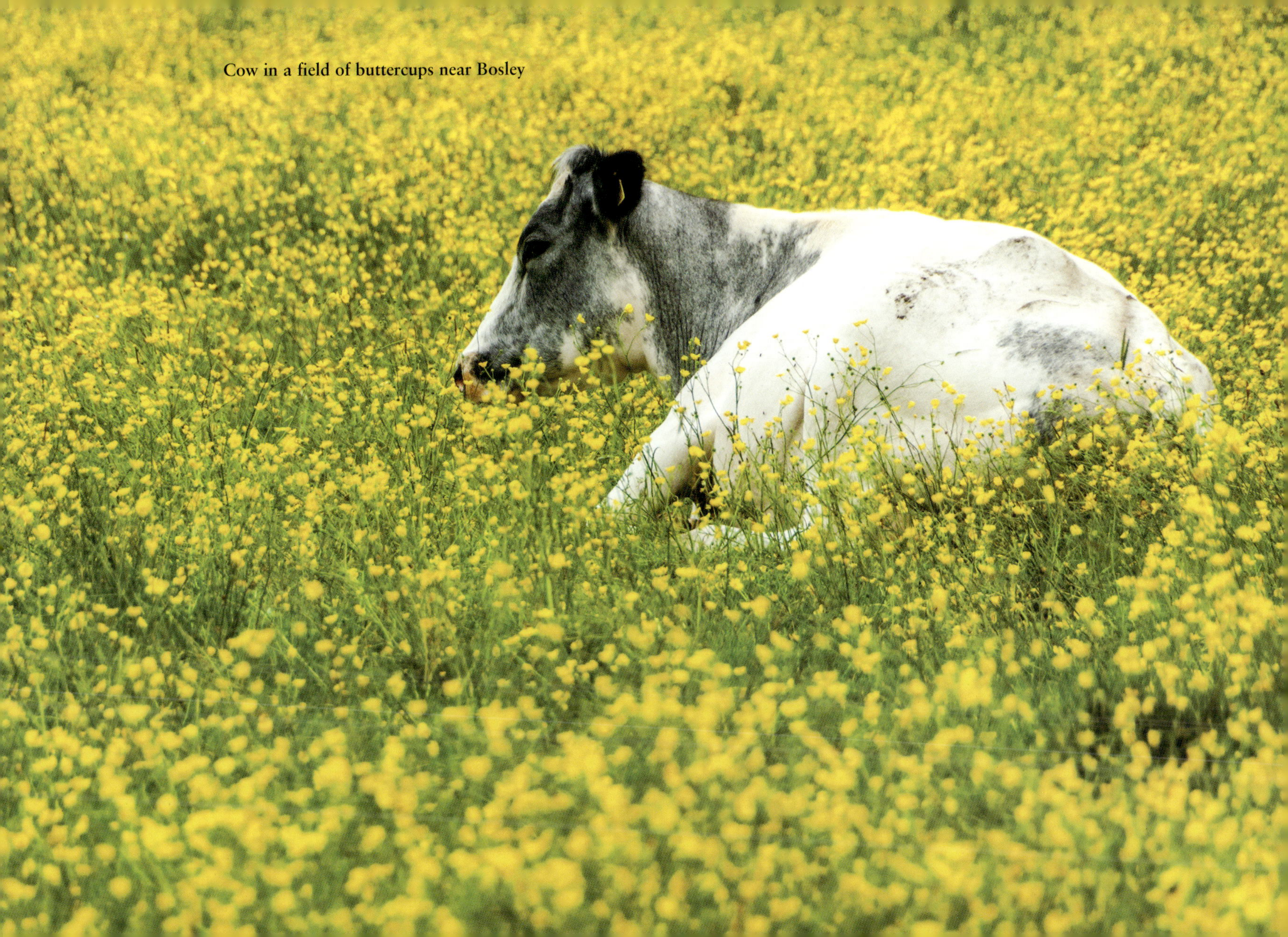

Cow in a field of buttercups near Bosley

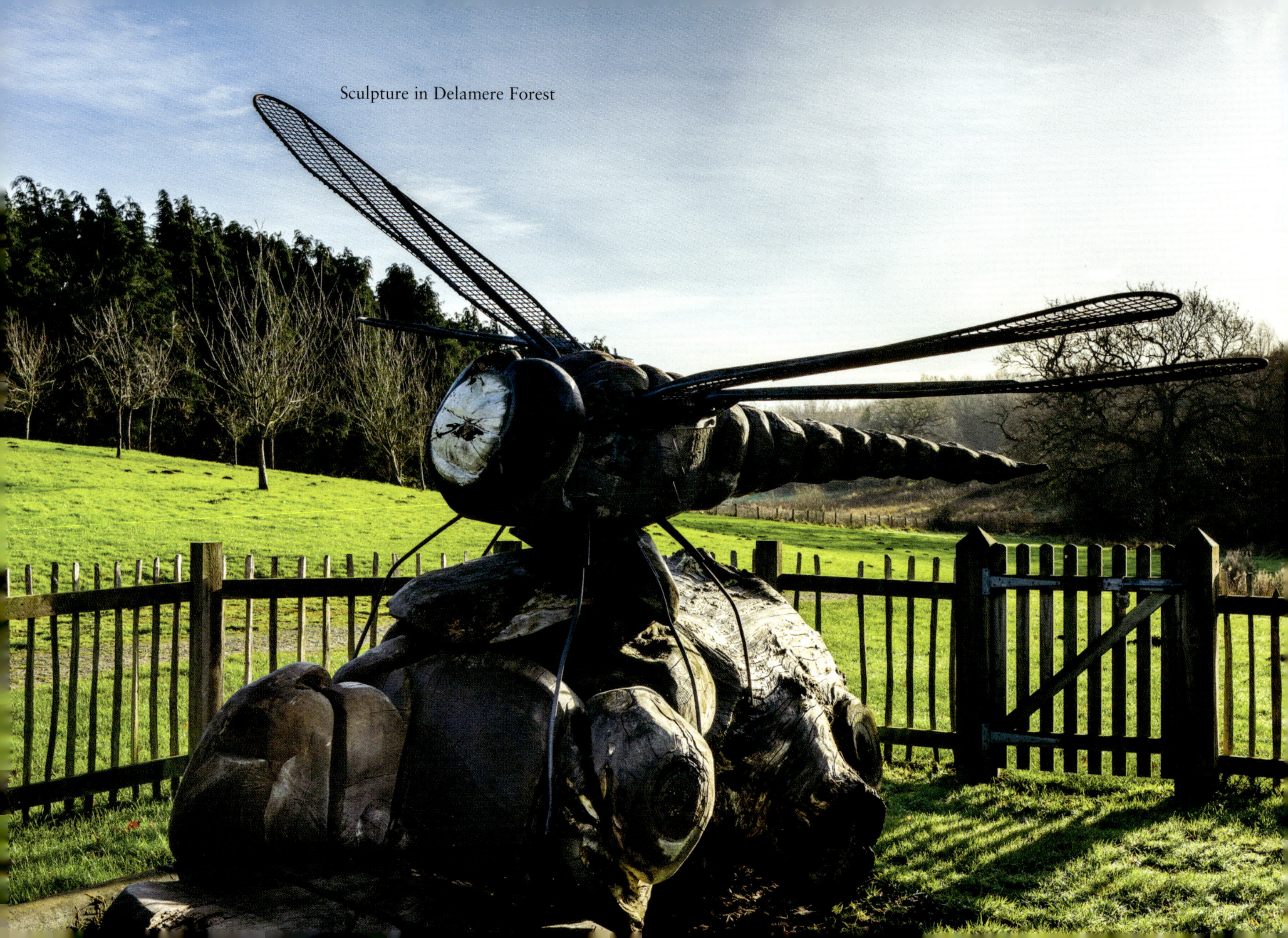

Sculpture in Delamere Forest

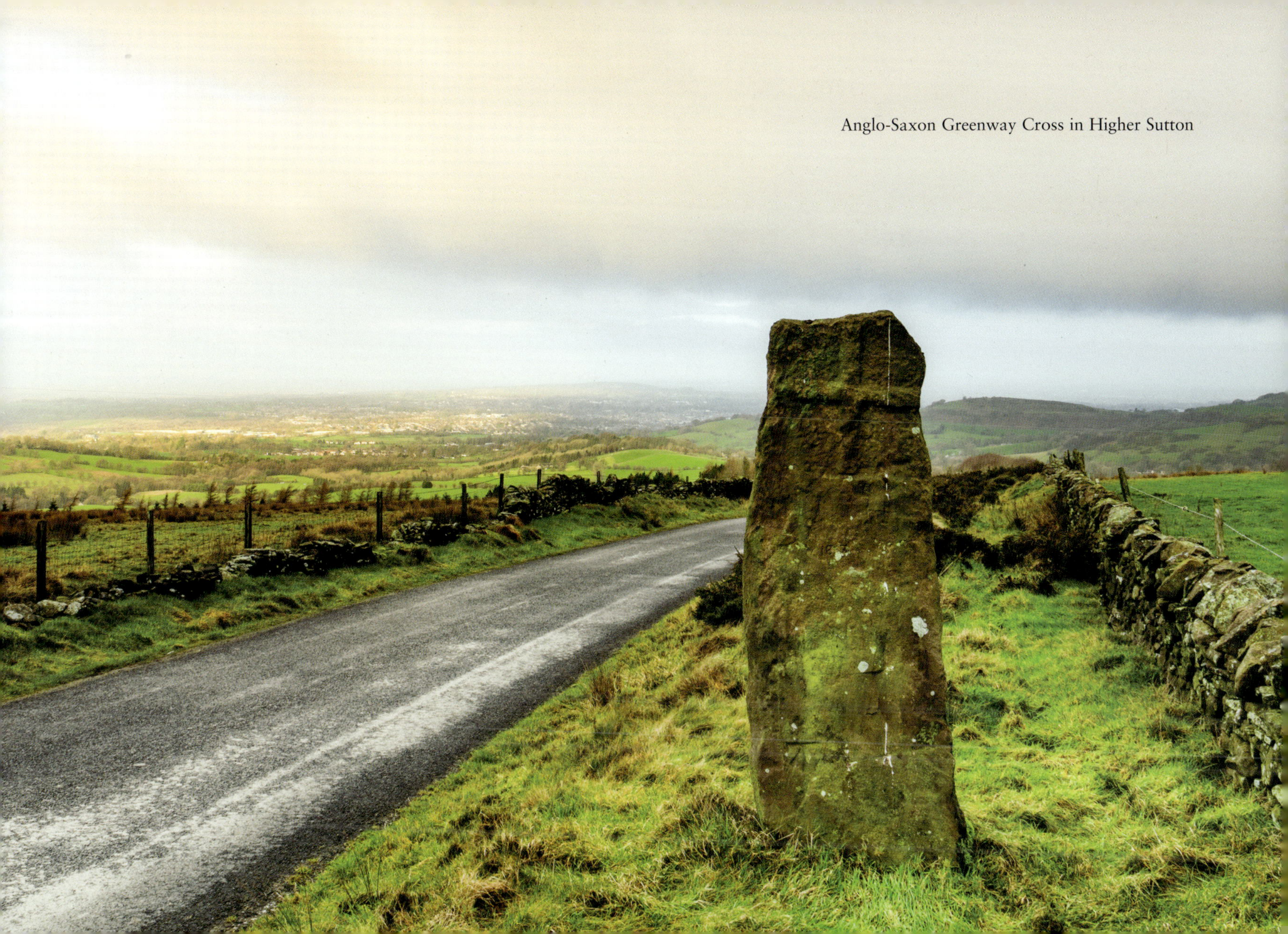

Anglo-Saxon Greenway Cross in Higher Sutton

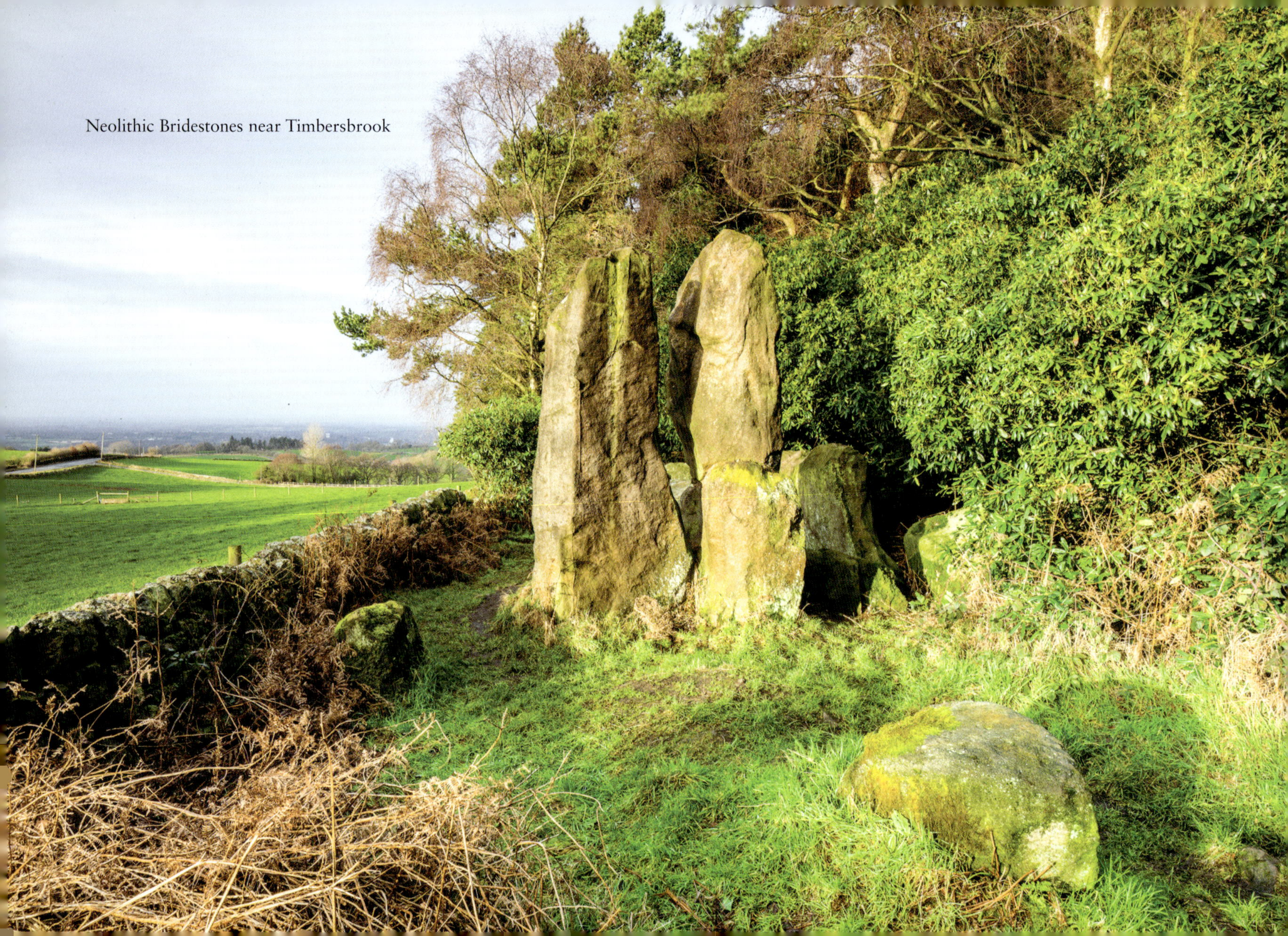

Neolithic Bridestones near Timbersbrook

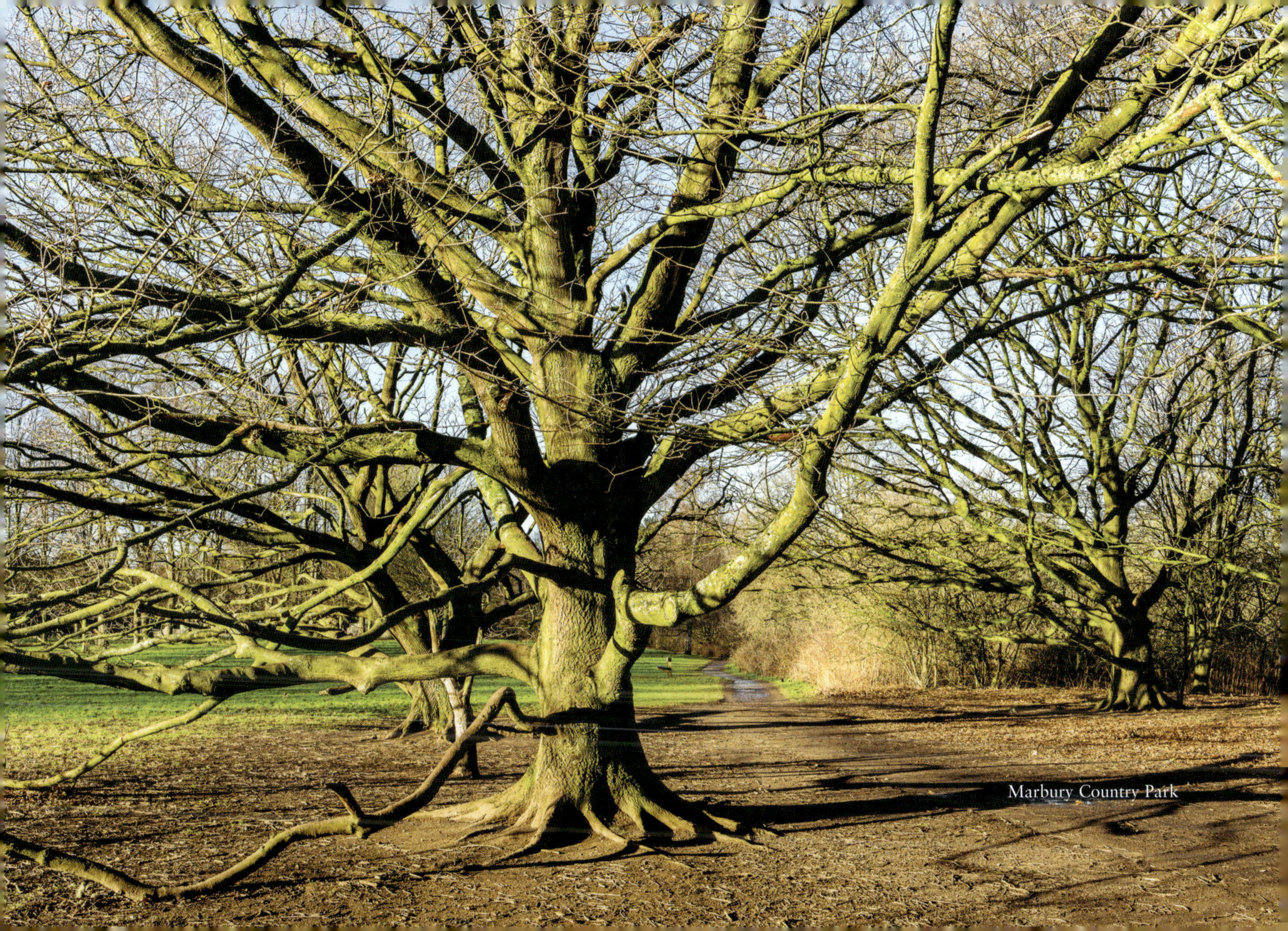

Marbury Country Park

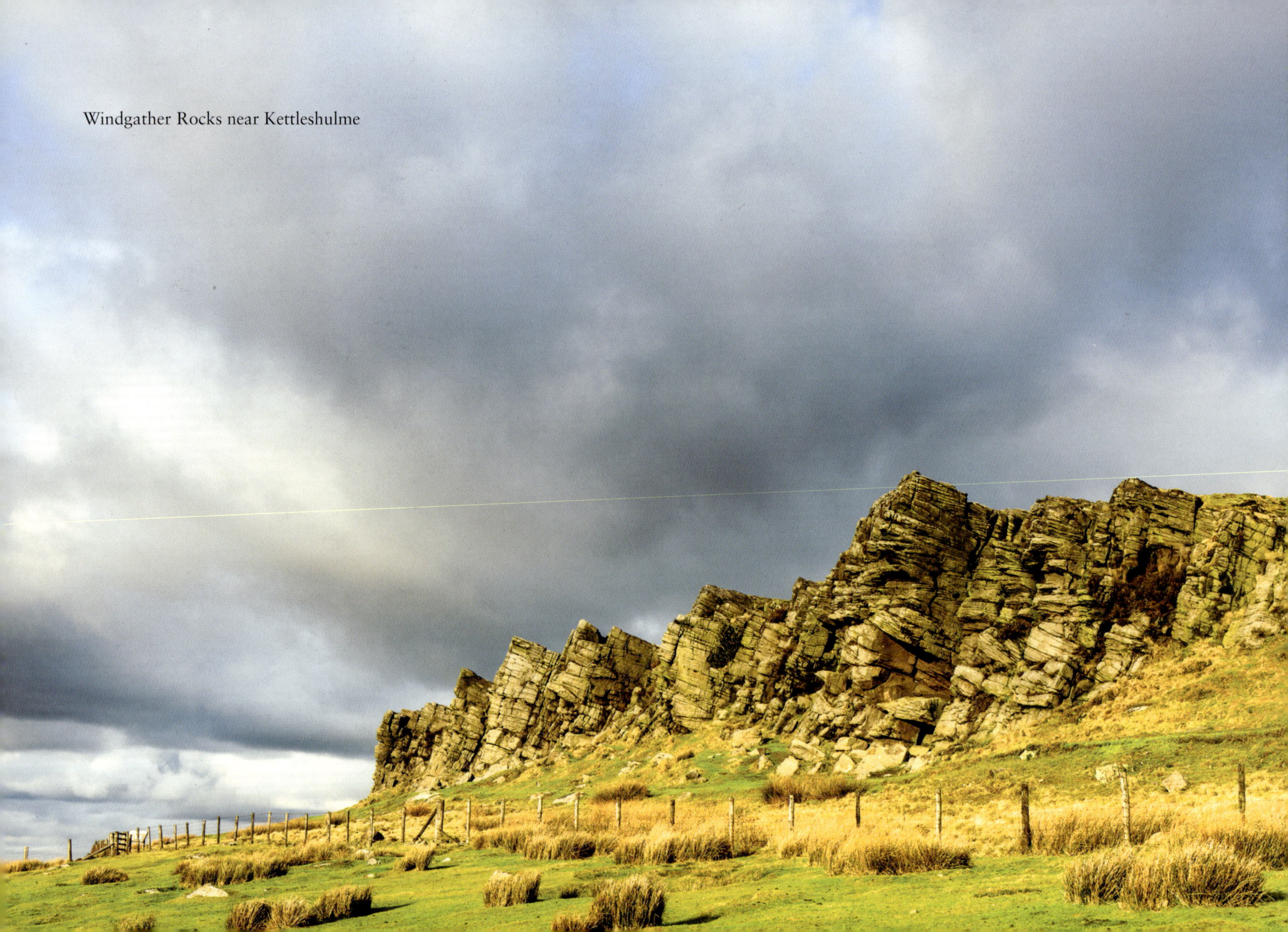

Windgather Rocks near Kettleshulme

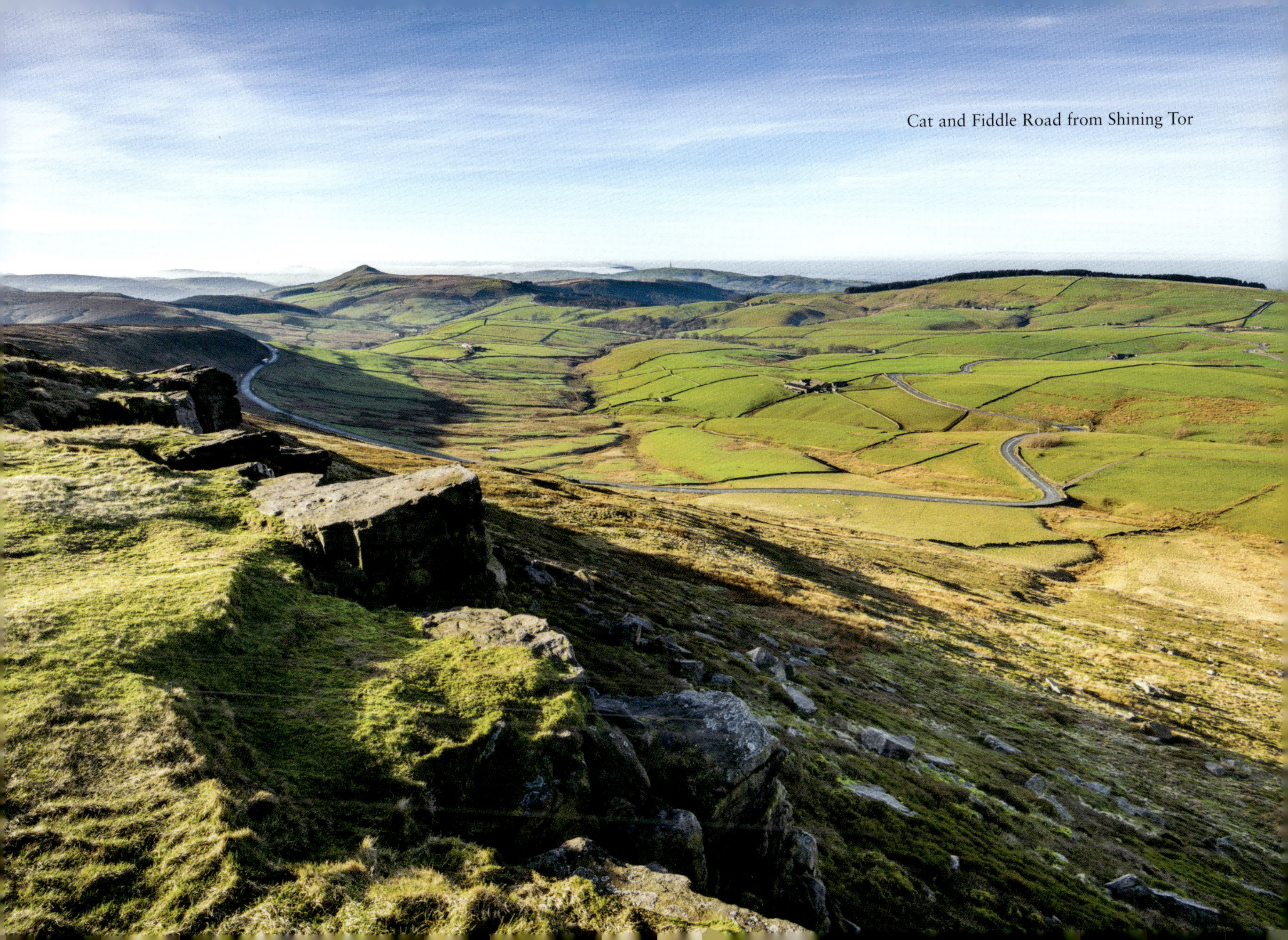

Cat and Fiddle Road from Shining Tor

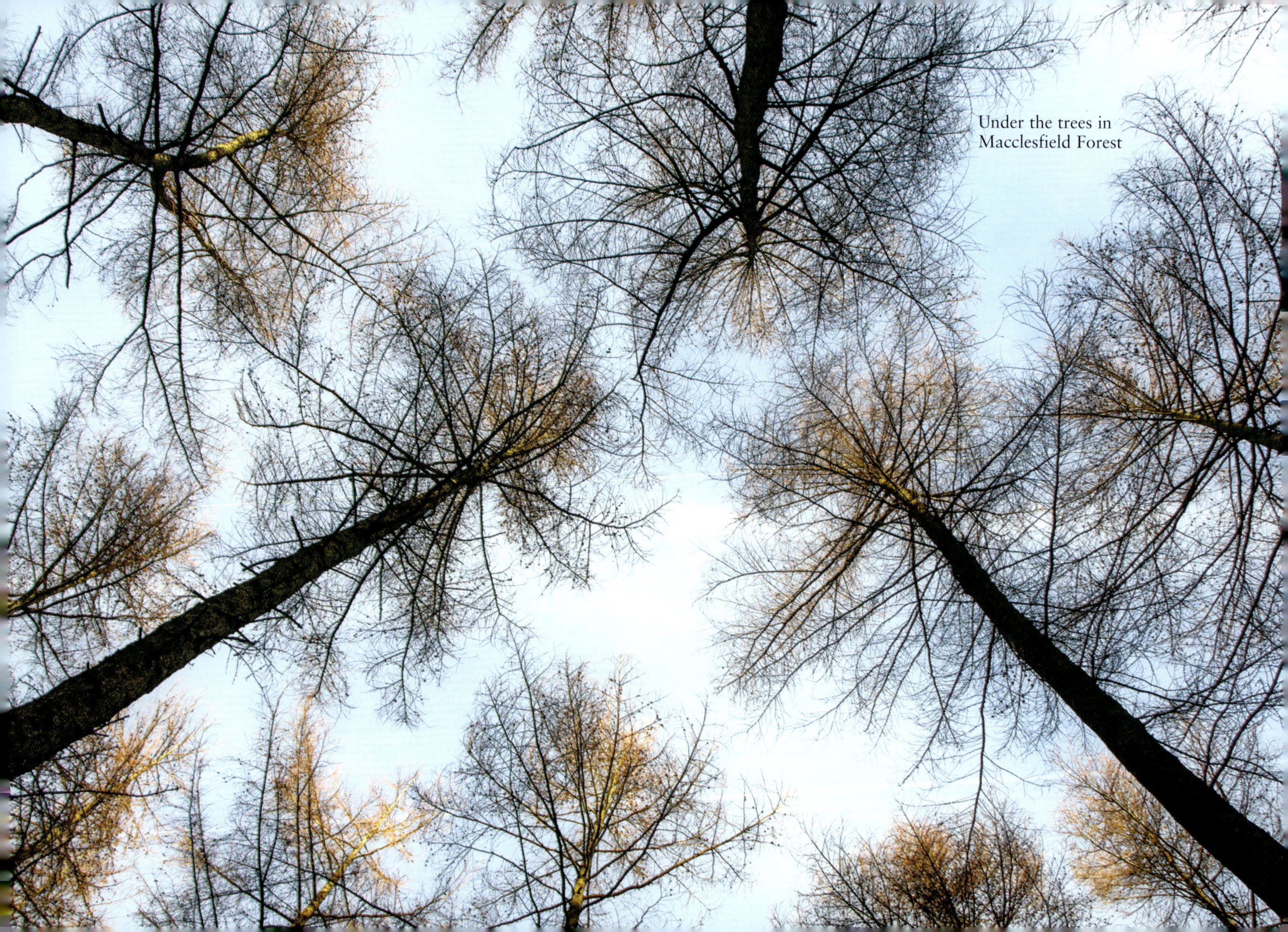

Under the trees in Macclesfield Forest

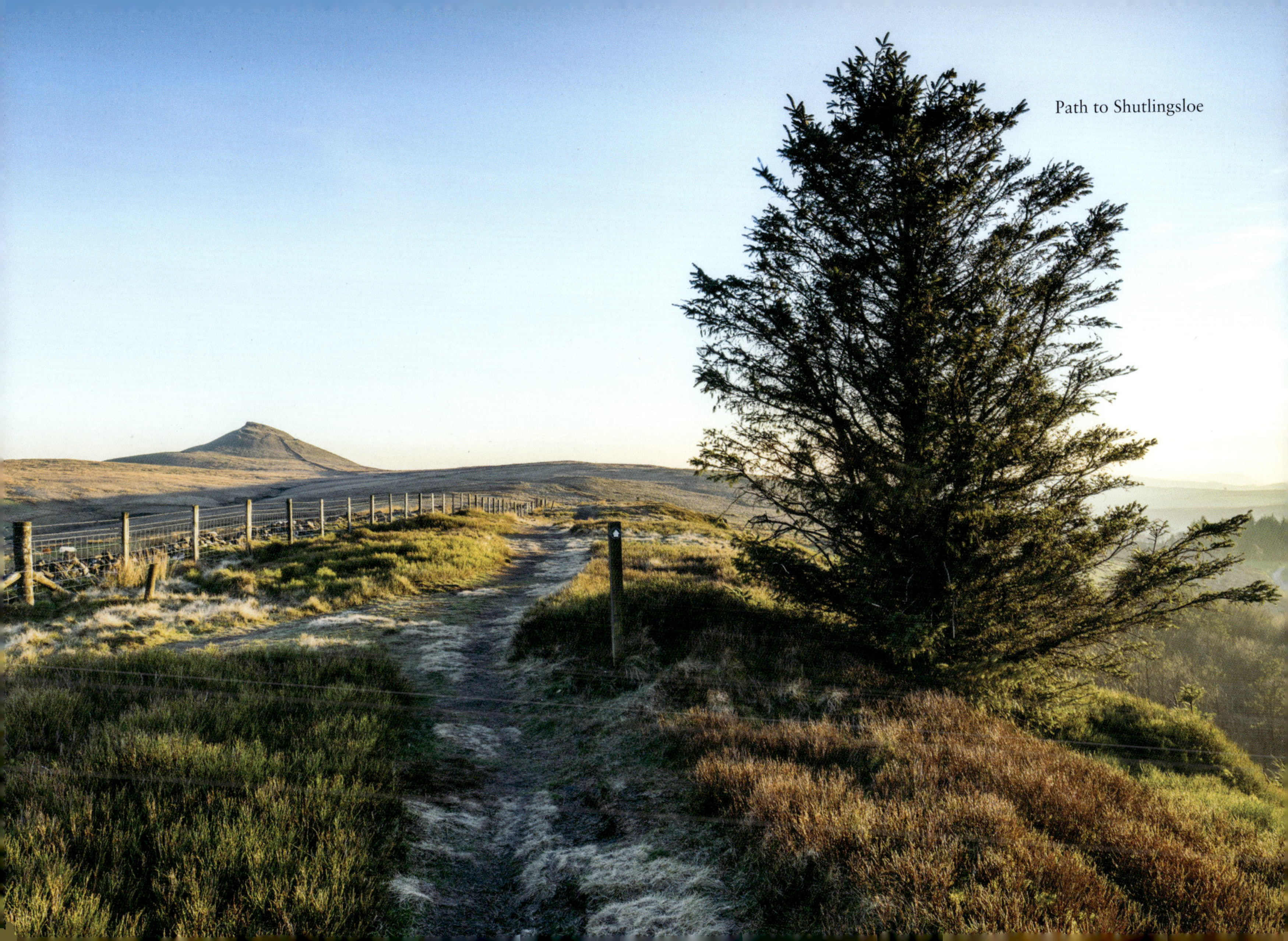

Path to Shutlingsloe

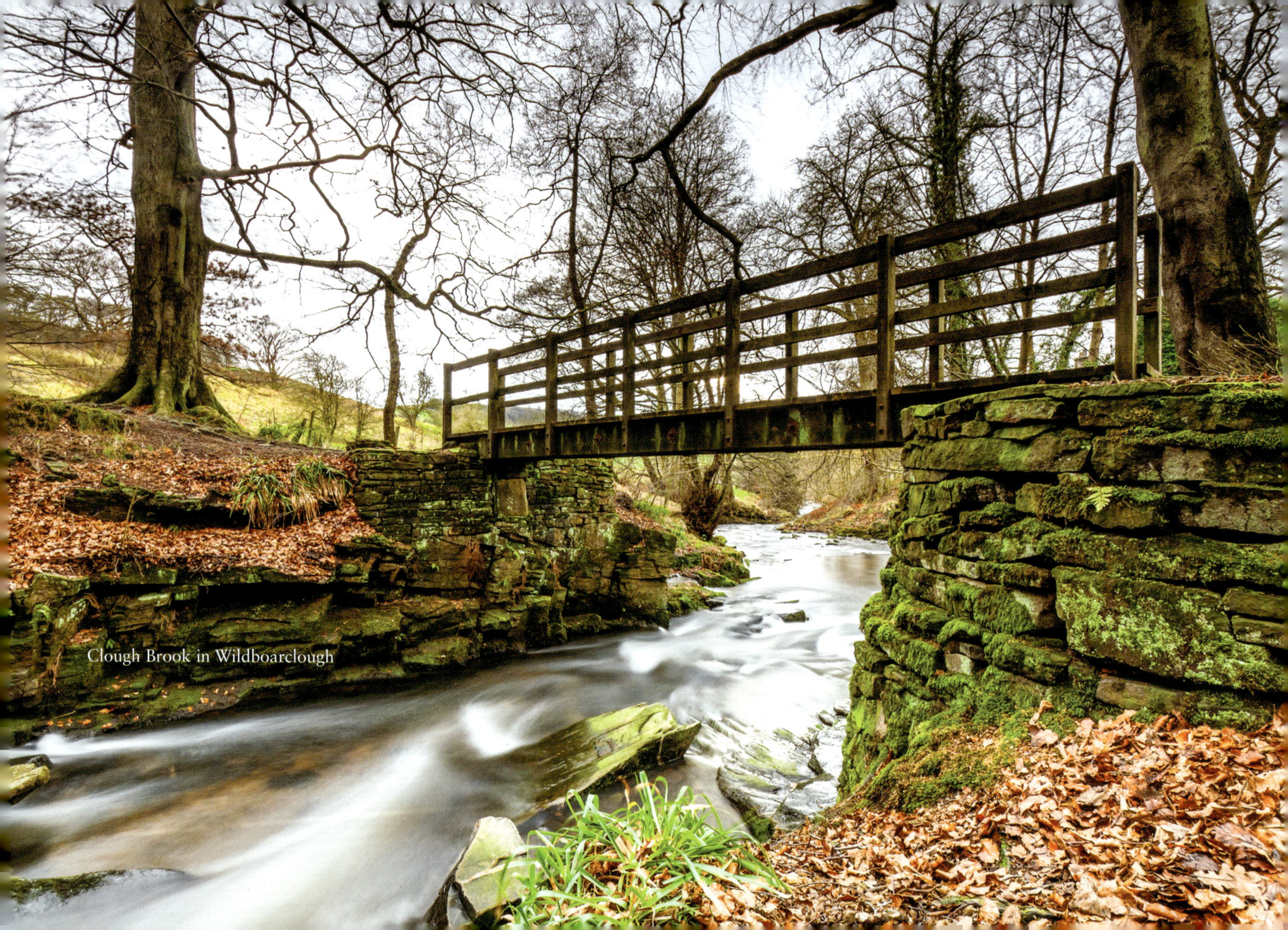

Clough Brook in Wildboarclough

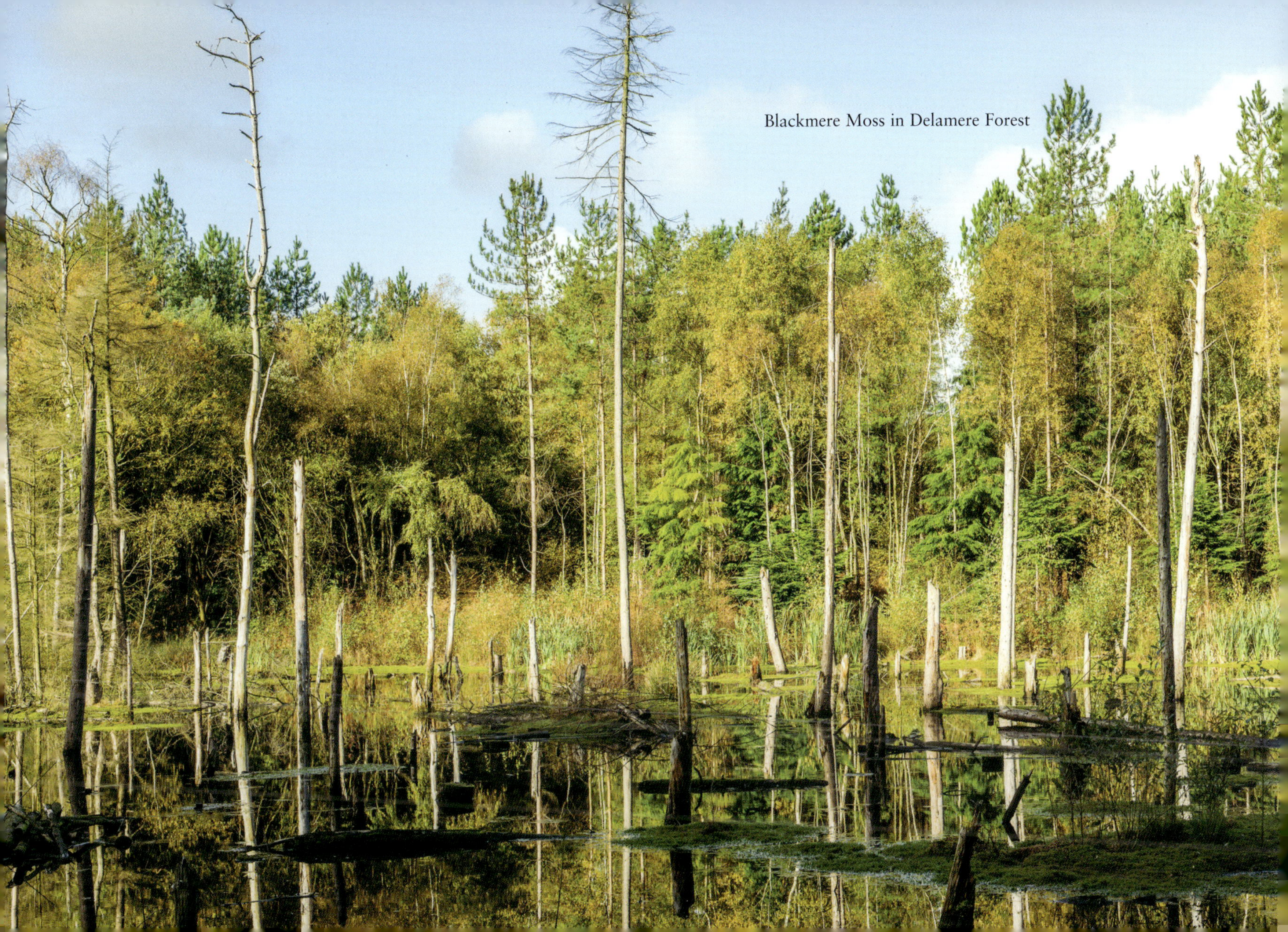
Blackmere Moss in Delamere Forest

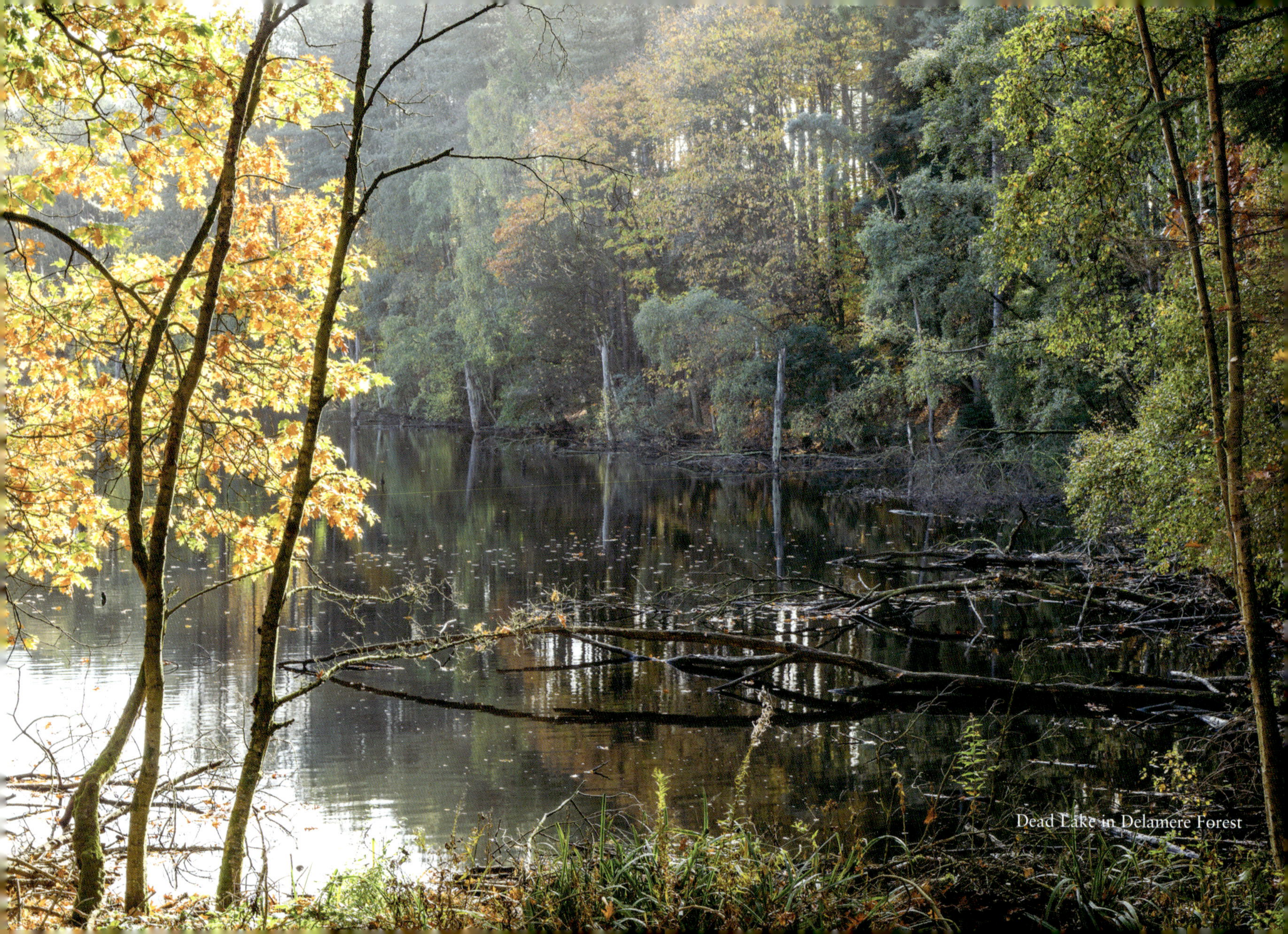

Dead Lake in Delamere Forest

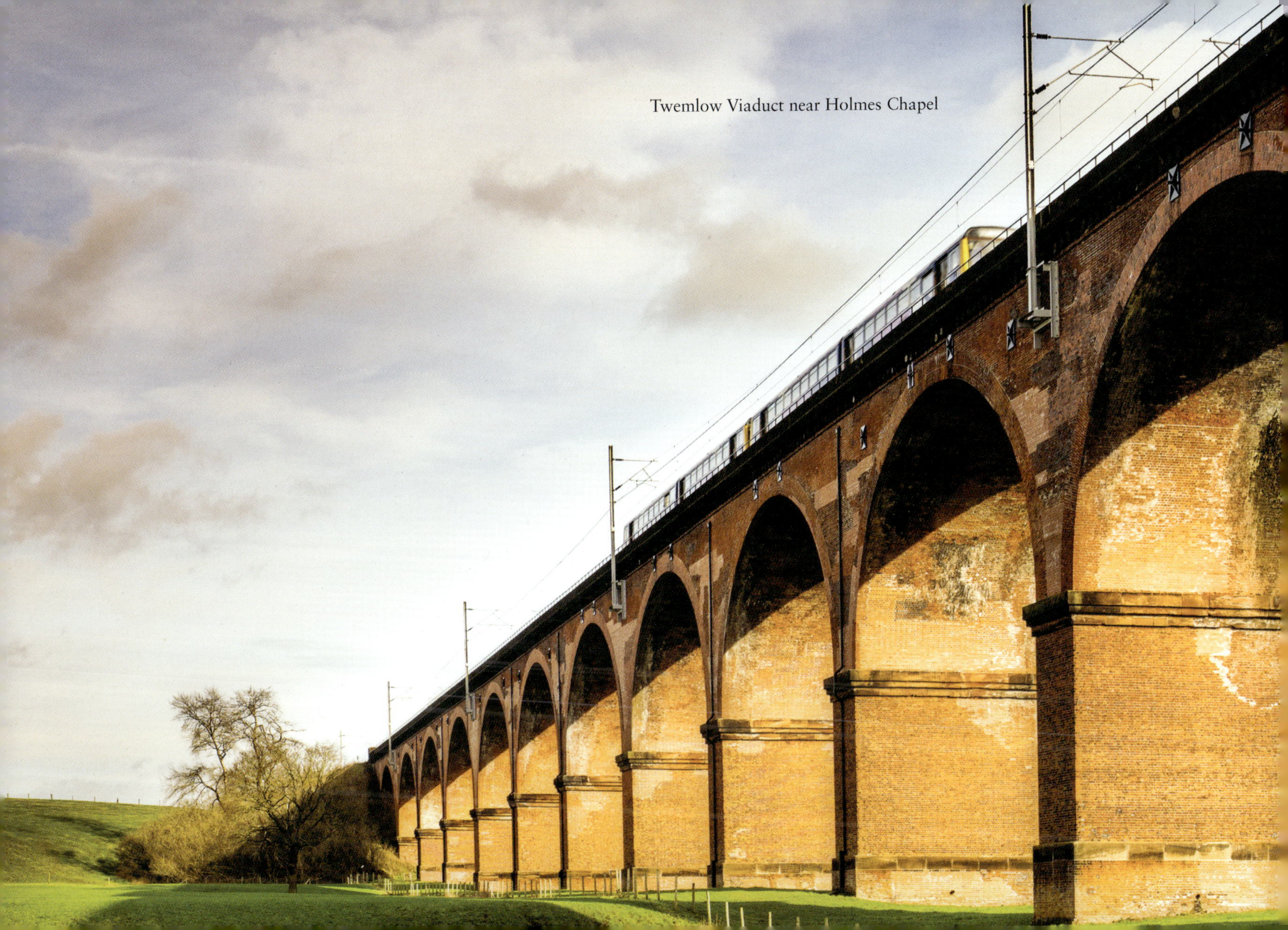

Twemlow Viaduct near Holmes Chapel

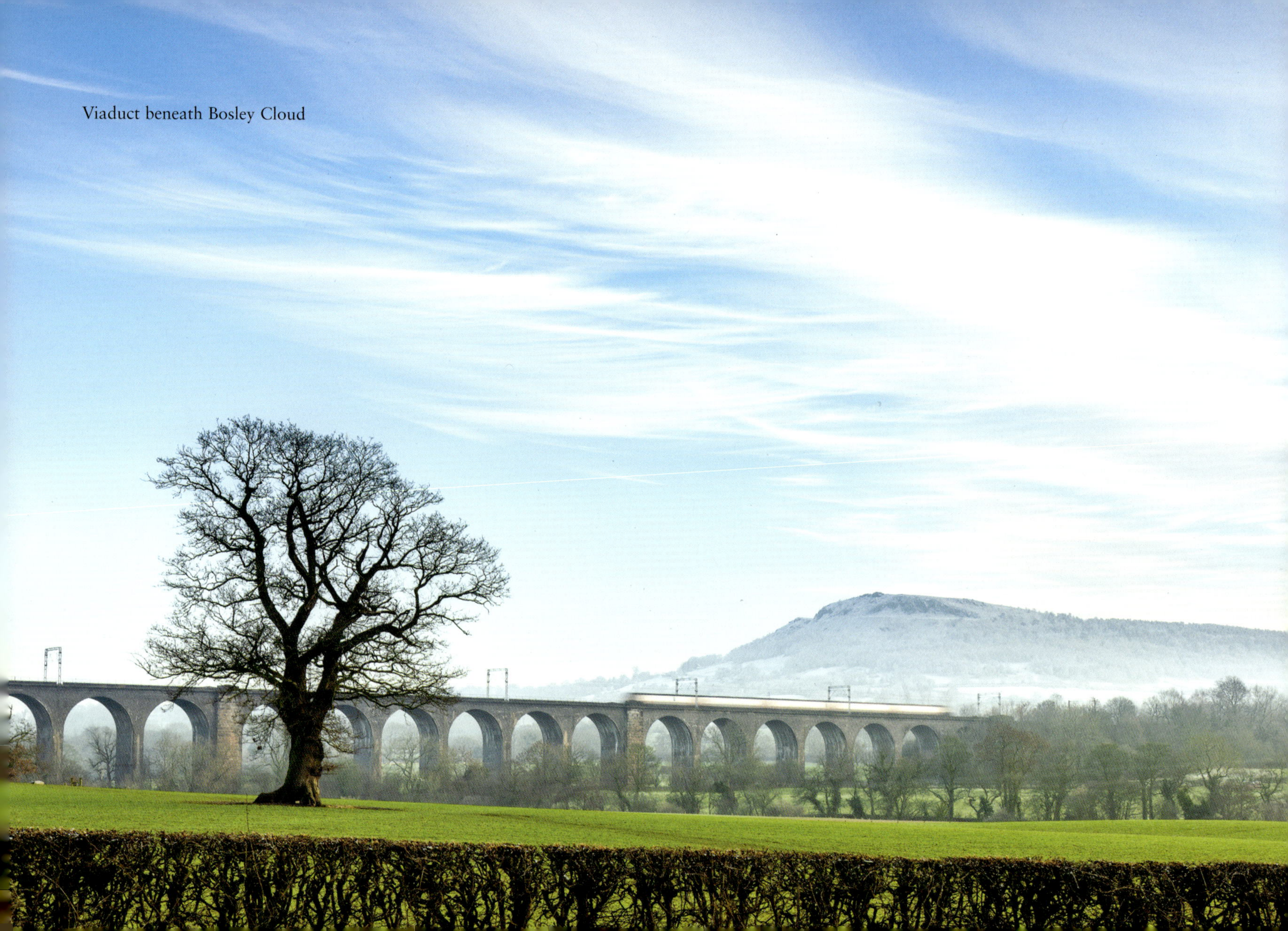
Viaduct beneath Bosley Cloud

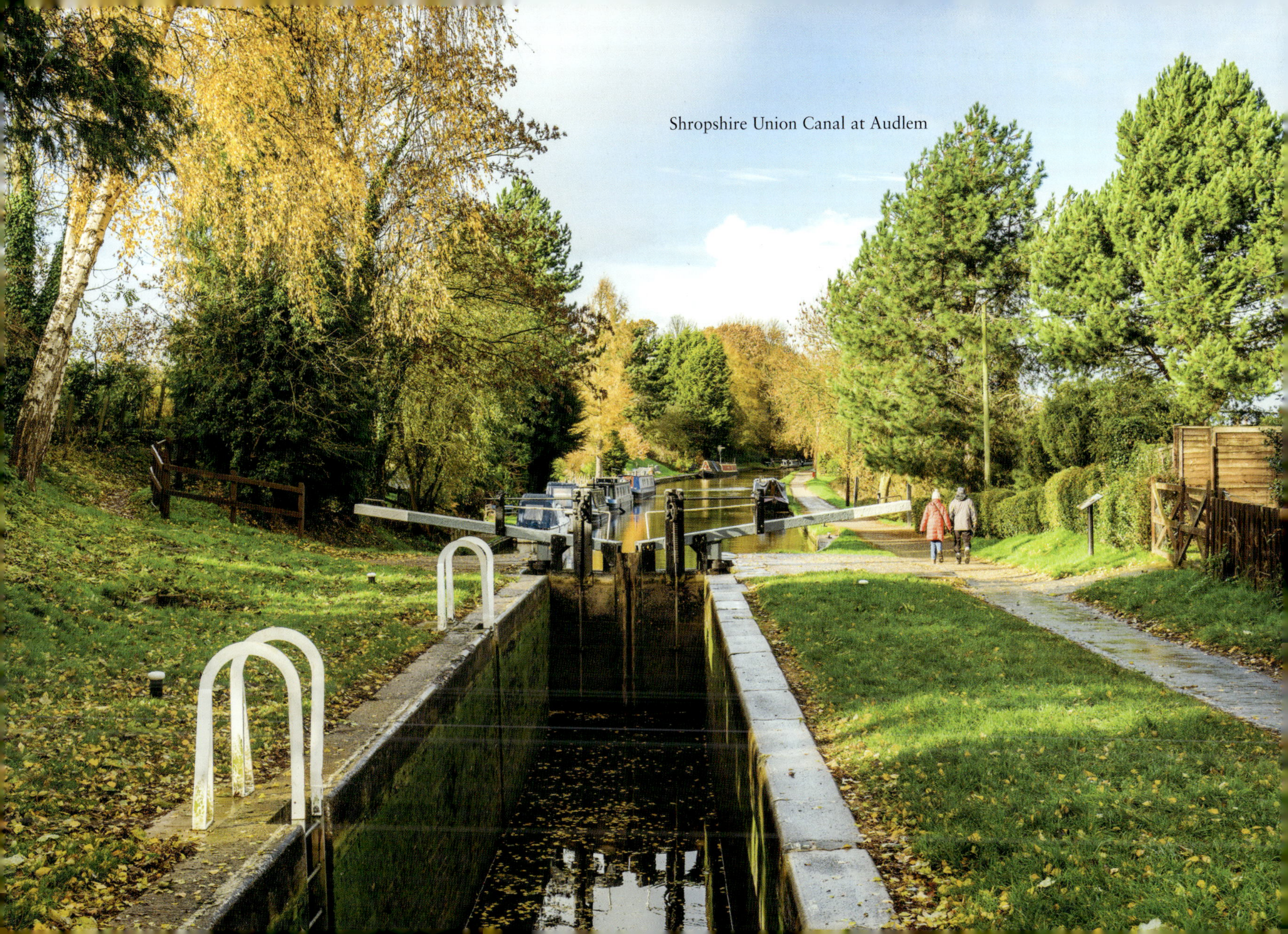

Shropshire Union Canal at Audlem

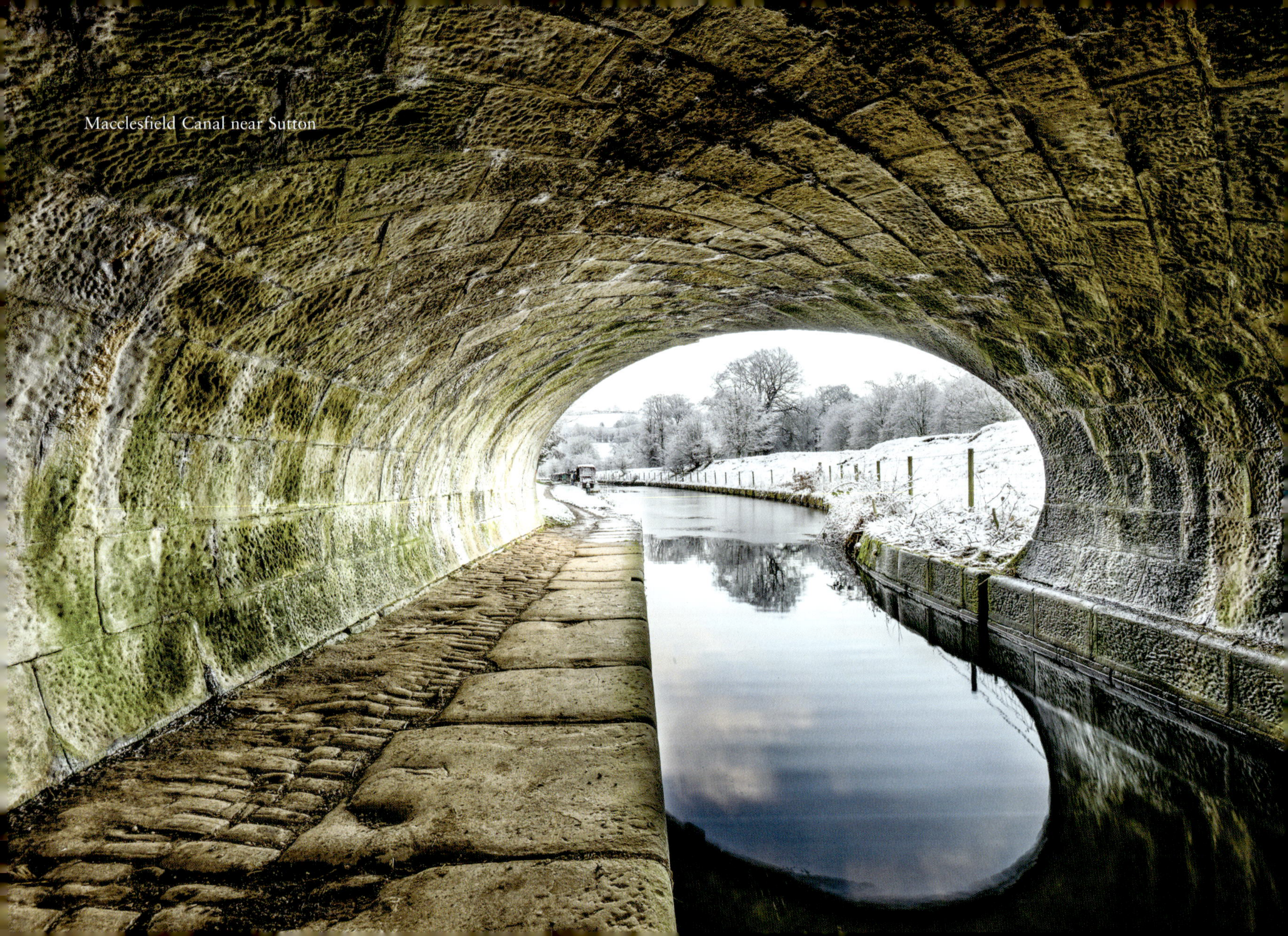

Macclesfield Canal near Sutton

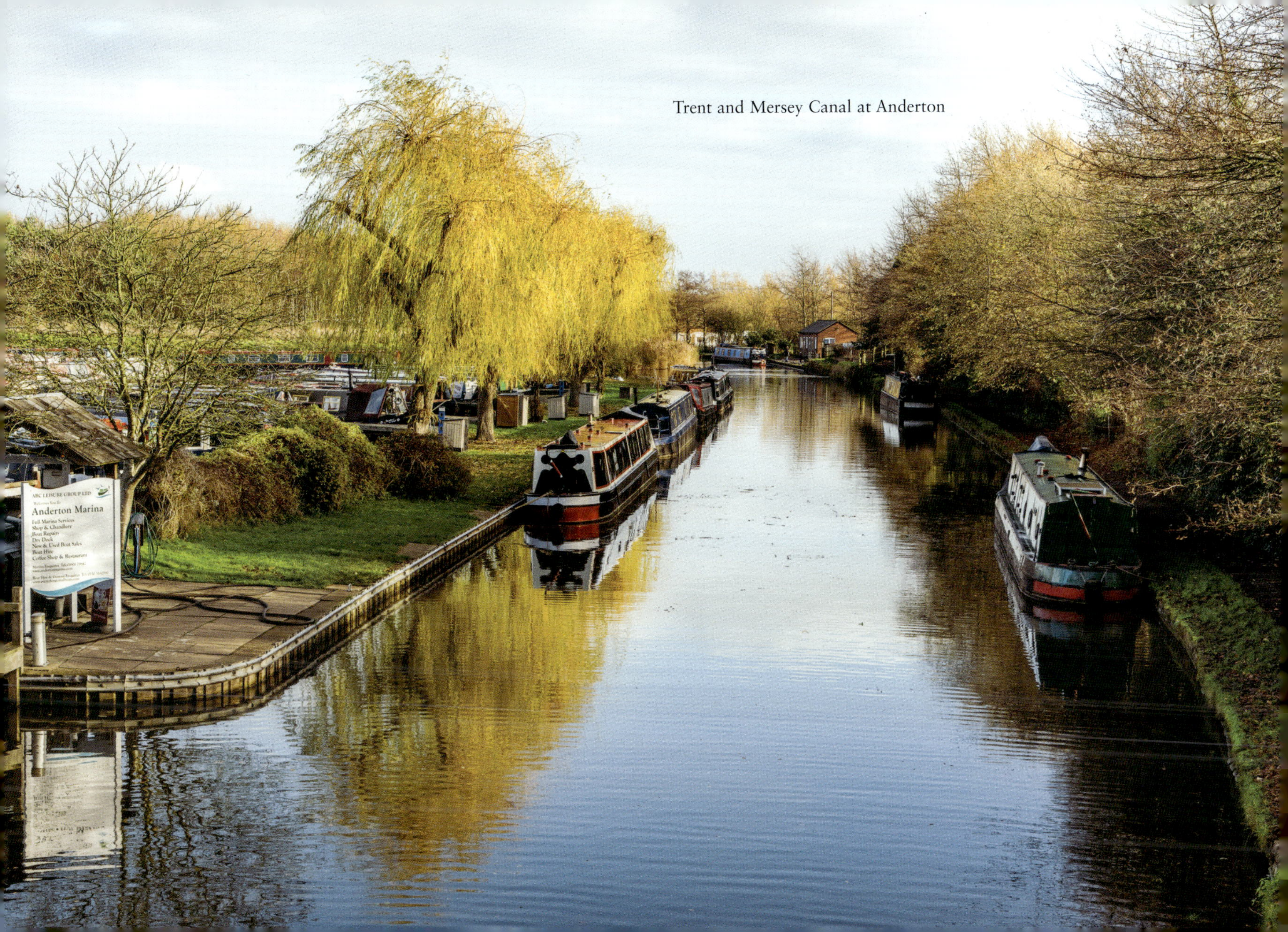

Trent and Mersey Canal at Anderton

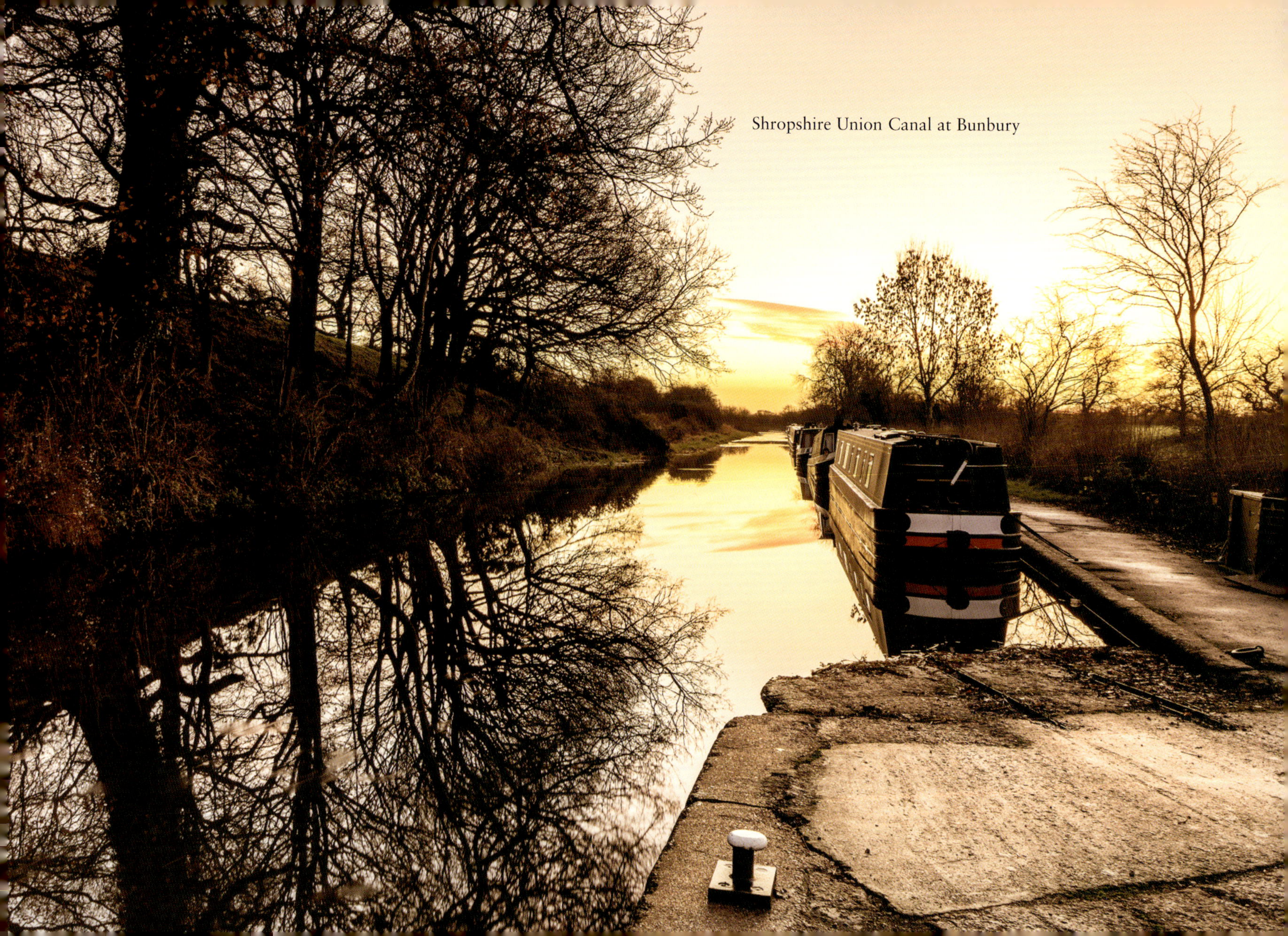

Shropshire Union Canal at Bunbury

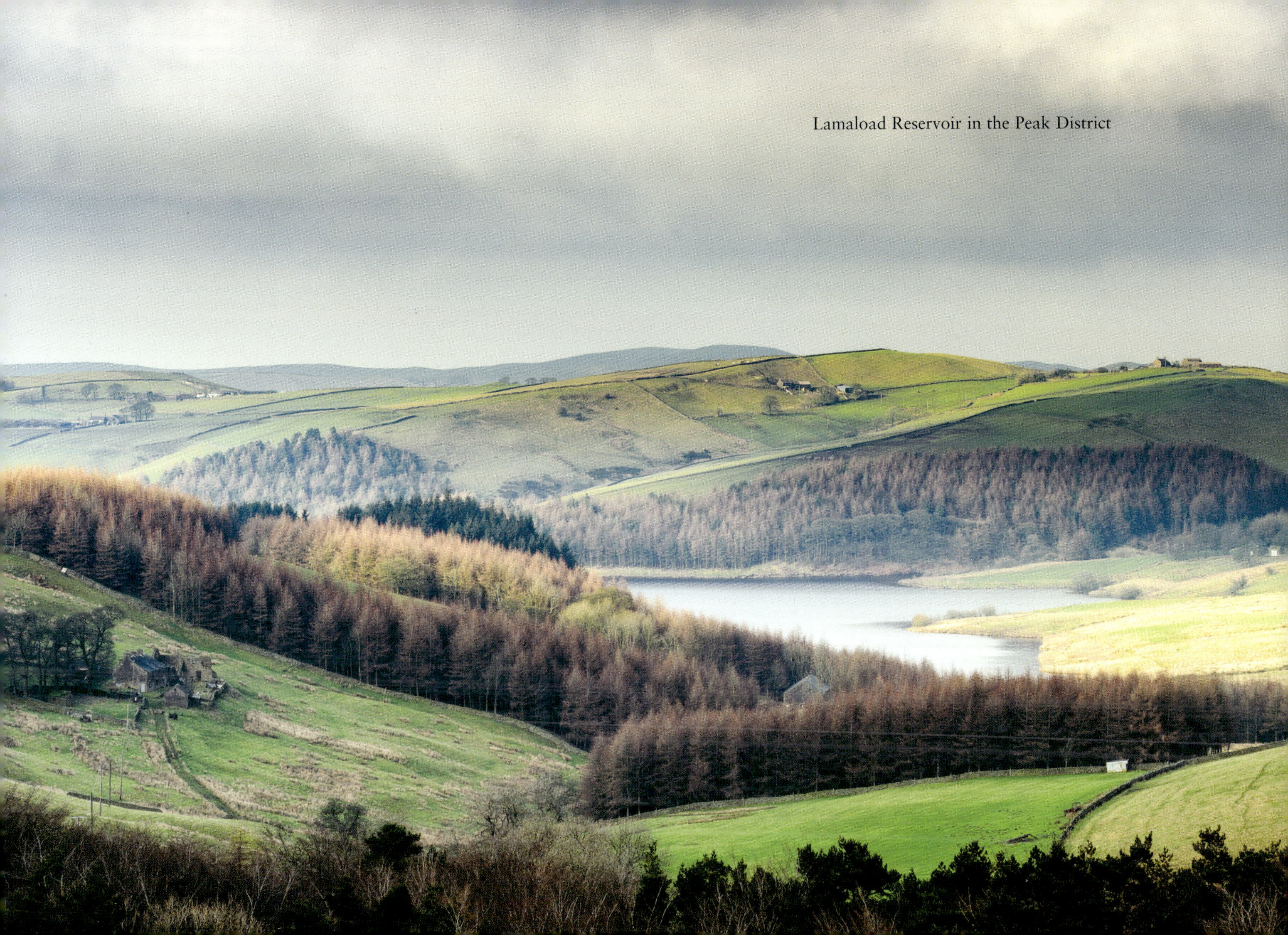

Lamaload Reservoir in the Peak District

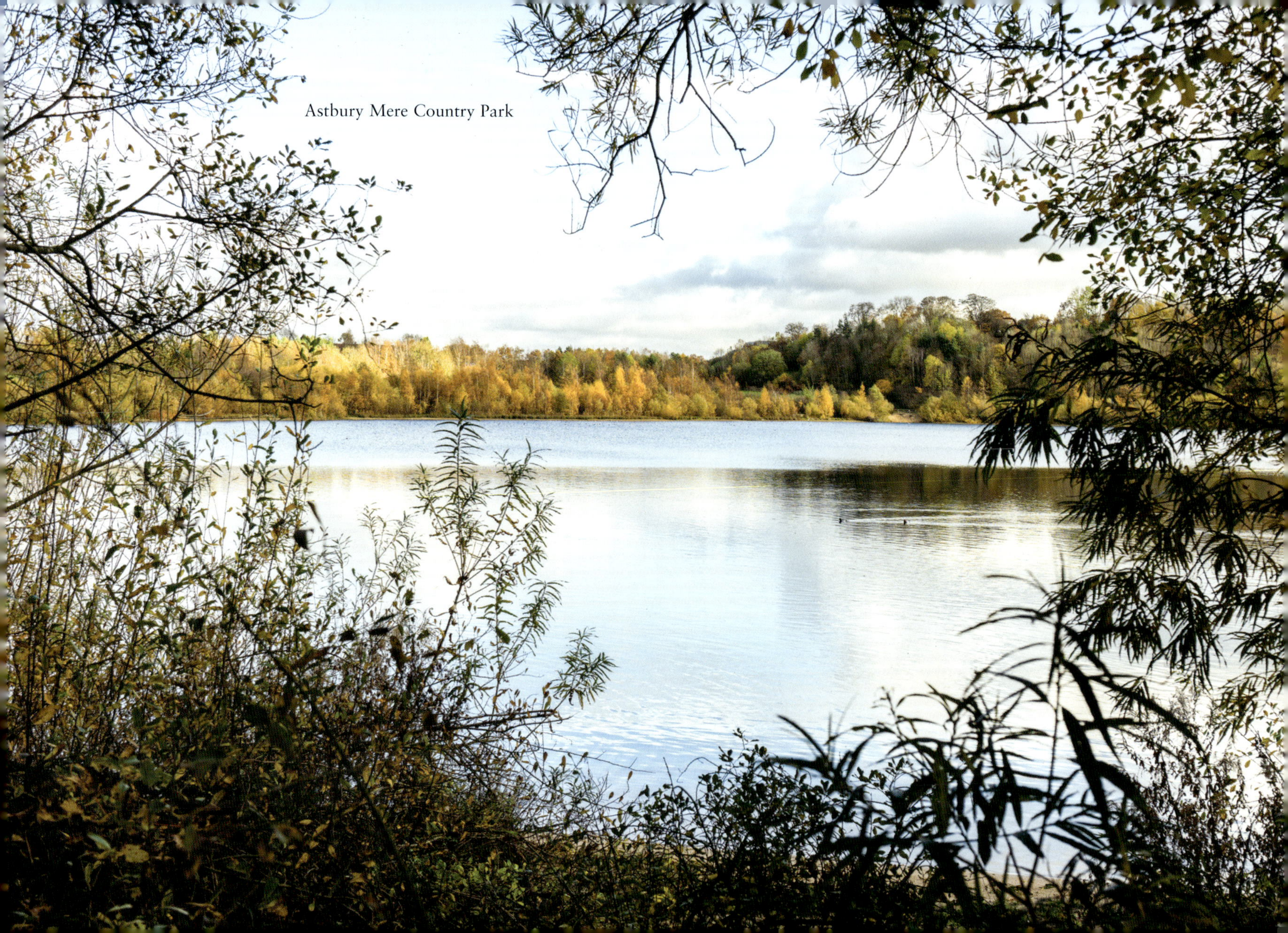

Astbury Mere Country Park

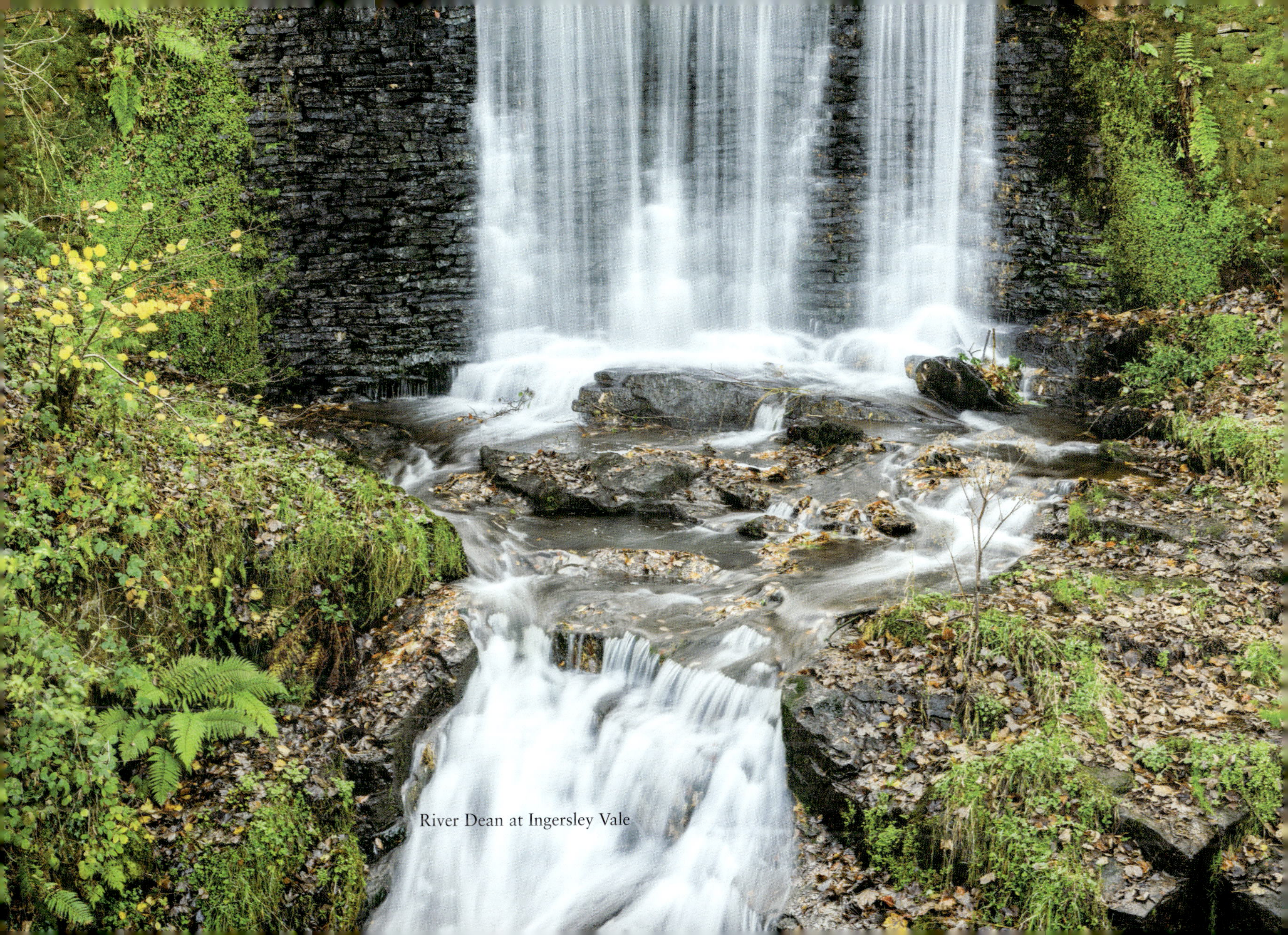

River Dean at Ingersley Vale

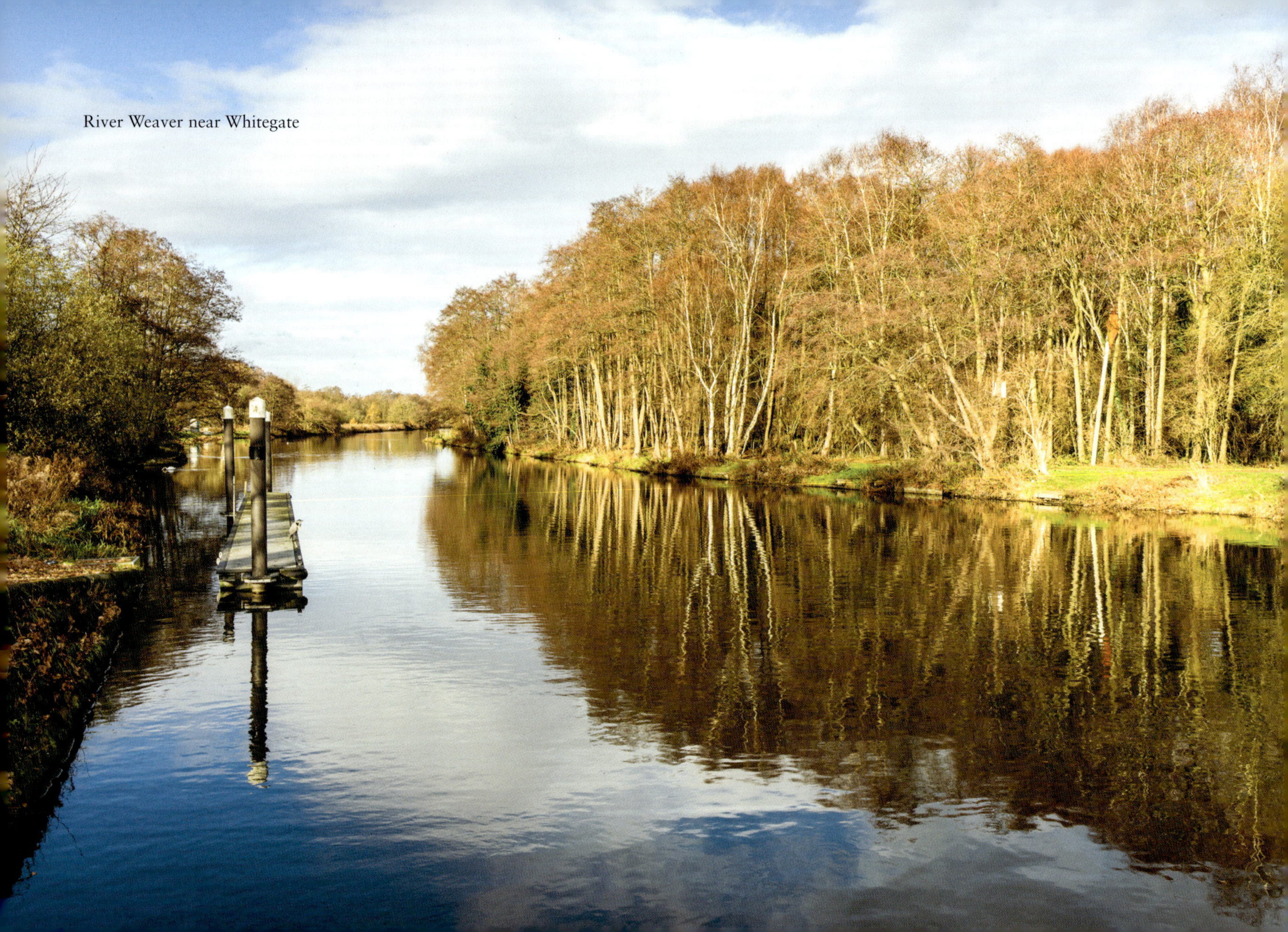
River Weaver near Whitegate

Acton Swing Bridge over the River Weaver

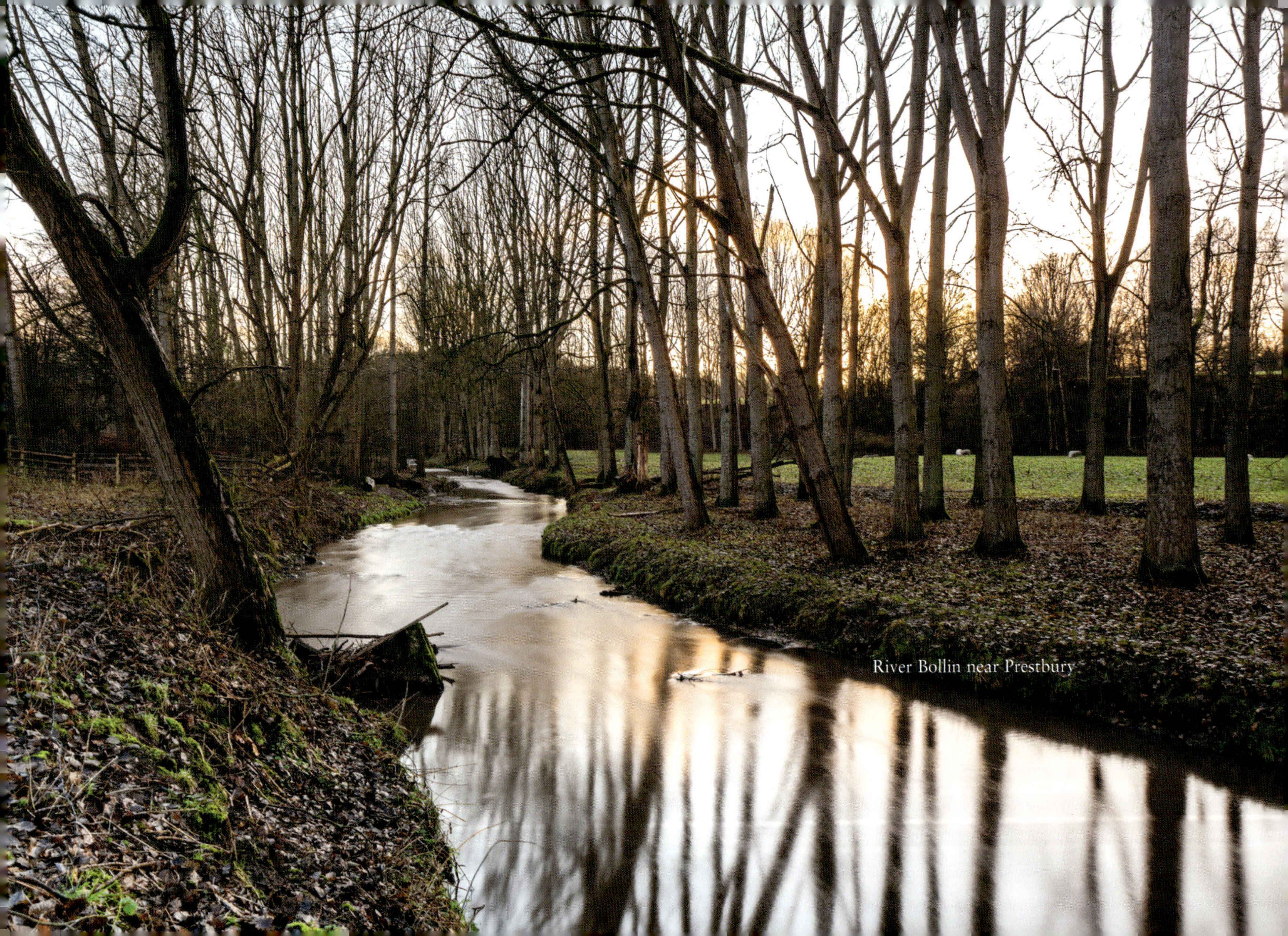

River Bollin near Prestbury

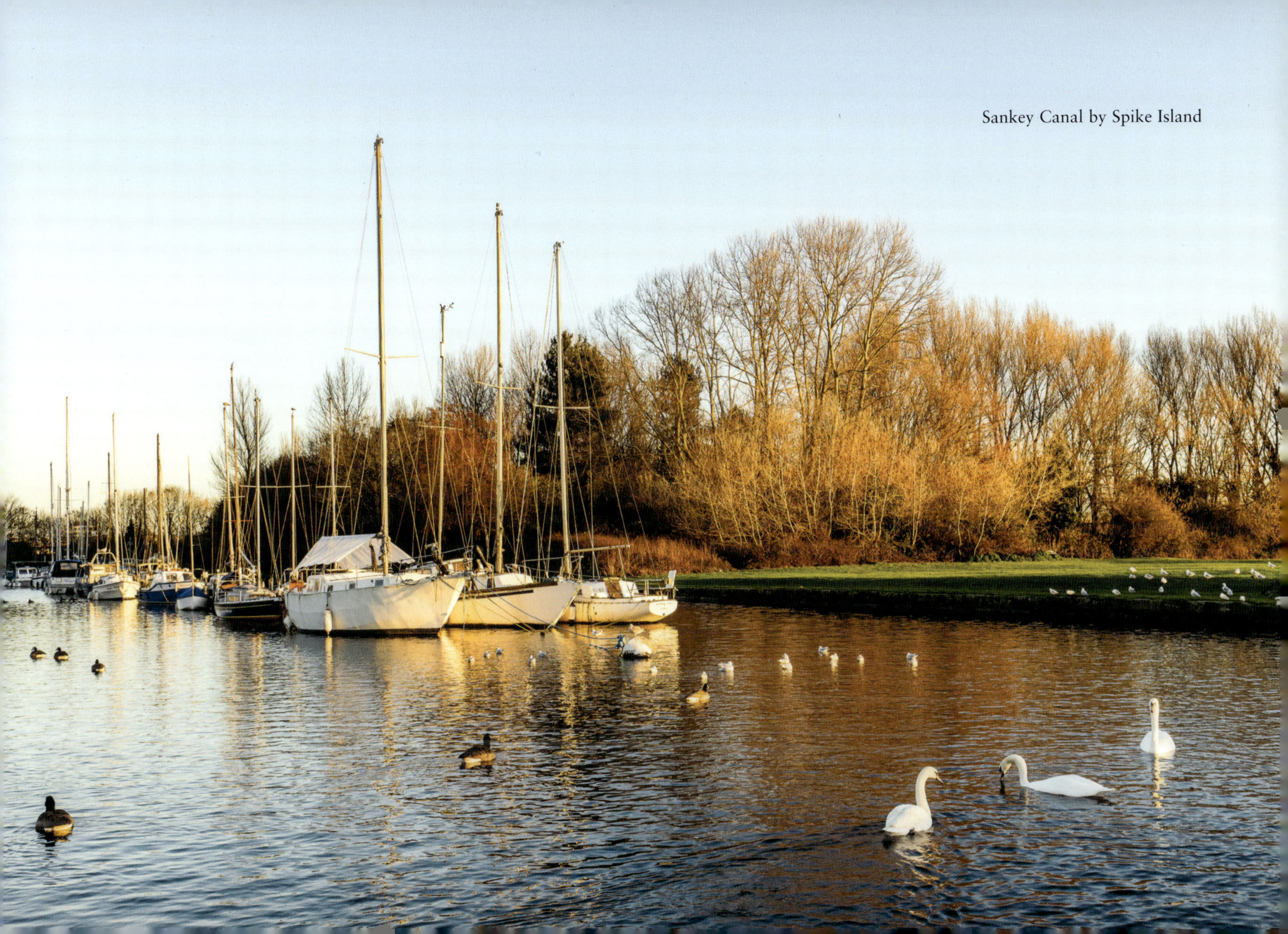

Sankey Canal by Spike Island

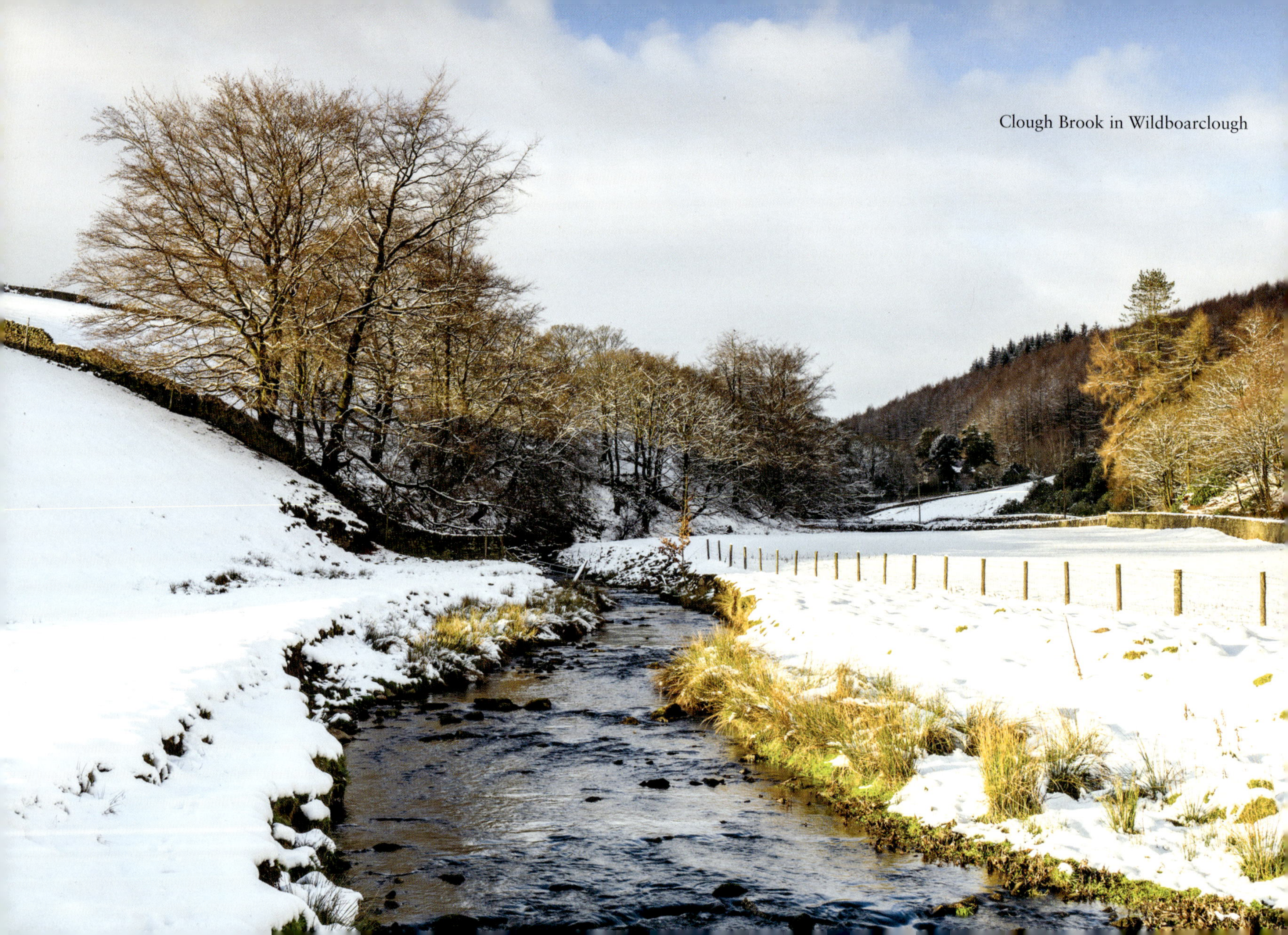

Clough Brook in Wildboarclough

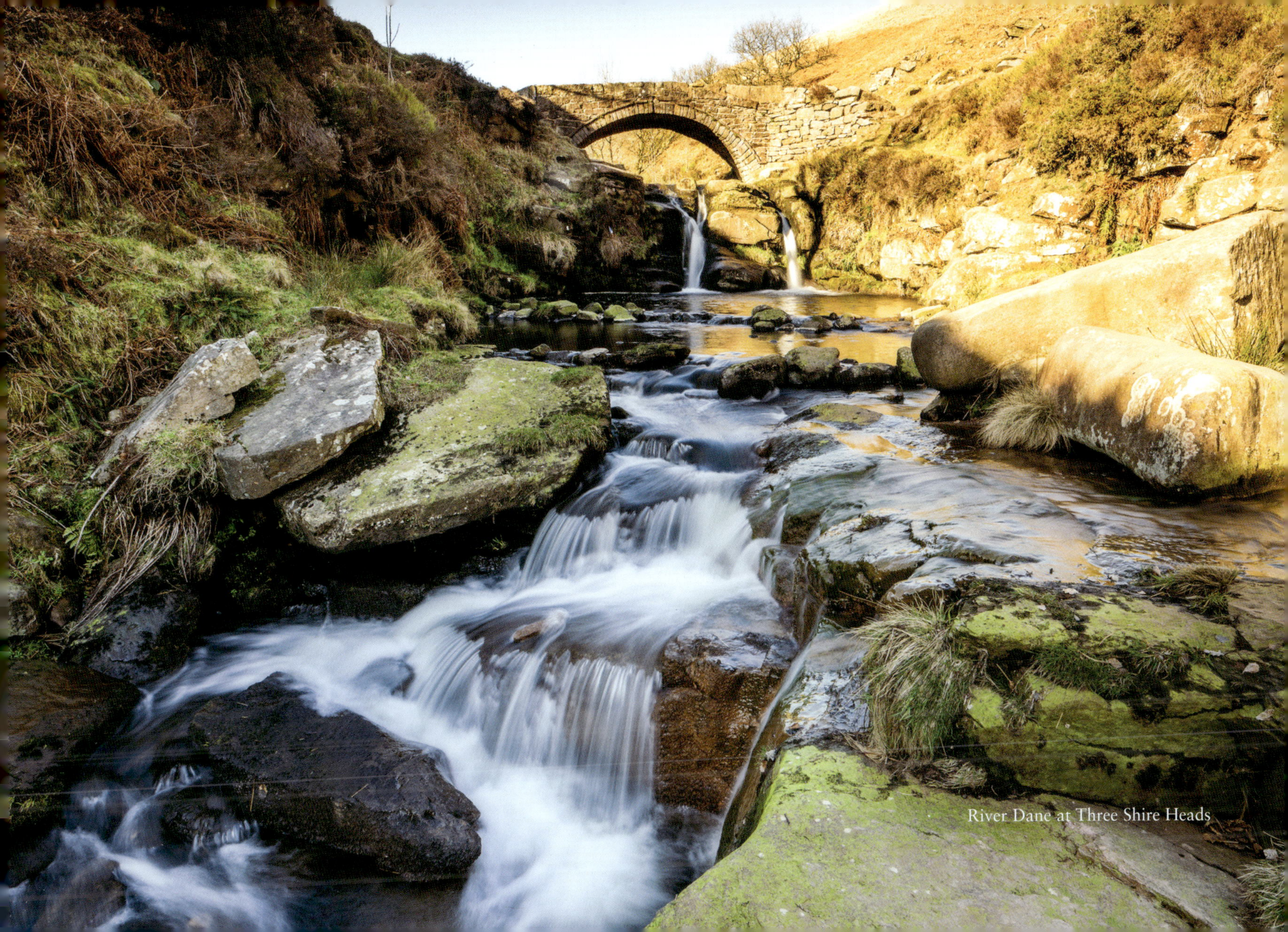

River Dane at Three Shire Heads

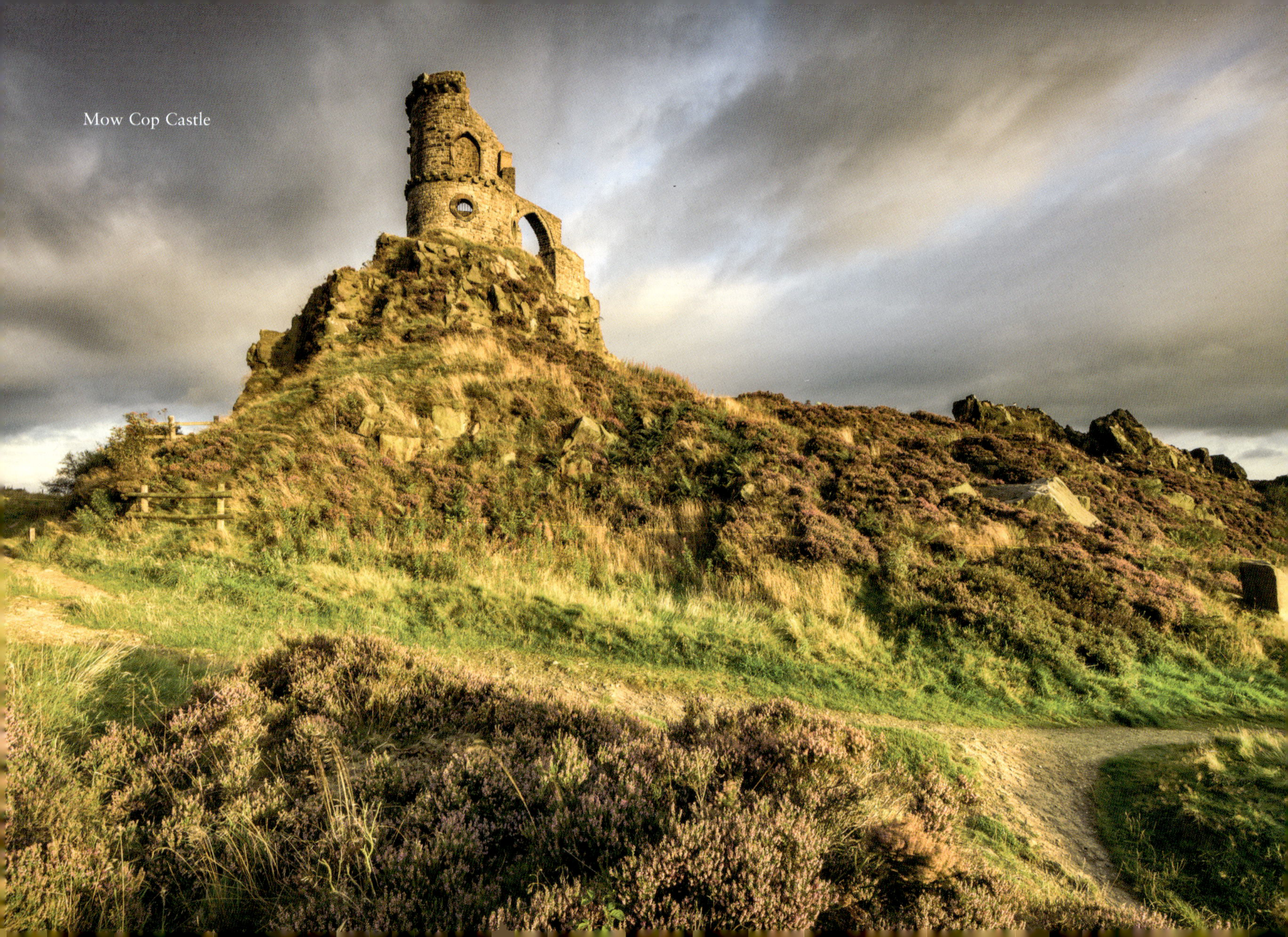
Mow Cop Castle

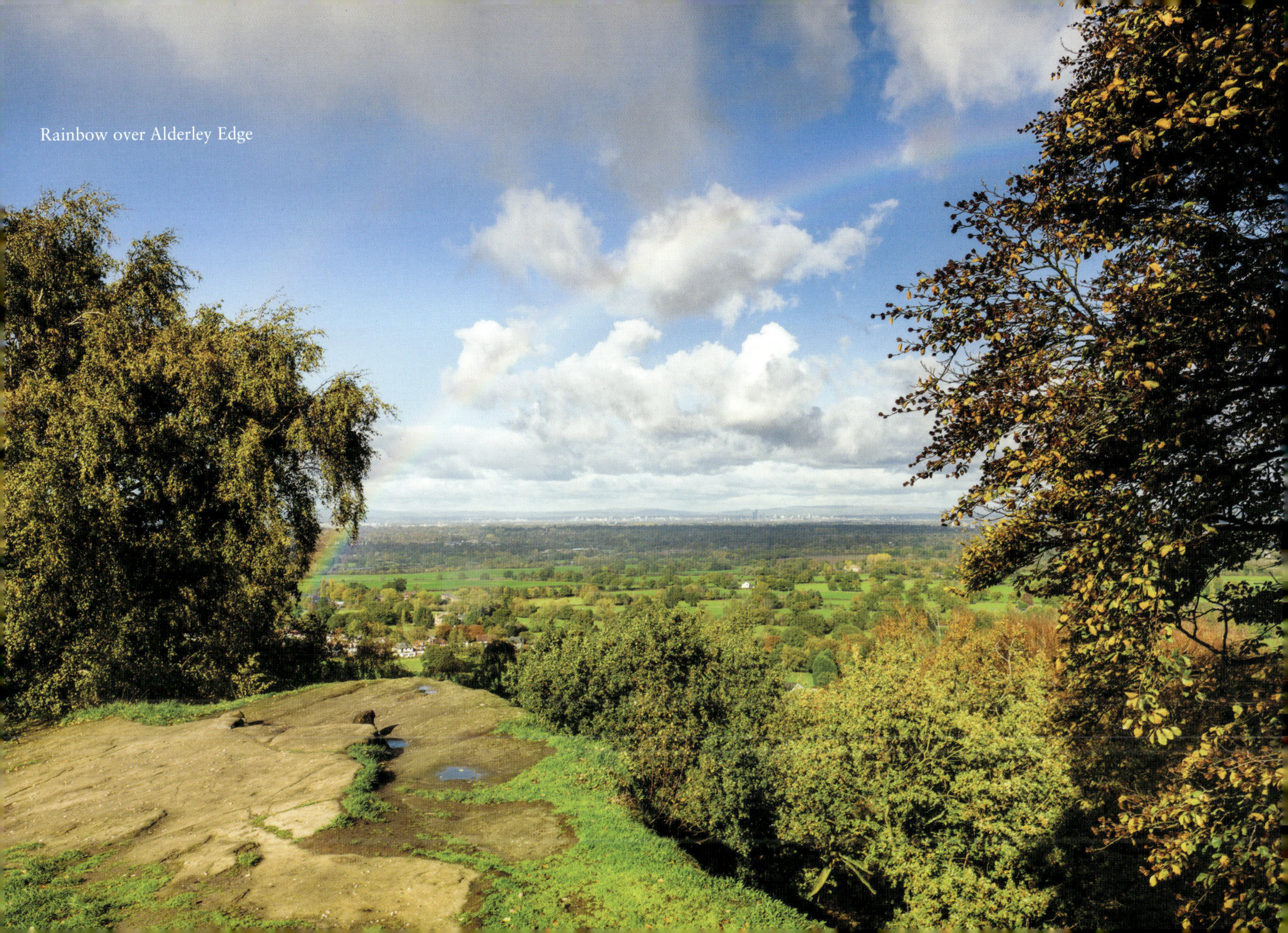

Rainbow over Alderley Edge

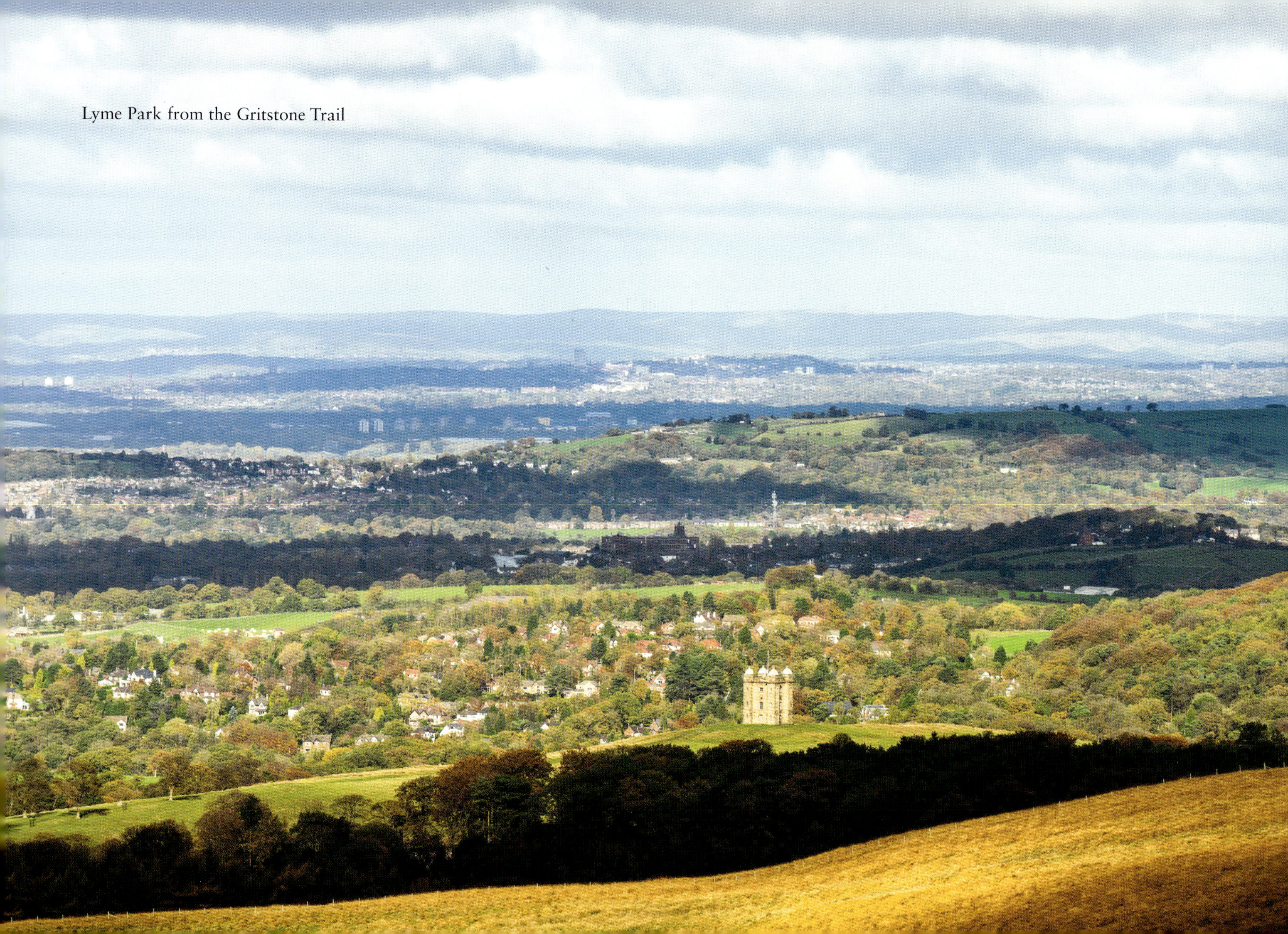

Lyme Park from the Gritstone Trail

VISITING CHESHIRE

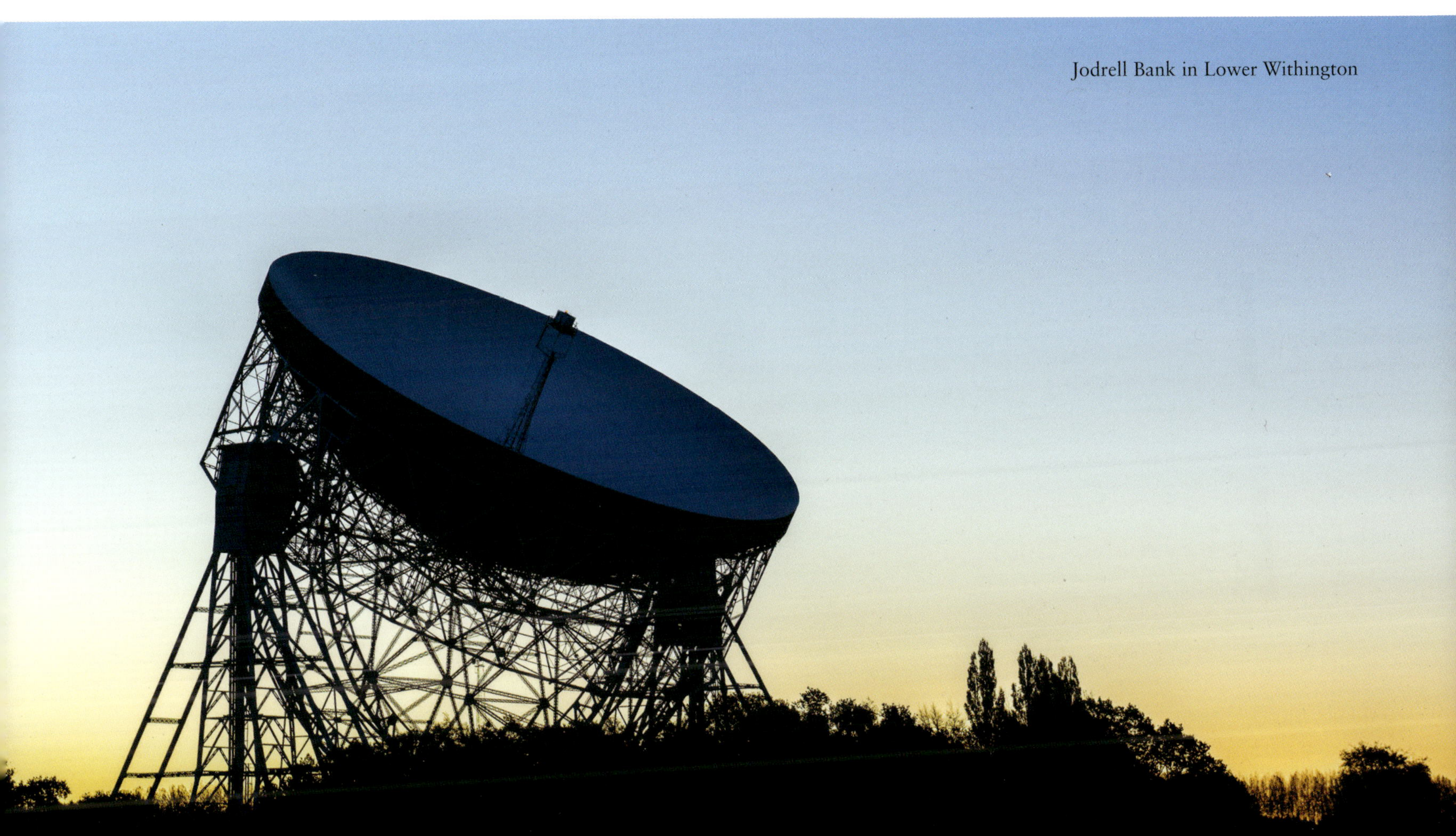

Jodrell Bank in Lower Withington

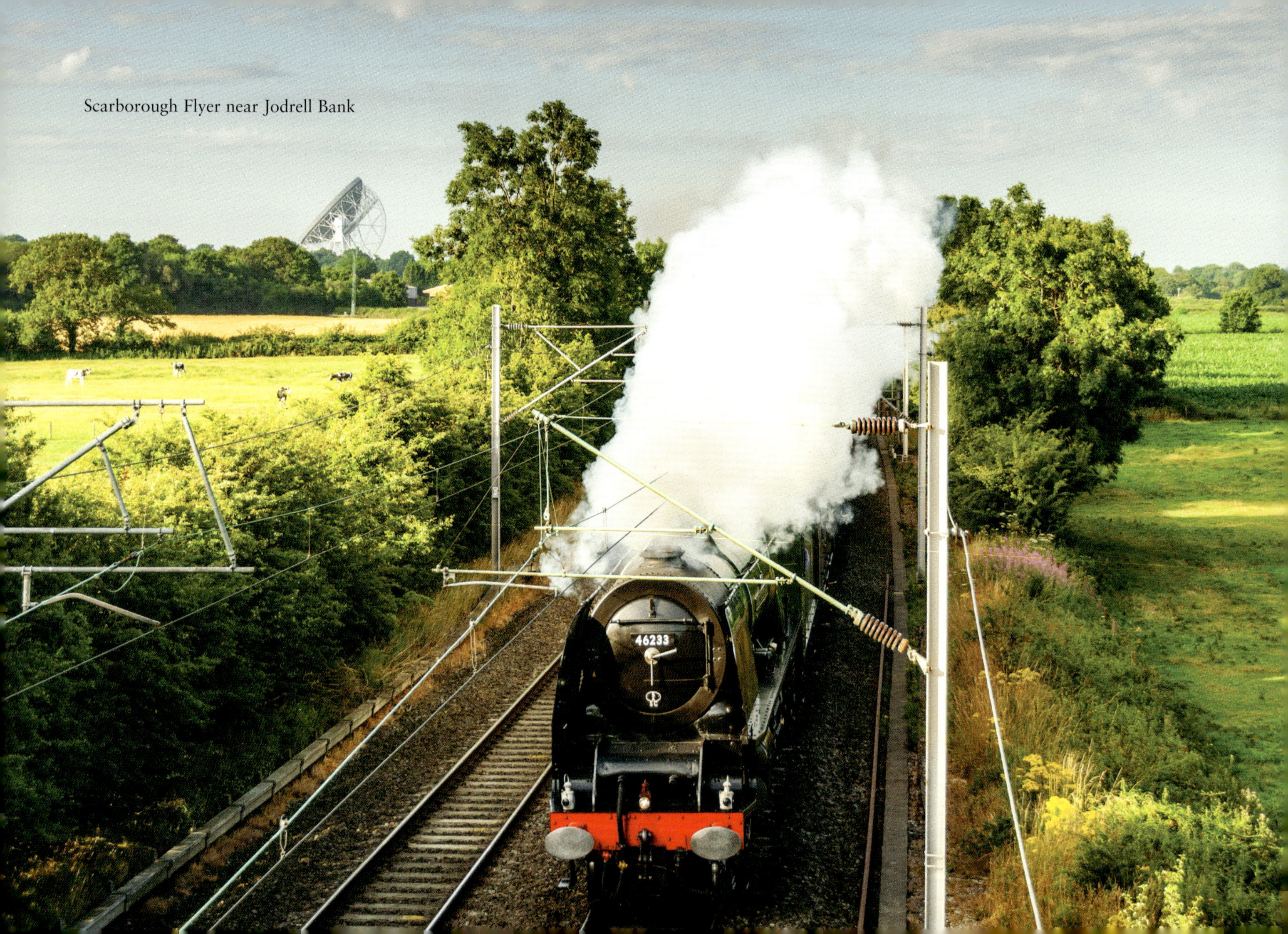

Scarborough Flyer near Jodrell Bank

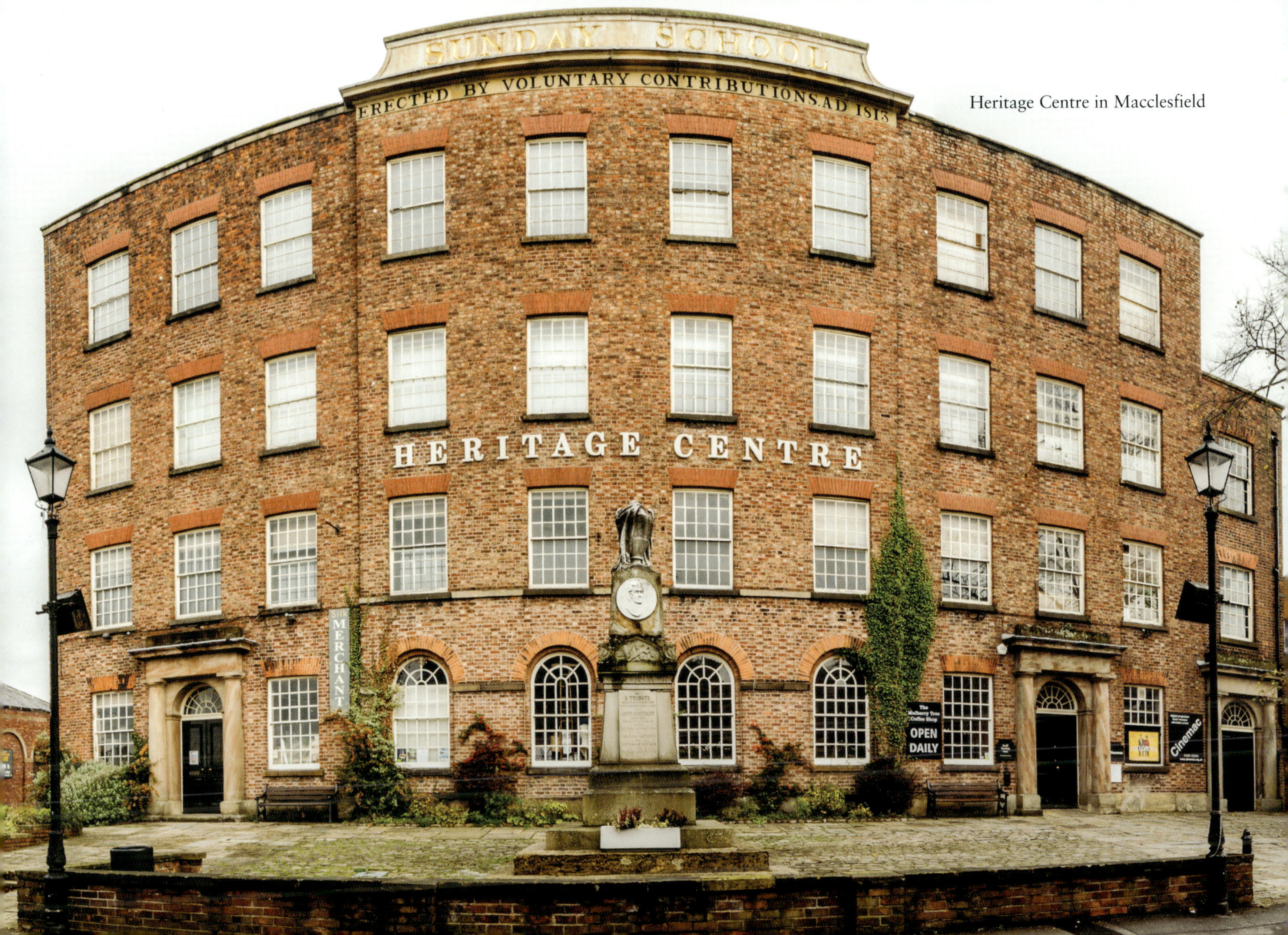

Heritage Centre in Macclesfield

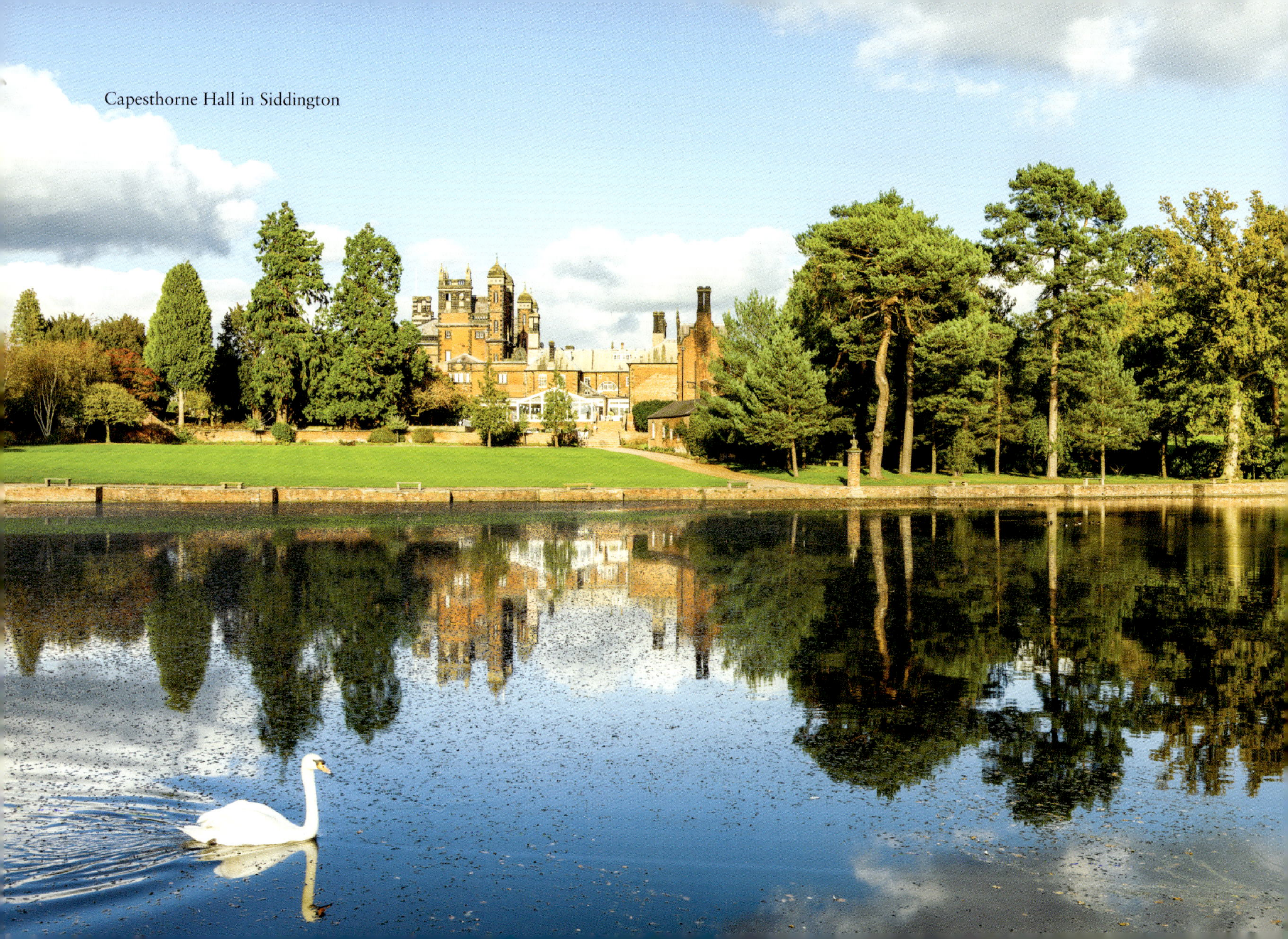

Capesthorne Hall in Siddington

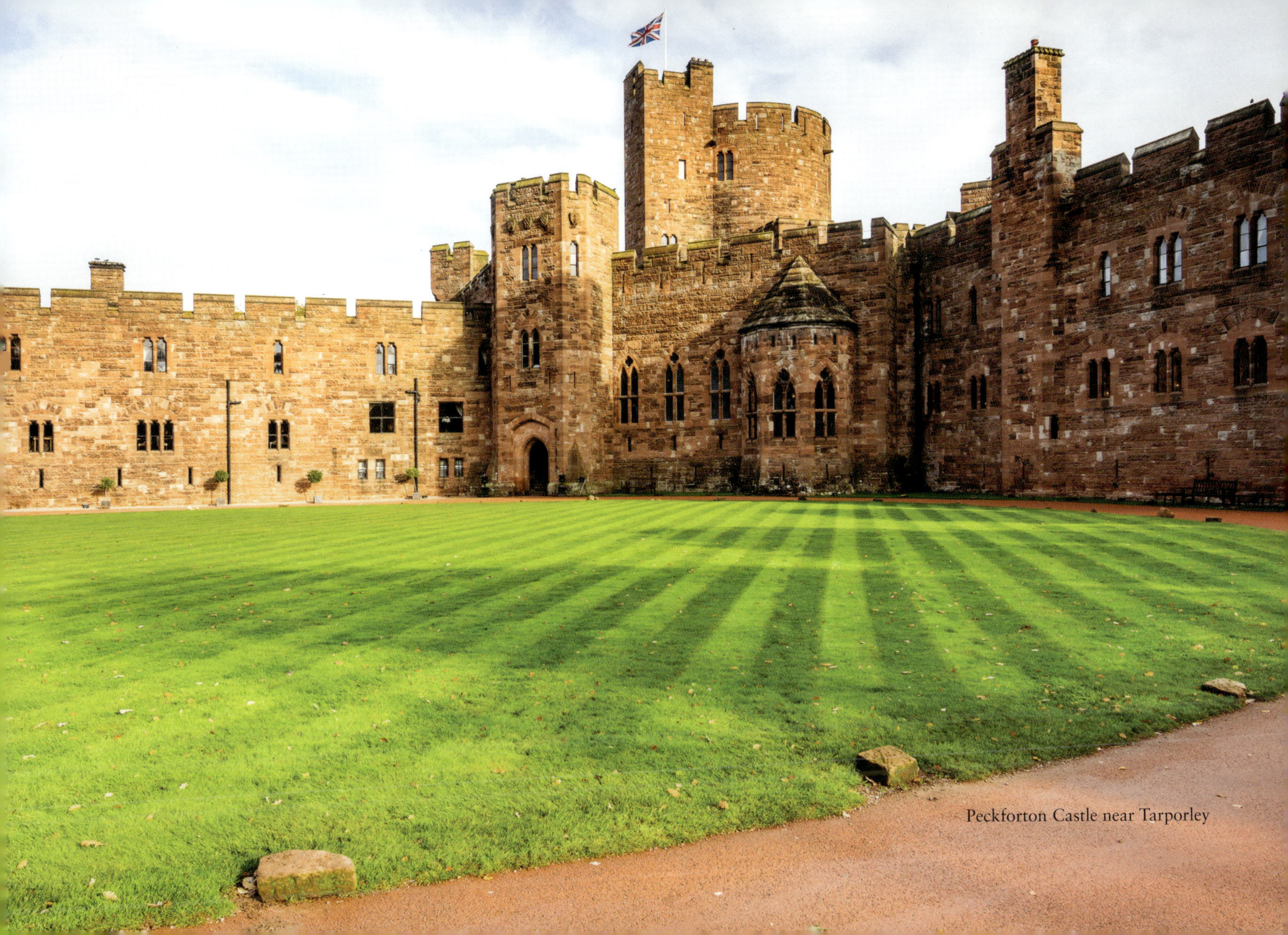

Peckforton Castle near Tarporley

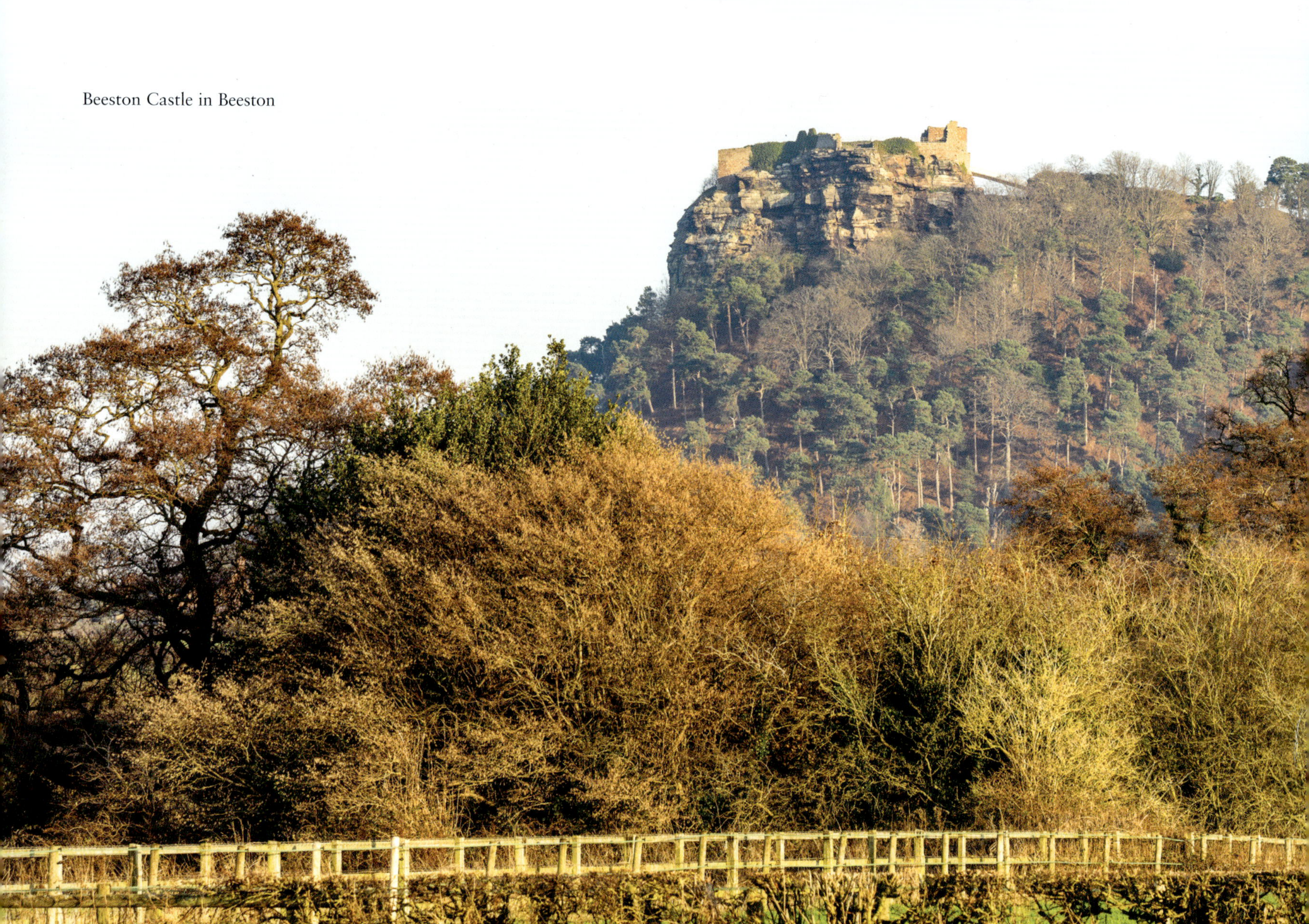

Beeston Castle in Beeston

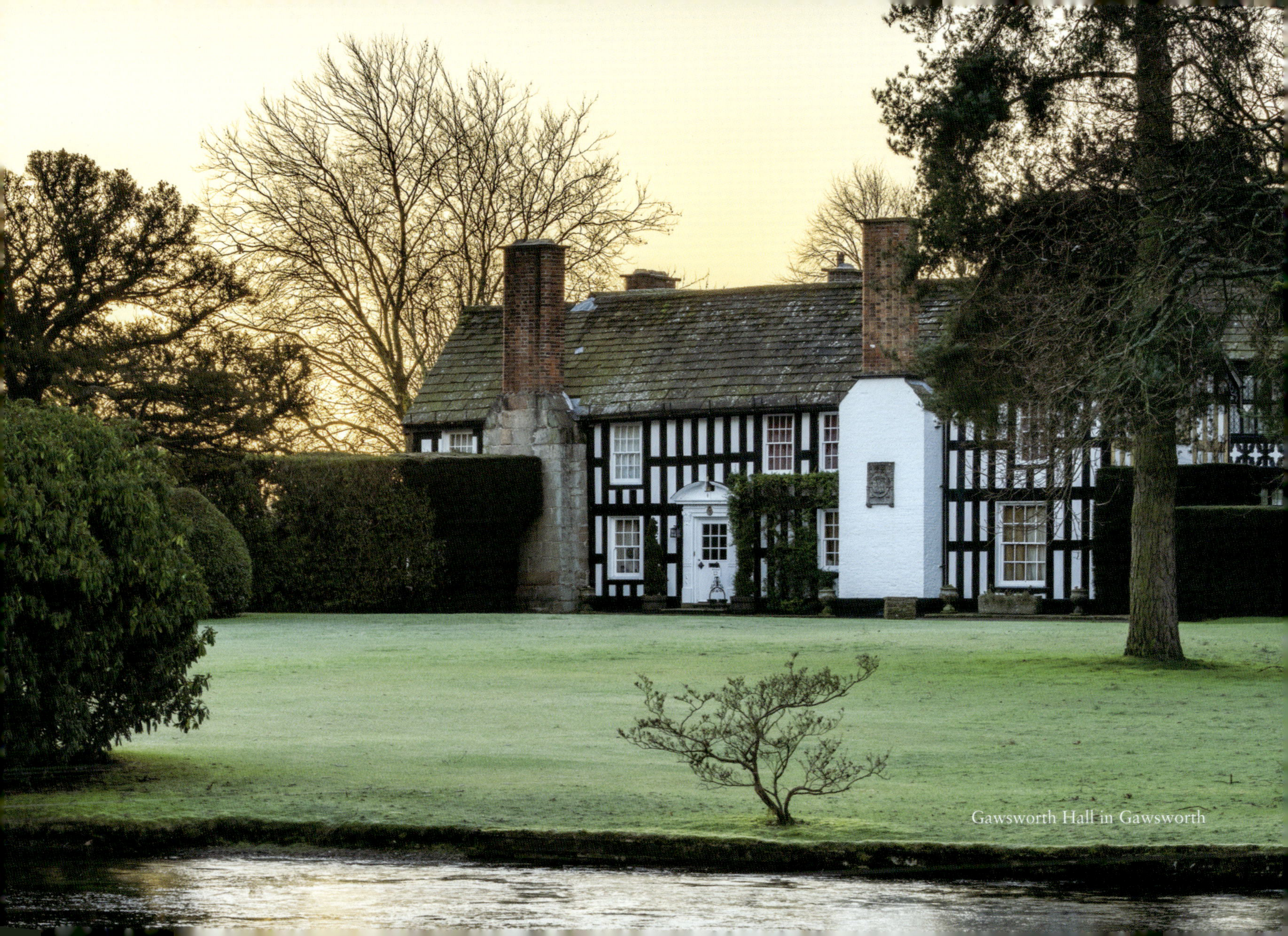

Gawsworth Hall in Gawsworth

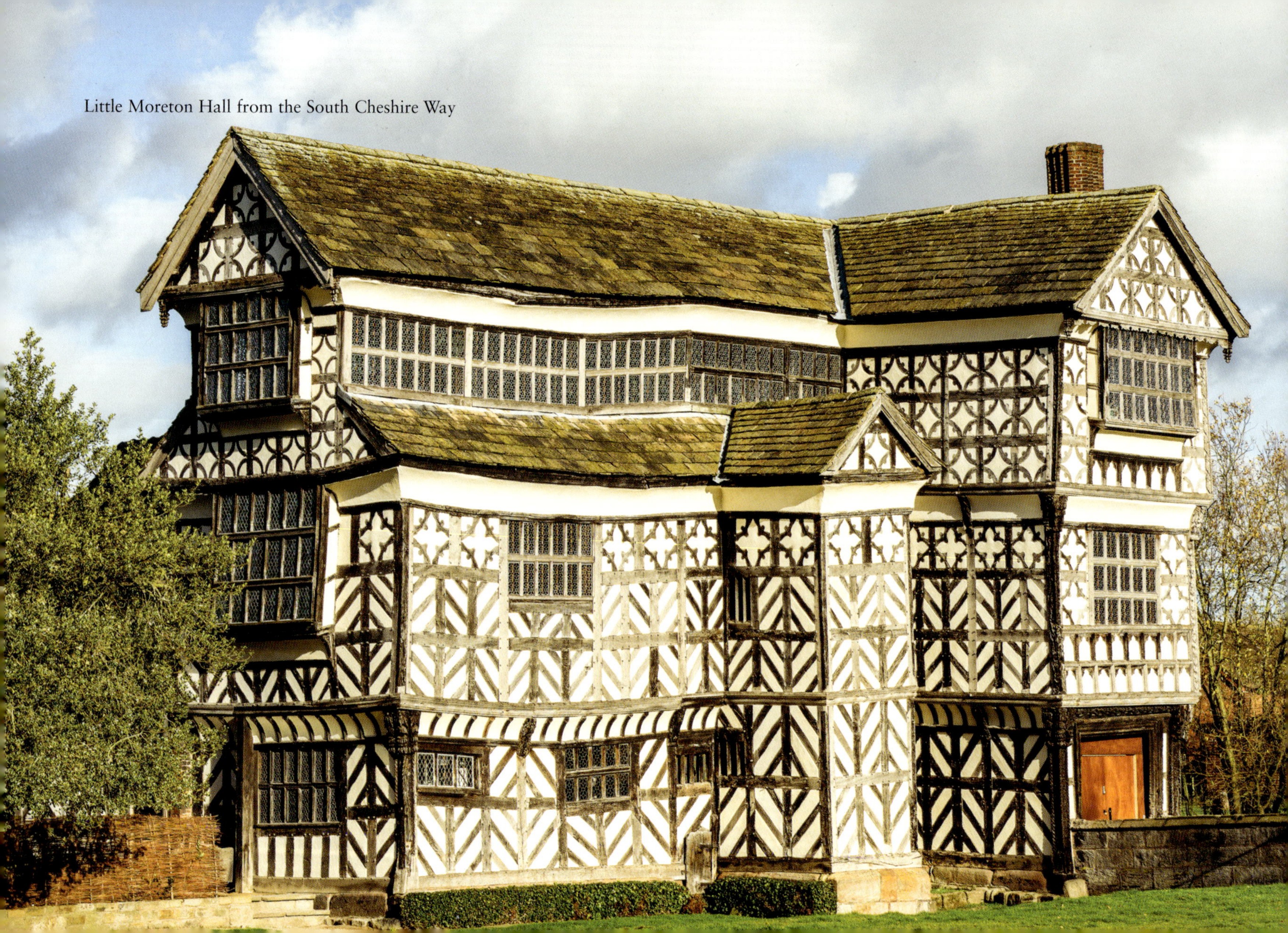

Little Moreton Hall from the South Cheshire Way

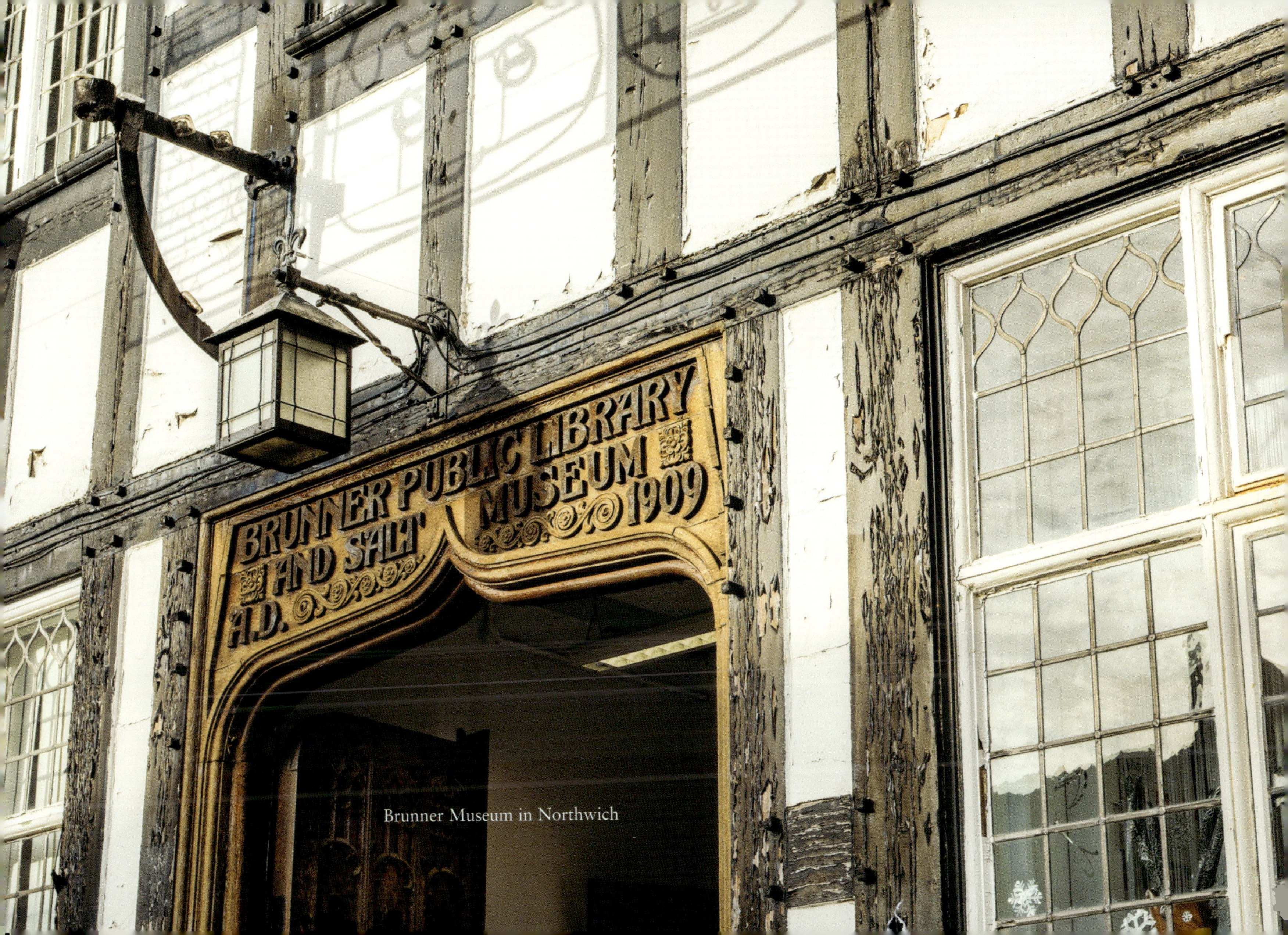

Brunner Museum in Northwich

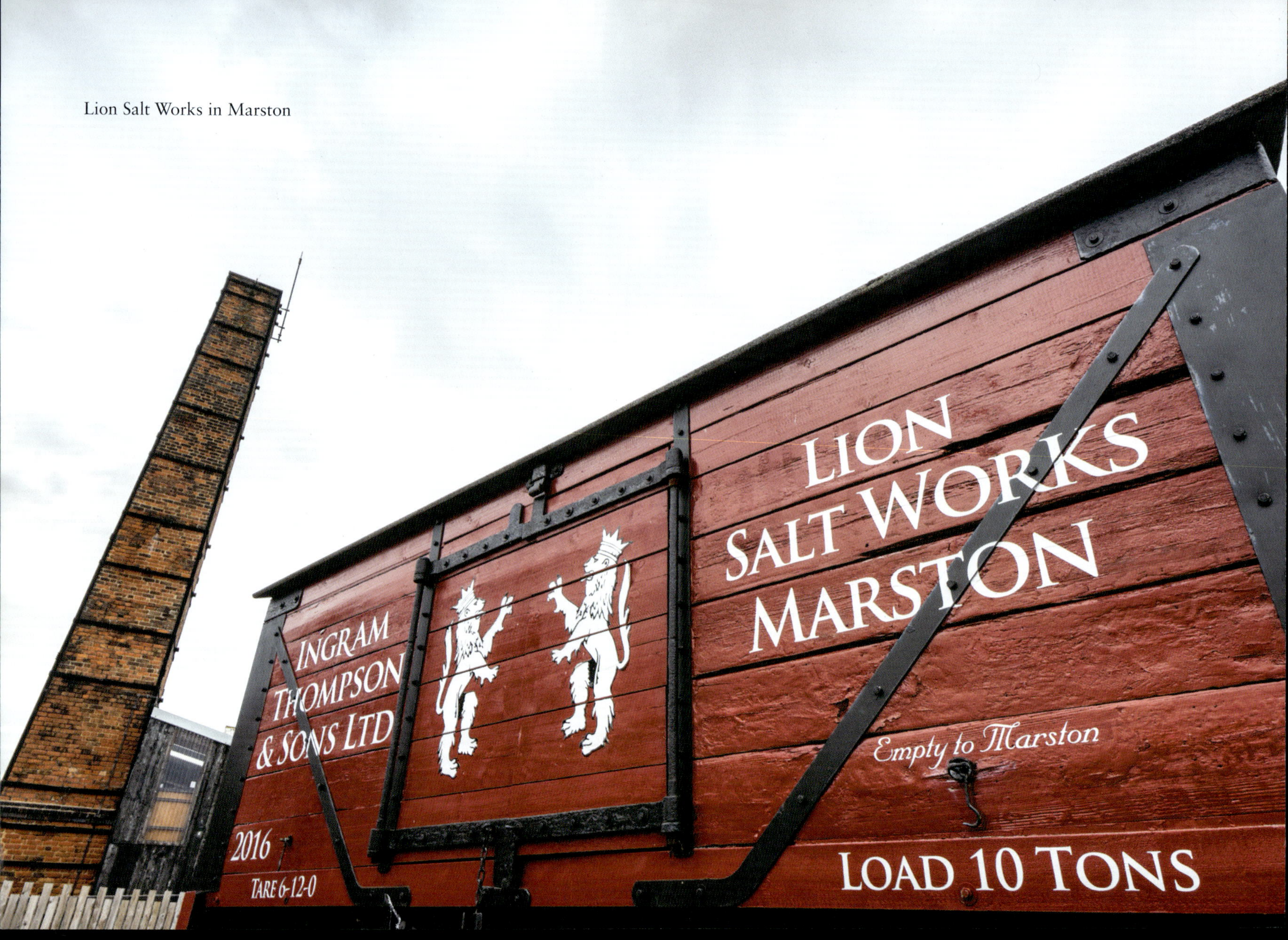

Lion Salt Works in Marston

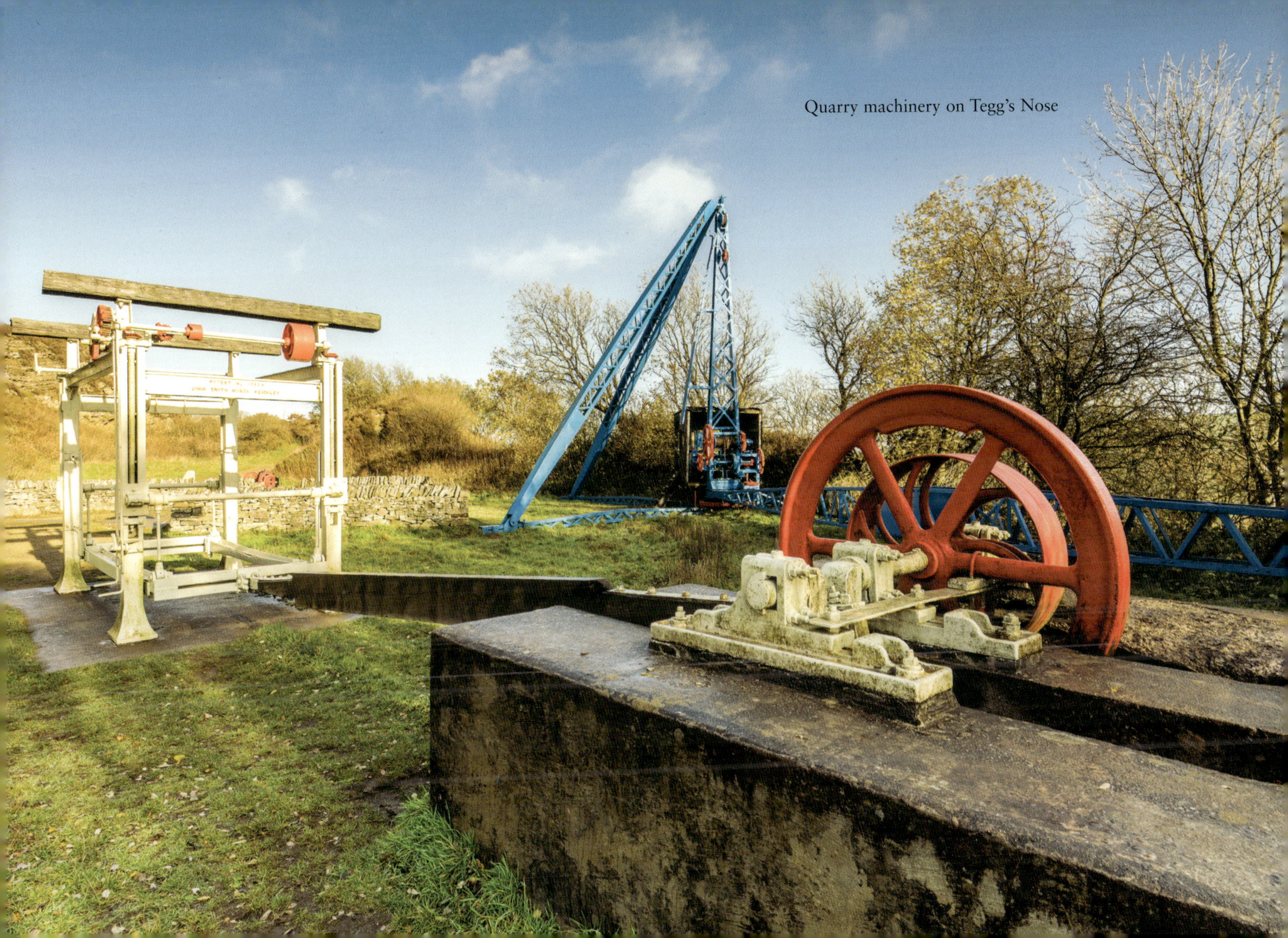

Quarry machinery on Tegg’s Nose

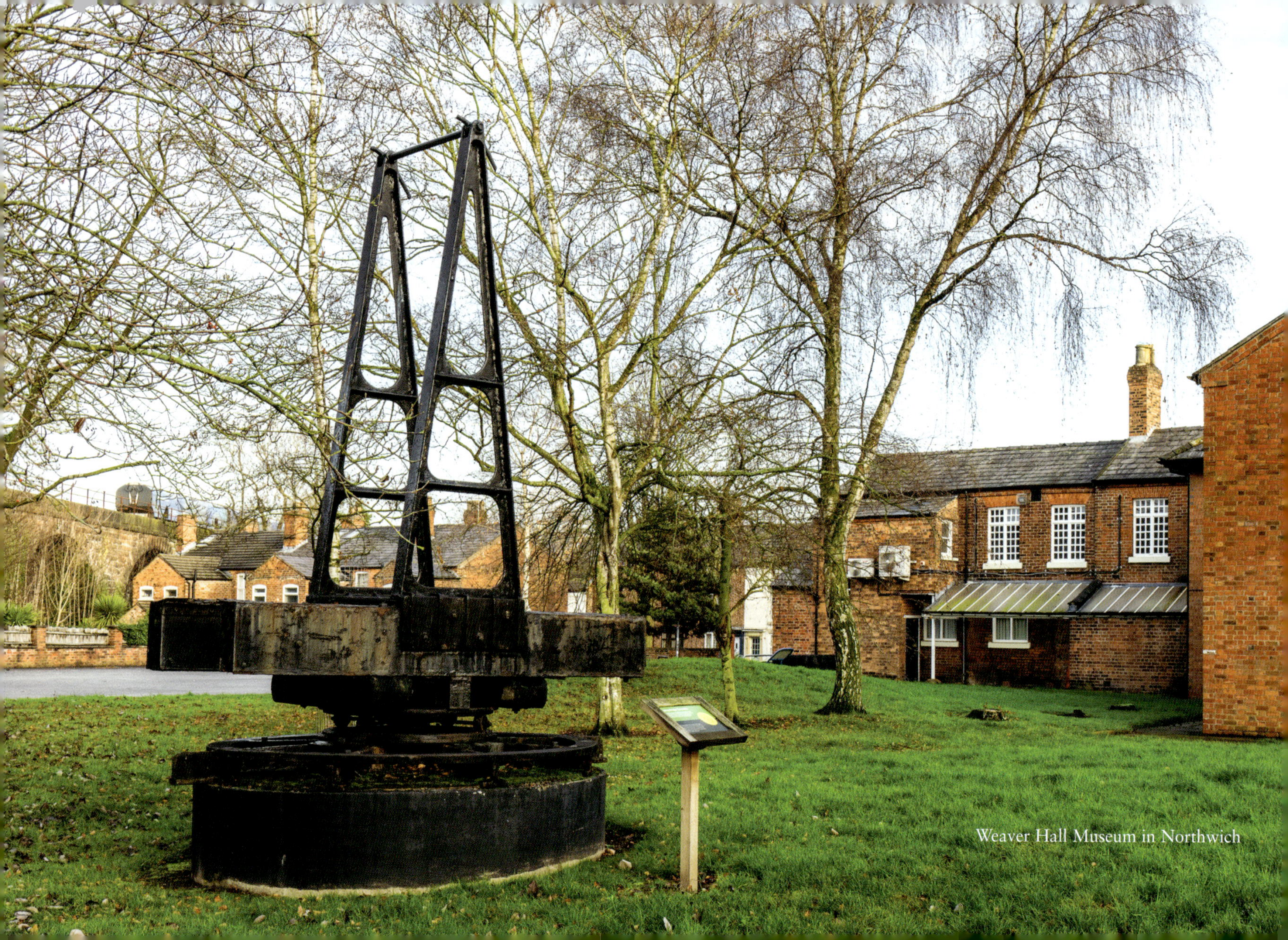

Weaver Hall Museum in Northwich

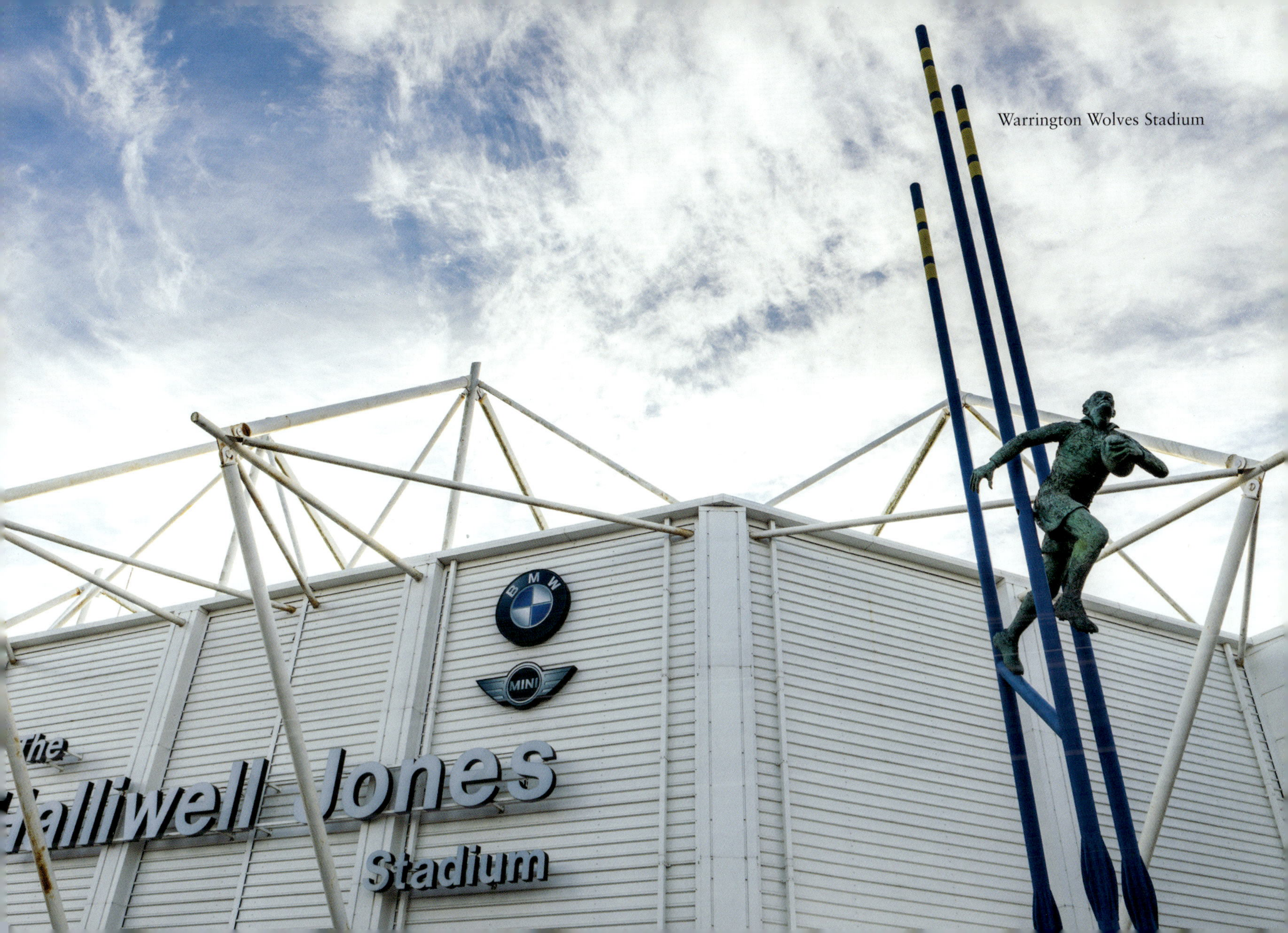

Warrington Wolves Stadium

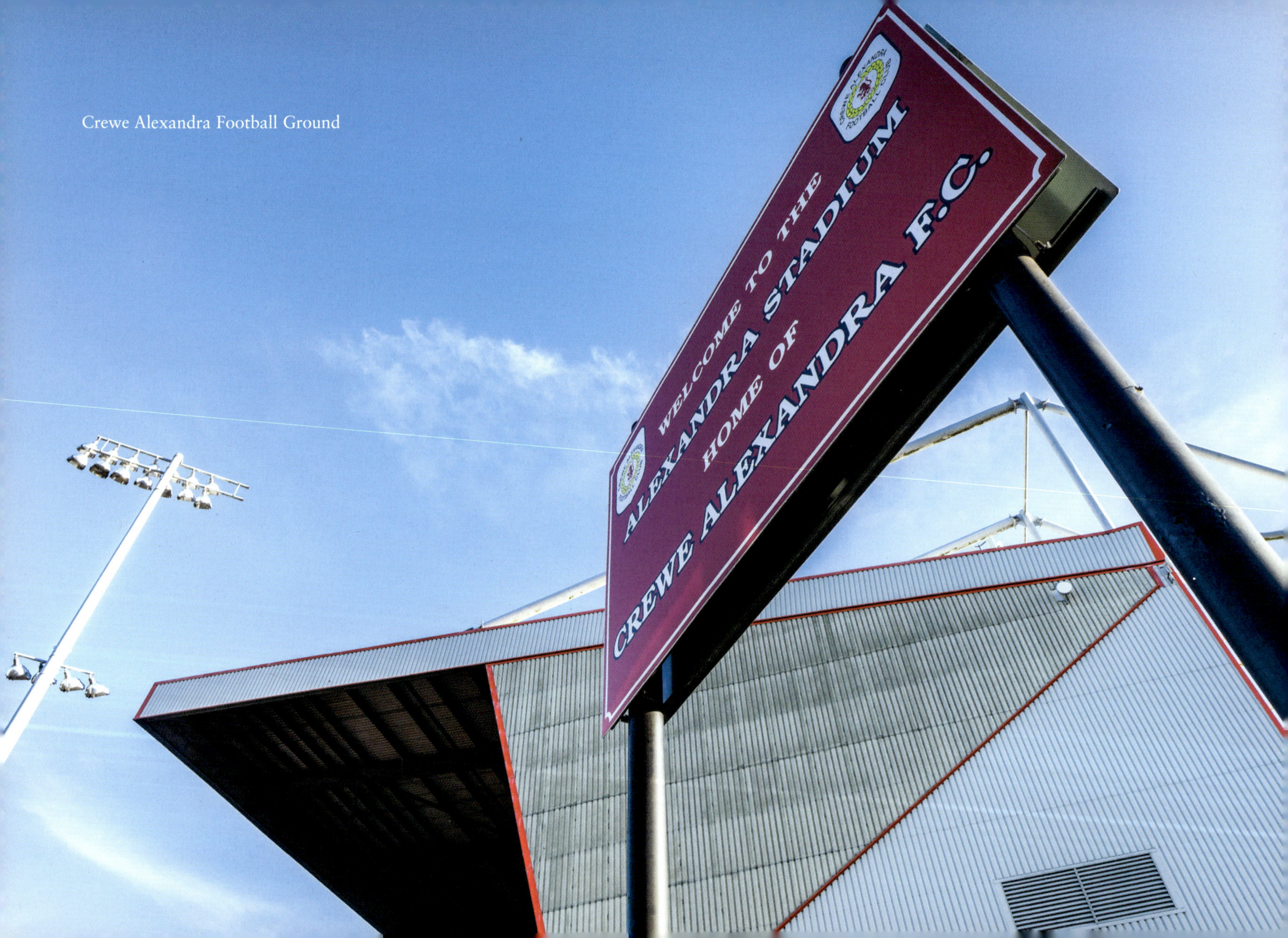

Crewe Alexandra Football Ground

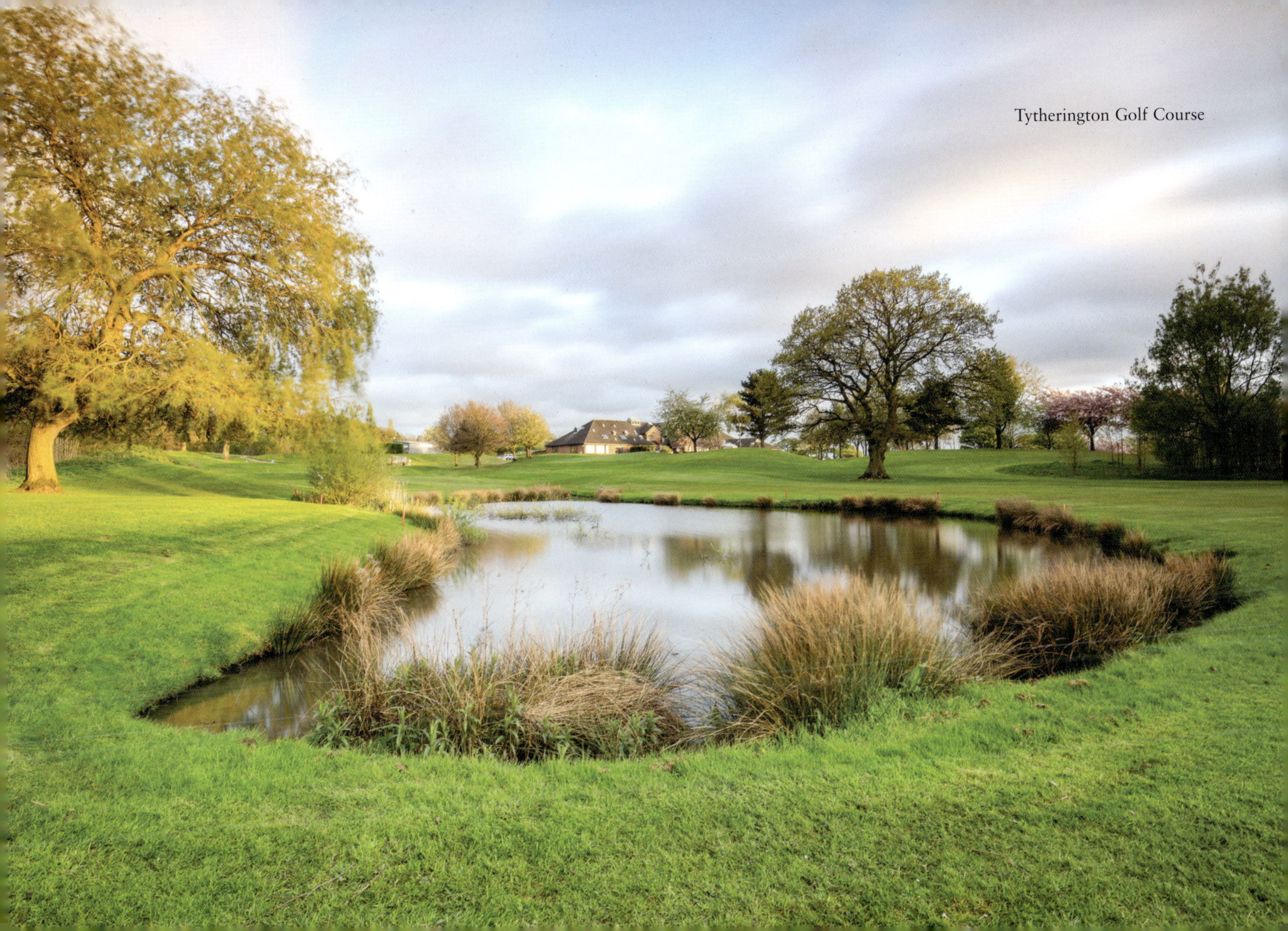

Tytherington Golf Course

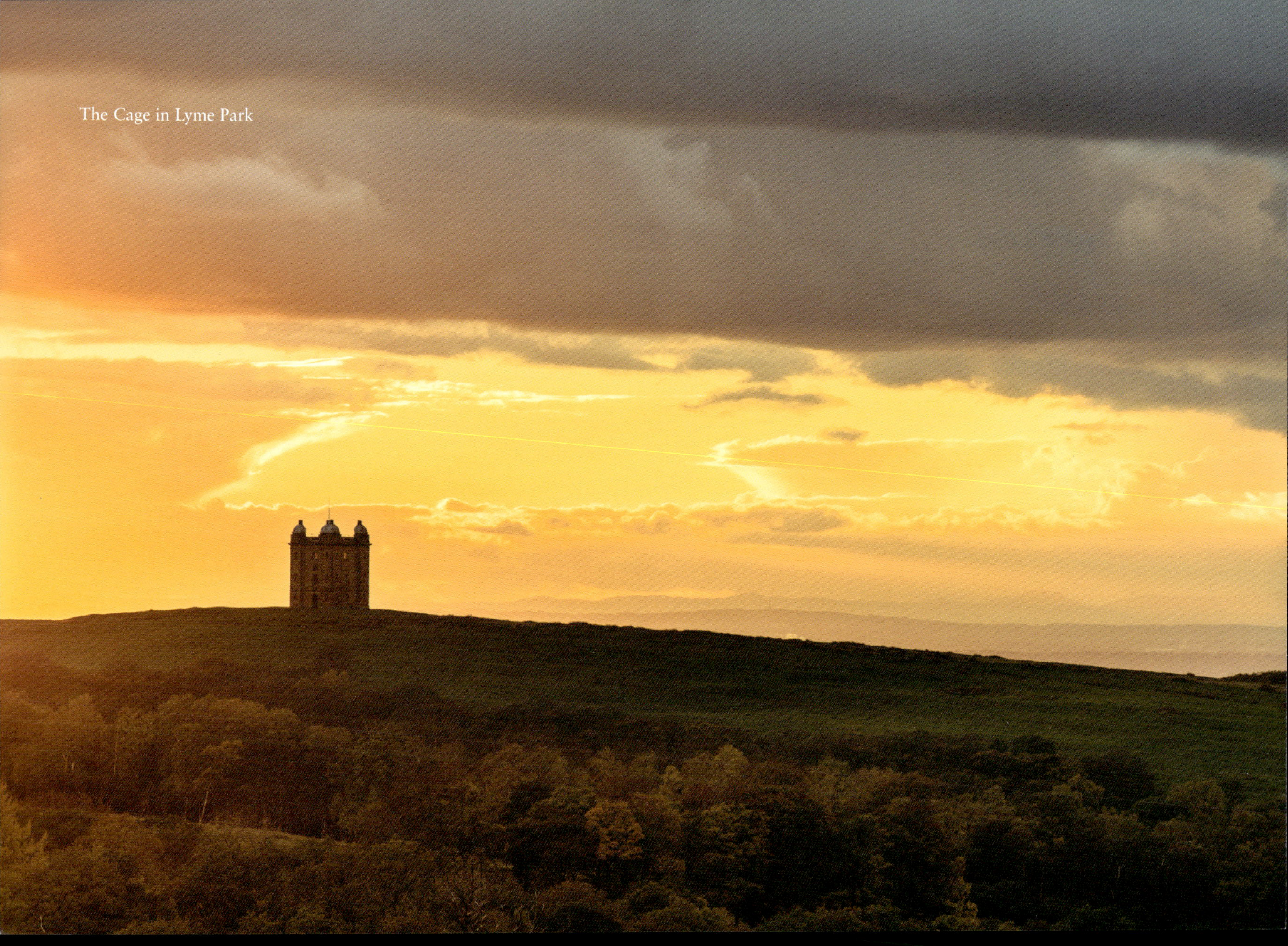
The Cage in Lyme Park

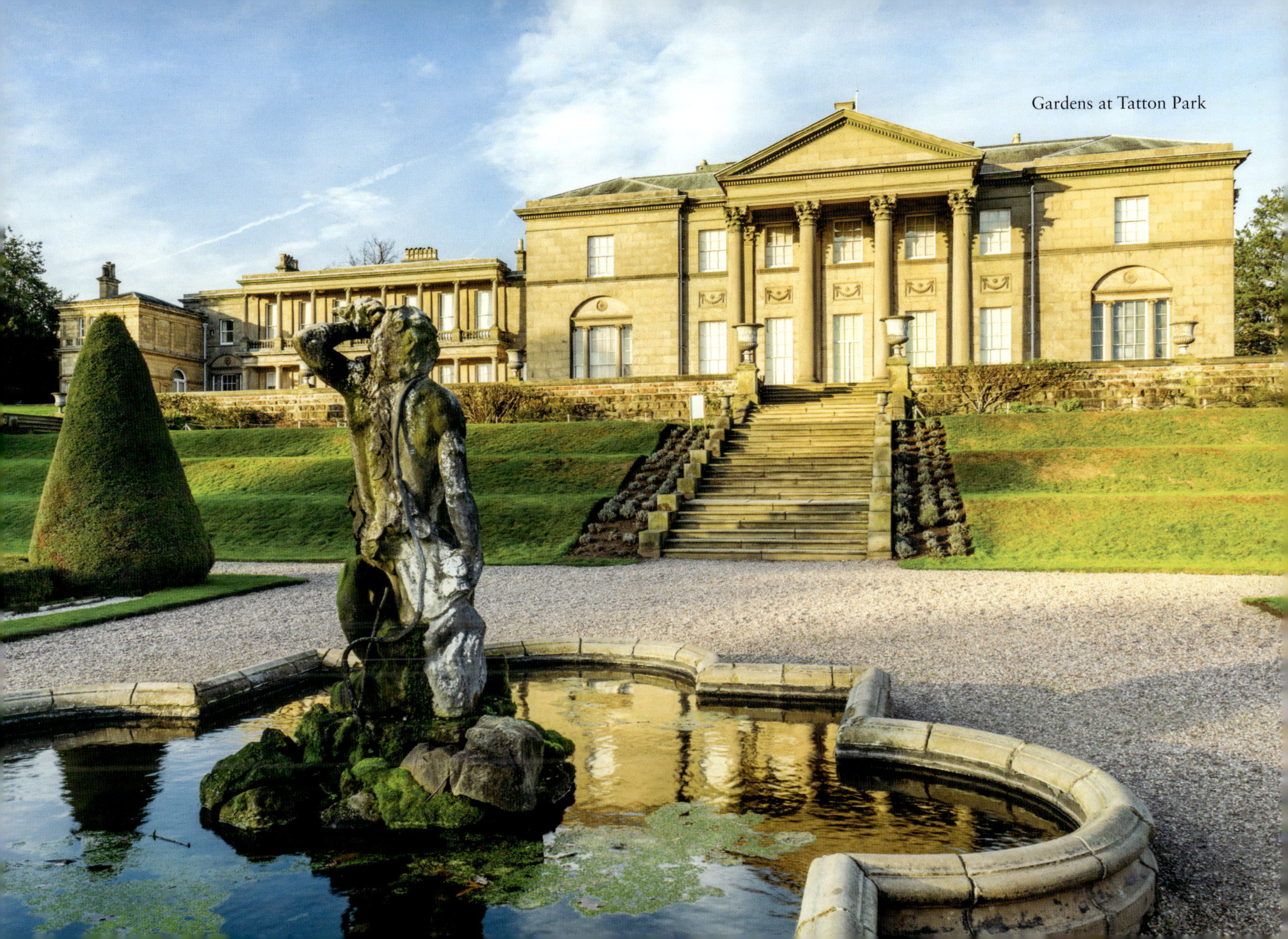
Gardens at Tatton Park

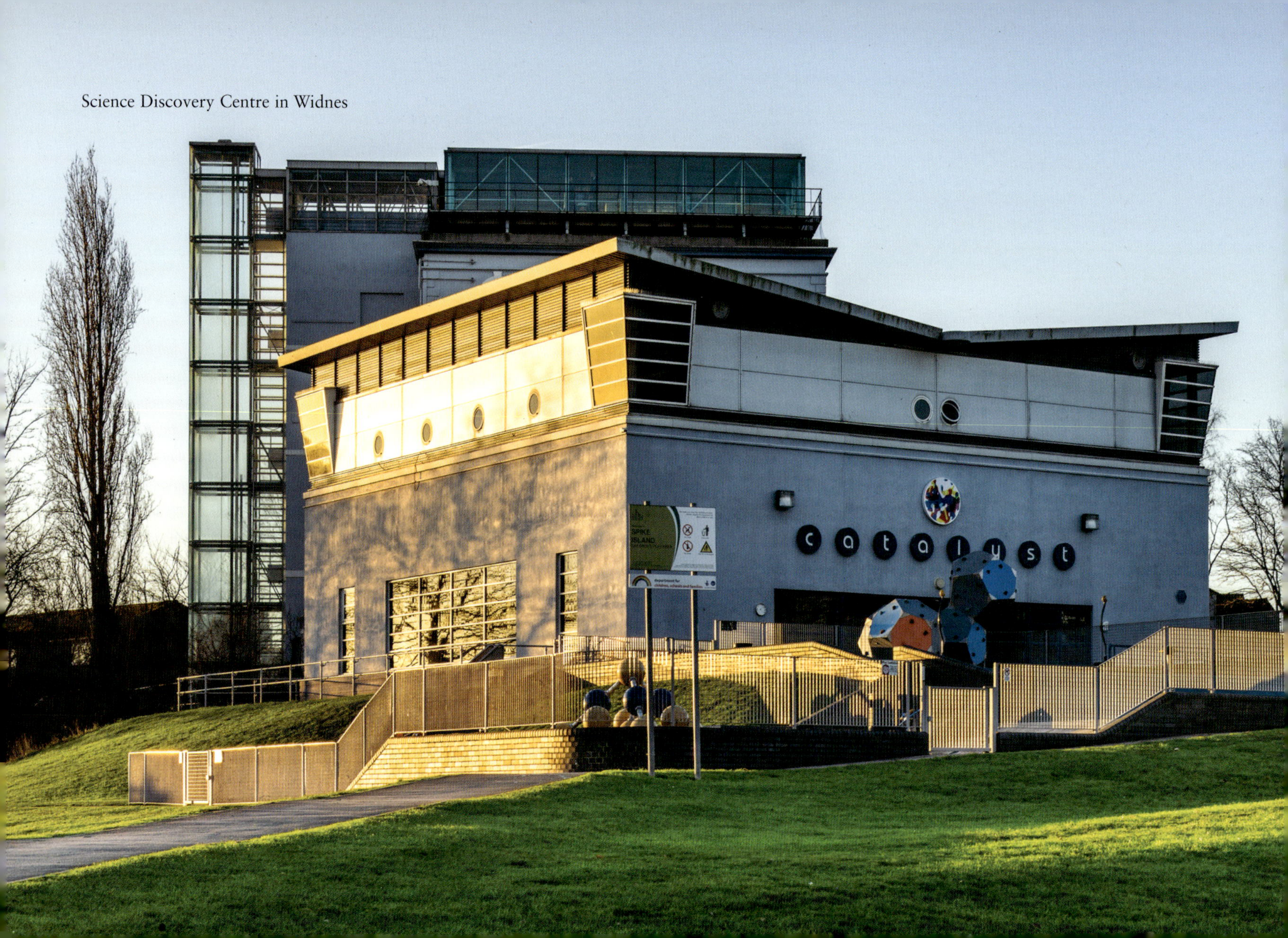

Science Discovery Centre in Widnes

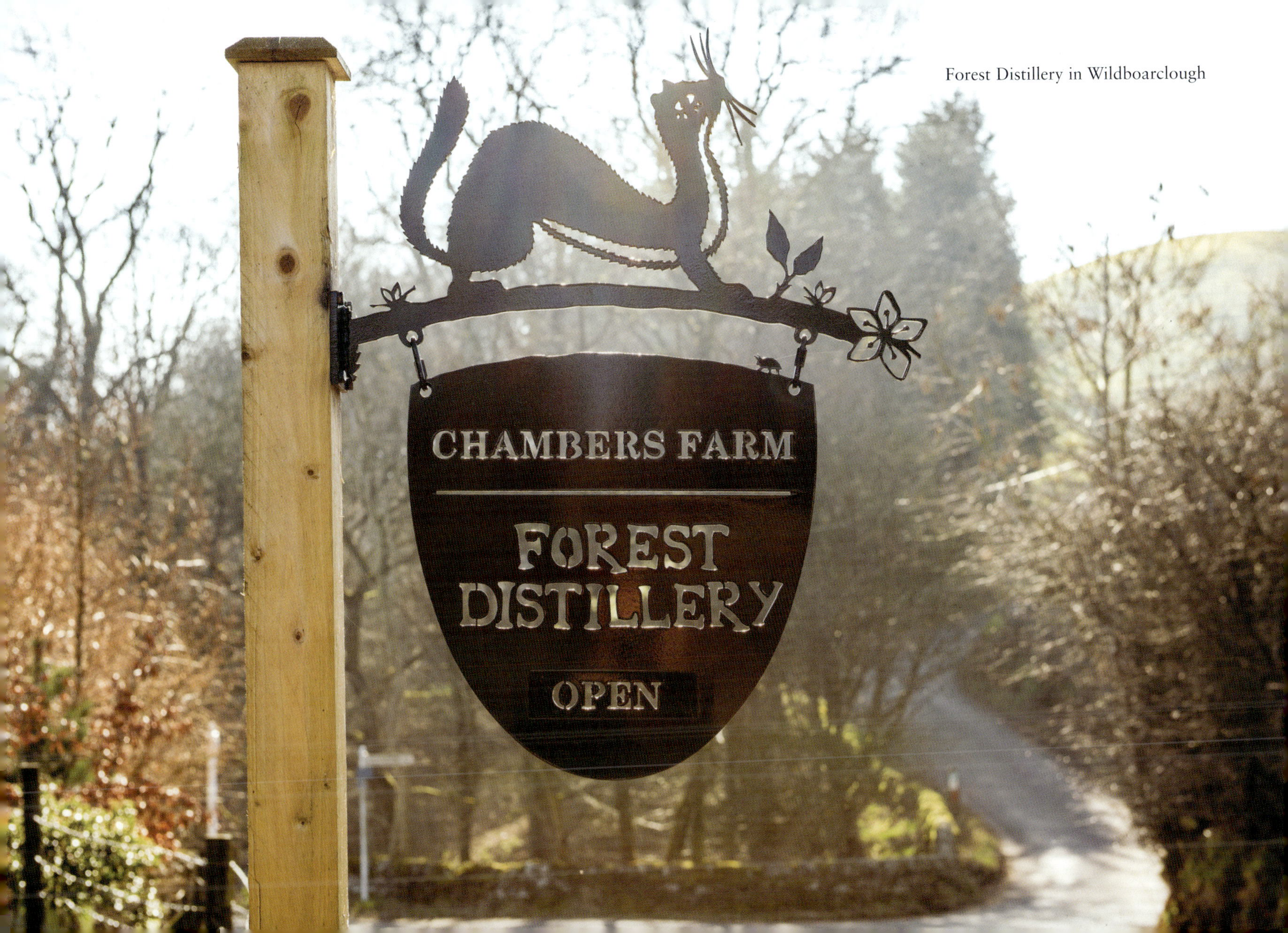

Forest Distillery in Wildboarclough

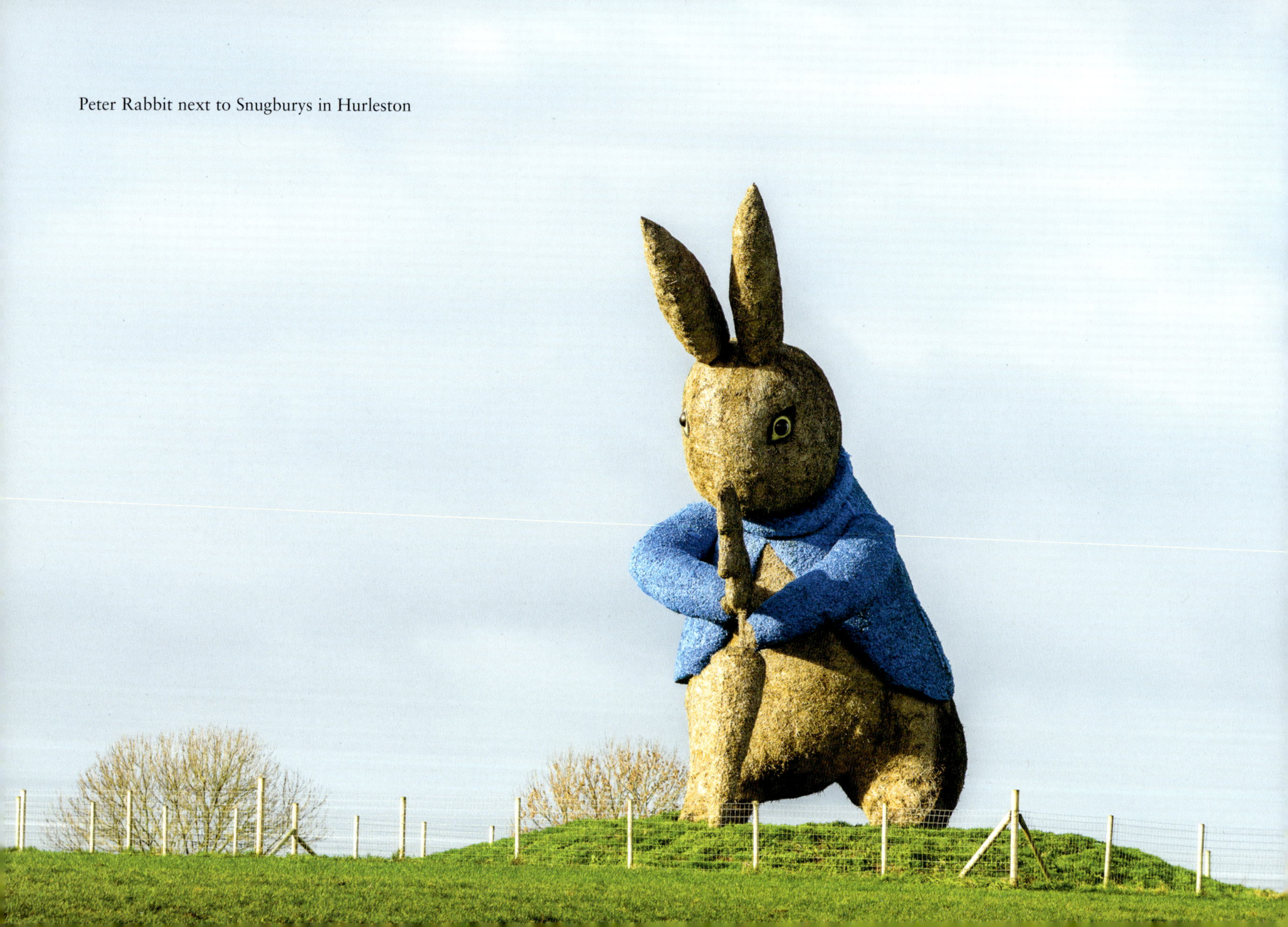

Peter Rabbit next to Snugburys in Hurleston

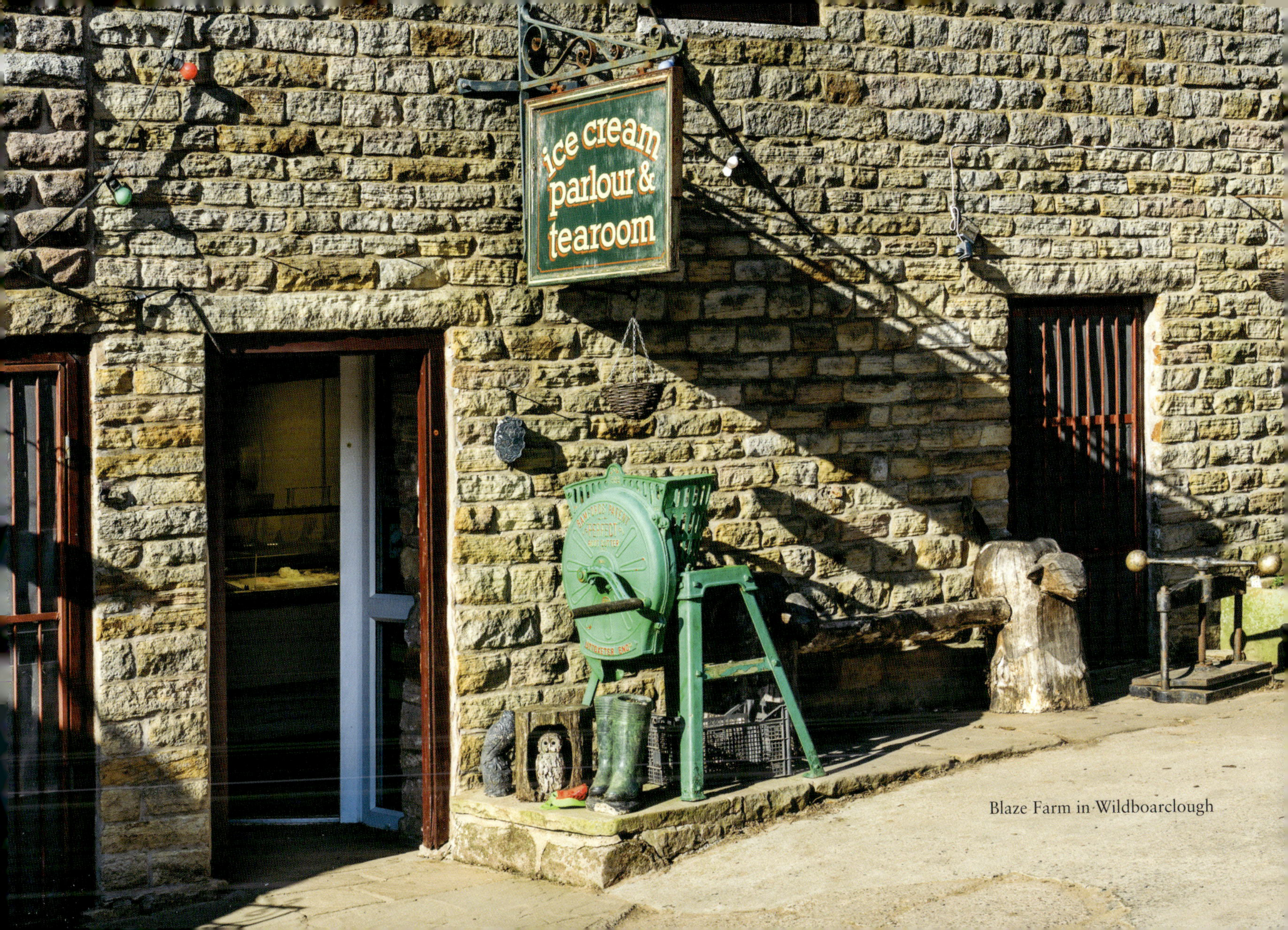

Blaze Farm in Wildboarclough

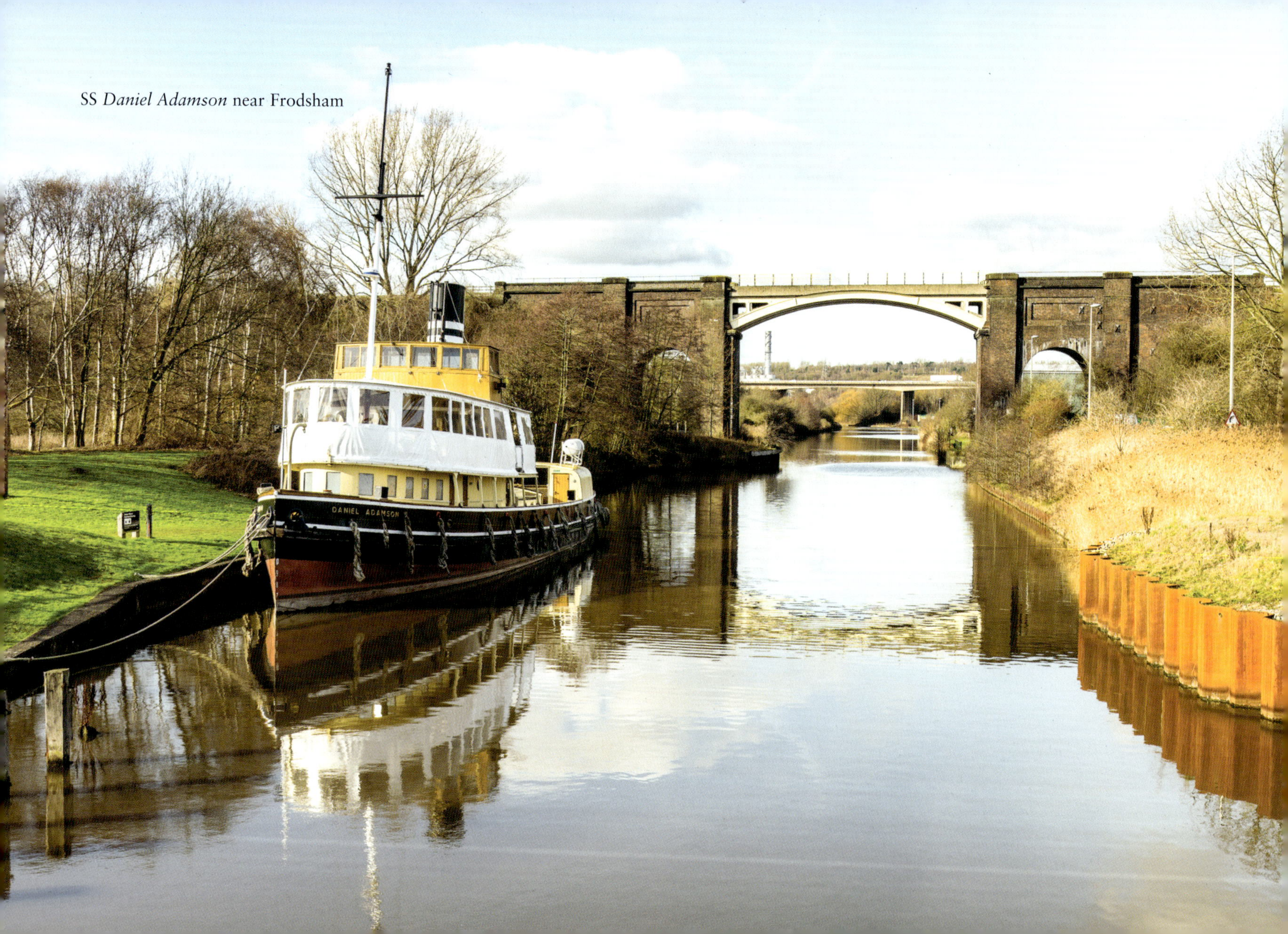

SS *Daniel Adamson* near Frodsham

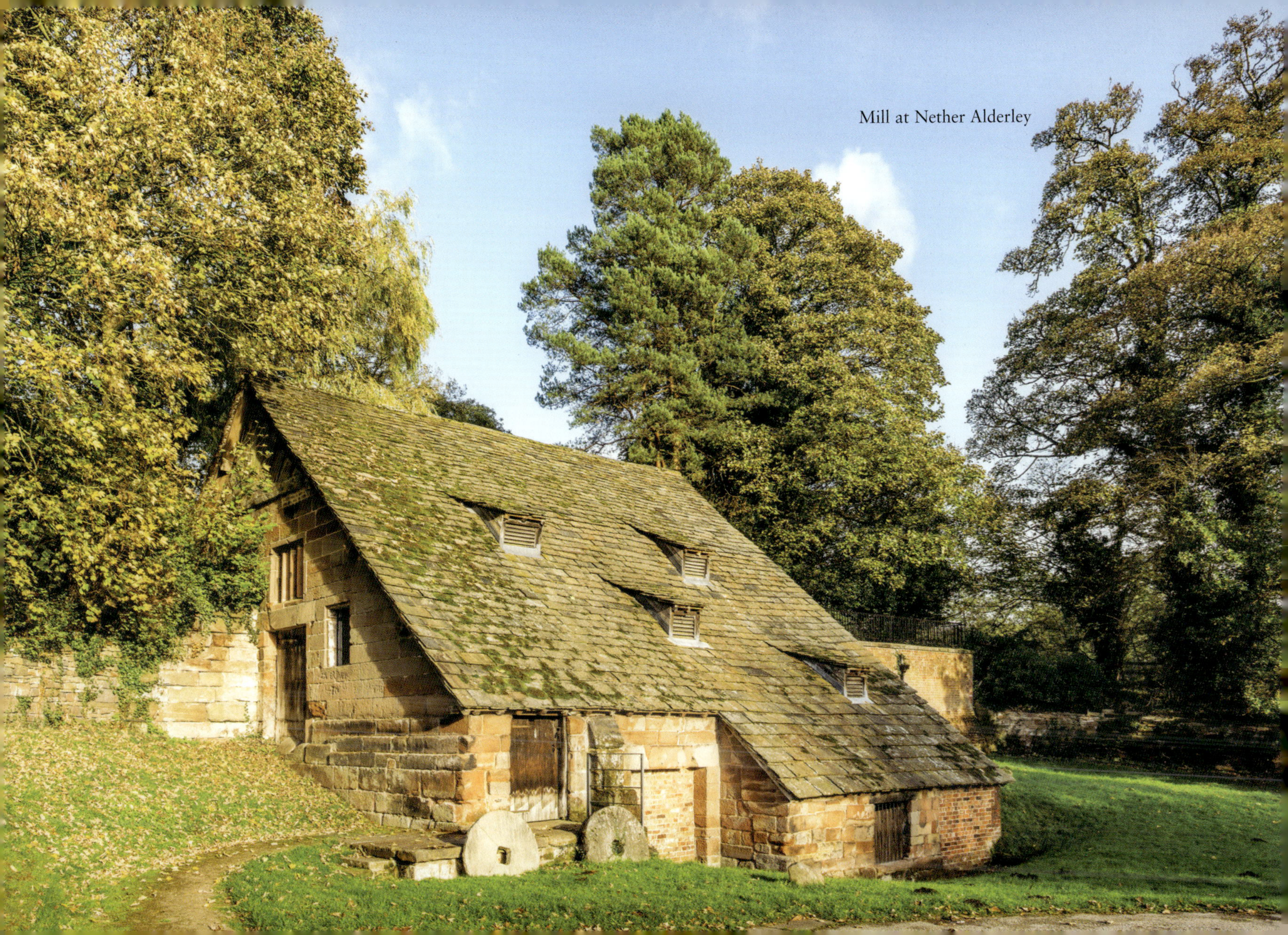

Mill at Nether Alderley

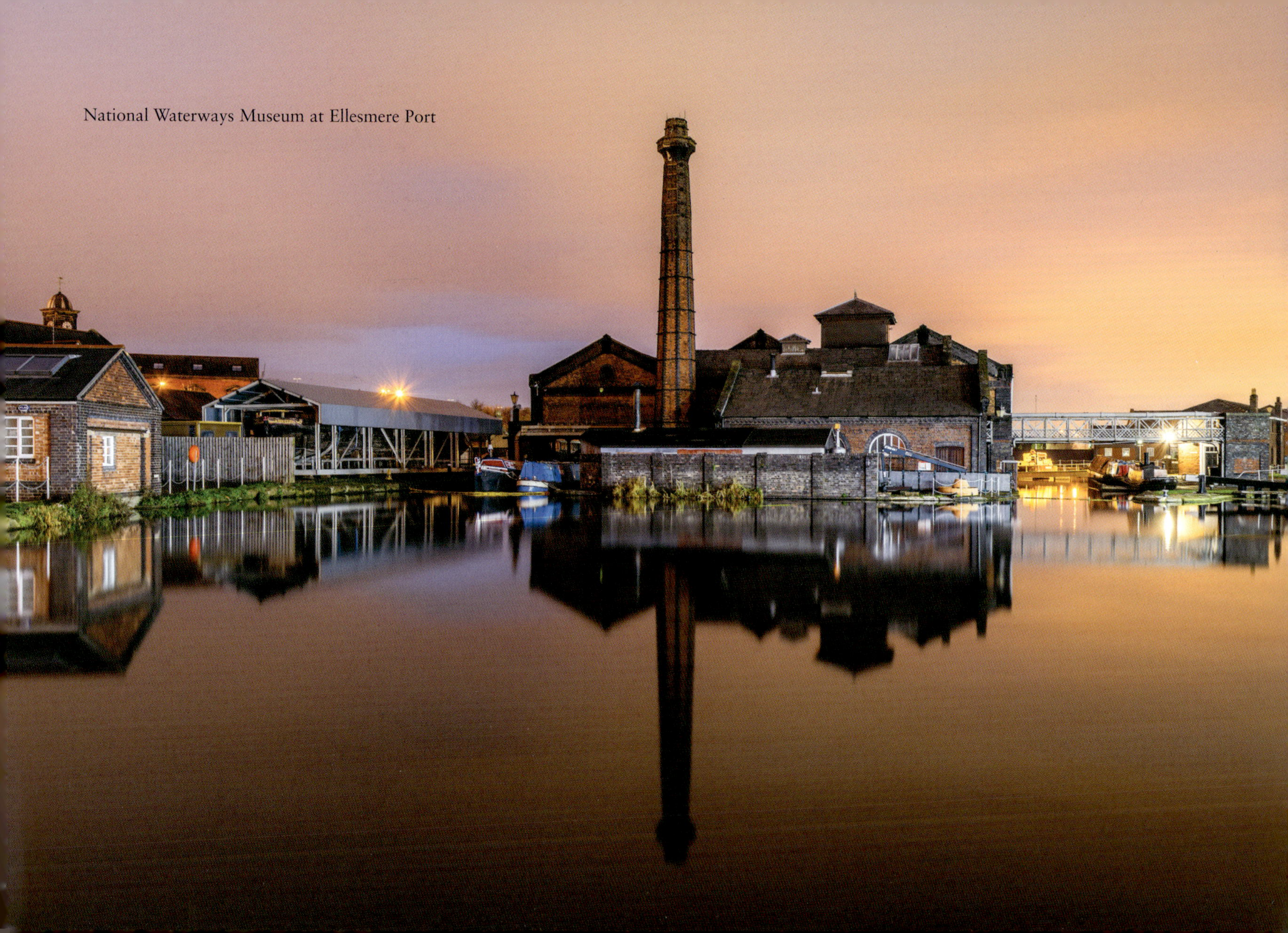

National Waterways Museum at Ellesmere Port